The

SERVANT CLASS

City

Globalization and Community

SUSAN E. CLARKE, *Series Editor*
DENNIS R. JUDD, *Founding Editor*

(continued on page 294)

The

SERVANT CLASS

City

Urban Revitalization versus the
Working Poor in San Diego

DAVID J. KARJANEN

Globalization and Community, Volume 25

UNIVERSITY OF MINNESOTA PRESS

MINNEAPOLIS · LONDON

Published by the University of Minnesota Press
111 Third Avenue South, Suite 290
Minneapolis, MN 55401-2520
http://www.upress.umn.edu

Printed in the United States of America on acid-free paper

The University of Minnesota is an equal-opportunity educator and employer.

22 21 20 19 18 17 16   10 9 8 7 6 5 4 3 2 1

Library of Congress Cataloging-in-Publication Data
Names: Karjanen, David J., author.
Title: The servant class city : urban revitalization versus the working poor in San Diego /
David J. Karjanen.
Description: Minneapolis : University of Minnesota Press, 2016. | Series: Globalization and
community ; 25 | Includes bibliographical references and index.
Identifiers: LCCN 2015036891 | ISBN 978-0-8166-9462-4 (hc) | ISBN 978-0-8166-9748-9 (pb)
Subjects: LCSH: Urban renewal—California—San Diego. | Poor—California—San Diego. |
Low-income housing—California—San Diego.
Classification: LCC HT178.D54 D37 2016 | DDC 307.3/41609794985—dc23
LC record available at http://lccn.loc.gov/2015036891

"The servant class is all around us. They just aren't on the household payroll. They've been outsourced."

—PHYLLIS PALMER, quoted in the *New York Times,* 1995

Contents

Acknowledgments

This book was a decade-long project, and I have many people to thank. This research began while I was working at the Center on Policy Initiatives, and some of the innovative methodologies that were developed to examine labor market outcomes and job creation owe a great deal to my colleagues there, particularly Murtaza Baxamusa, Sarah Zimmerman, and Sundari Baru. I also thank Donald Cohen, as well as colleagues at partner organizations LAANE and the Partnership for Working Families, whose research staff contributed to much of my thinking about urban revitalization and accountable development. Other community organizations, particularly the Environmental Health Coalition, have also provided important insights, as well as the Urban League of San Diego, among other organizations.

In San Diego I benefited greatly from the accommodating and patient staff at numerous city offices, including the Redevelopment Agency, Centre City Development Corporation, and Planning Department. While a visiting fellow at UCSD I was offered time to begin drafting what would become the framework for much of this book, particularly the data analysis of immigrant and Latino populations in San Diego County. Portions of this manuscript were presented at the Institute for Labor and Employment at UCLA. I thank the participants and my copanelists, and especially Chris Tilly for somehow always being free enough to answer the odd question about labor markets and career ladders, no matter how busy he was. I also thank participants of the Spatial Justice conference held at the Paris West University Nanterre La Défense in 2008, especially Edward Soja and Peter Marcuse.

Over the years, subsequent research trips have been generously supported by the University of Minnesota, Department of American Studies, the Office for Equity and Diversity, and the Imagine Fund. Also at Minnesota, I have had the fortune of generous support to write at the Institute for Advanced Study, and I greatly appreciate the feedback from my colleagues there.

Since arriving at the University of Minnesota, I have had an incredibly supportive group of colleagues, mentors, and readers: Evelyn Davidheiser, Rod Ferguson, Riv-Ellen Prell, Kevin Murphy, Elaine Tyler May, and Kale Fajardo. I owe an especially great debt to Jennifer Pierce and Lary May, who read the manuscript and provided crucial feedback. Thanks to the "it's never too late social club," David, Josh, Jimmy, and Clint.

Over the years, I have benefited from feedback from a number of colleagues, Murtaza Baxamusa, Enrico Marcelli, and Abel Valenzuela. As I neared the completion of this manuscript and looked toward future projects, Peter Marcuse provided words of encouragement for which I thank him sincerely.

Years ago, my intellectual trajectory was forged with the graciousness and generosity of Steve Reyna, Nina Glick Schiller, and Les Field, and I am eternally grateful to them. My thinking about political economy, property, and economics has been profoundly influenced by too many people to list, but I must acknowledge Katherine Verdery, whose work continues to inspire and provoke me into thinking about these issues in new ways, as well as David Harvey, and the late Rolph Trouillot and Sharon Stephens, whose presence I have dearly missed.

This manuscript would never have reached full fruition without the remarkable and tireless work of the people at the University of Minnesota Press, particularly the support of Richard Morrison (who is sorely missed), Pieter Martin, and Kristian Tvedten, and all the rest of the staff who brought this work to life. Susan Clarke has been an especially supportive series editor, and I am grateful for her assistance. I owe a great debt to the two anonymous reviewers of the book; their contributions have been remarkably helpful. Thanks to Taylor Long for cartography and map production.

For more than a decade I have probed into people's lives, been to birthdays, funerals, and Quinceañeras. Friends and families of Sherman Heights, Grant Hill, Logan, Southcrest, Mountain View, Stockton,

Mount Hope, and elsewhere have come and gone, but I will always be privileged to have so much support and interest in this effort. Gracias a Marcia, José, Marta, Teresa, Brian "Lucky," and Jefe "Accion," and to Ving, Van, and Terry. And to the many families who invited me in and shared their stories; to the pan dulce champions, Maria and Donna; and Ricky, Terrance, and Brandon, thank you.

Thanks to my dear friends Antony and Jess.

Finally, I thank my family: my parents, Edward and Louise, and my tirelessly supportive wife, Bianet, and my wonderful girls, Lucia and Sofia.

Introduction

THE IMAGE OF the urban poor conjured in American popular discourse raises the unfortunate specter of lazy welfare abusers, idle ethnic minorities on street corners, and urban blight. This stereotype has been widely dismantled, and in more than a decade of my own research in San Diego's inner city, the figure of the welfare queen or vast swaths of career criminals lining street corners goes wanting for lack of evidence. There are very few people who fit this profile. Indeed, the vast majority of residents in San Diego's urban core have experienced dropping unemployment and crime rates for over a decade. In fact, the area has seen massive investment, both public and private, creating jobs and housing, and even new public services. There are challenges, however: despite the job creation, poverty remains high, the portion of working poor is staggering, and for these predominately Latino and African American communities, getting ahead economically is daunting. To illustrate these challenges, take the typical hard-working inner-city couple, Raymond and Monica, whom I have known since this research began over a decade ago.

Raymond is an enterprising thirty-year-old. He barely finished high school, but that does not prevent him from being a model entrepreneur, hardworking and determined. He gets up at 6 a.m. three days a week to drive his partner, Monica, around central and southwestern San Diego as they pick up four other people in his overcrowded, aging Ford Taurus. The last person to get in, Tony, is seventeen and small framed, so he sits in the luggage area in the back of the station wagon. They each pay Raymond five dollars for their ride to work at two downtown San Diego hotels. With the twenty dollars, Raymond pays for gas and pockets the rest. Each of these workers prefers the informal taxi service most mornings because it is more reliable than the bus system, and they get to work quicker (the bus ride for some is over an hour, but in Raymond's car it is only fifteen to twenty minutes depending on who gets picked up first). After dropping Monica and their other co-riders off downtown, he drives across town to work part time at a car garage/gas station, where he does minor repairs like rotating tires and sometimes works at the cash register. After taxes, he typically earns $900 a month from the garage, but he adds to that the $60 he makes as an unregistered taxi during the week, for another $240 tax free per month. In addition, he works for himself doing odd car repairs, washing, detailing, and bodywork for people in the neighborhood.

This work has grown somewhat over the past few years since he began. In a good week, he'll earn $75 from this work, but he says he averages about $150 a month from his side jobs, again tax free as it is paid cash in hand. Thus, his total income runs around $900 after taxes from his regular part-time job; with his cash-in-hand work of being an informal cab driver and doing odd car repairs, he earns another $390 or so, bringing his monthly income to around $1,290, or $15,480 per year. He often does not file taxes, because his official earnings are so low, and when he does he uses the 1040EZ—"What I've always used, even since working in high school." He is too wealthy and has too much in assets (a car) to qualify for most public assistance, and he does not rely on any. He pays a premium to get coverage with his partner for health insurance through her job, but it is so high that some months he stops paying, and then reinstates it later when they have enough money.

When I first spoke to Raymond about his job prospects he described looking for work at temp agencies, in factories, and even the shipyard, but his limited specialized skills kept him bouncing from job to job until he settled in on his current "entrepreneur" approach. As he puts it, he likes the freedom of working independently and earning his own money, being his own boss. On the downside, however, he will never get health insurance through his job or be able to afford it, he relies on MediCal, he does not have any real career ladder he can climb, and there is no real "on-the-job training" offered; he is going it alone, and most of all, he engenders a great degree of economic risk. If his car needs a major repair, then his informal taxi business is bust; if he gets injured or is somehow unable to do his side repairs, then that income stream is at risk; he does not qualify for unemployment insurance through his cash-in-hand work, and he has no retirement funds. The greatest problem, from his perspective, is that his income is limited. He can't become a cab driver full time, nor can he do more car repairs or charge more for them (his clients are mostly poor themselves and can't get the work done at a regular repair shop), and he can't rely on full-time work at the gas station. As a result, he is, in his own words, "stuck": "I'm thirty now, sort of settled, I'm not going to get a computer job or go to school, so . . . unless something comes along I'm kind of stuck."

When looking at his options in the labor market, I raised the option of an apprenticeship program at the shipyard, not far from where he lives. He had considered it and even applied twice, but the first time he was rejected for an unknown reason, and the second time he was approved to start, but then declined because he wasn't going to be paid enough during the training program. Moreover, he feared investing a lot of time and effort to get tied to a specific career, which might leave him without a job if the defense industry cut back or the shipyard closed. Citing past rounds of defense industry cuts that cost thousands of jobs in San Diego in the 1990s and saw some major defense contractors fold up shop and leave the city, he said it was just too risky.

To some observers, Raymond's situation and outlook is frustrating; he obviously is a hard worker, why doesn't he just learn a trade or start his own business? The barriers to either, however, are multiple. During a spell of unemployment he fell behind on bills, damaging his credit rating, and he can't get any money to start a business, he explained. He pays in cash for everything now. Going to school is similarly problematic. The time involved and the costs are too great, as is the lack of a clear reward. He cited a friend who went to tech school for an electrician program. After paying several thousand dollars and spending a year studying, forgoing a lot of income at the same time, he could not find work. "Everyone wanted someone with experience, with the construction in the hole, there are experienced electricians everywhere. . . . Why hire someone out of school with no experience when you can get someone at the same price, but with years of work?"

Raymond could be the face of economic hardship in any American city. What is significant, however, is that he lives in a revitalized urban area with beautiful new apartment buildings, art galleries, shops, and lofts. This is not simply a product of gentrification or urban revitalization, but the very restructuring of the economy. Geographically he is in the middle of it. He is not isolated to a poor, inner-city ghetto; he lives in the midst of urban renewal. The barriers he faces are not spatial, nor are they racial discrimination in the labor market (he is white), but they are economic. The structures of opportunity have shifted, making it very difficult to attain any level of economic security or move up economically through greater income. This is not the result of lack of trying; indeed, Raymond and his partner do not receive any public assistance, even though they qualify for several programs. Rather, they are stuck by economic barriers that have been erected as the economy has shifted. Raymond stuck in a growing servant class economy of working poor in the inner city. In this volume, I expand our understanding of the urban poor and working poor, and critique efforts at urban revitalization for being driven by a set of ideological priorities rather than demonstrable outcomes that will improve the lives of those in a large inner city, and as such question the conventional wisdom widespread among planners, policy-makers, residents, and even many scholars that declining crime rates, booming downtowns and "creative class" enclaves of offices and espresso bars, and new sources of tax revenues represent progress. This is progress for certain economic interests in the urban economy; it is not widely shared, and indeed, it produces new types of inequalities and problems.

Raymond is no longer isolated in a poor urban neighborhood, but he has become less visible as new luxury condos and Starbucks expand into and around his tiny apartment building. As he and other low-income residents face displacement, move further to the fringes of the inner city, or find ways to remain where they are by stuffing themselves into more and more overcrowded housing, they are simultaneously more connected to urban revitalization, and yet more disconnected from it. They are more integrated in the sense that they face a more daunting, more contingent, and less rewarding housing market, labor market, and in many cases educational opportunities. But at the same time, these new realities of the changing economy of the inner city also push them to the margins. In short, it is like saying: "You can stay in the city, but you will find fewer housing options, less affordability, and fewer good jobs with decent pay. Get used to more low-wage service work. Enjoy!!!" Urban revitalization with its attendant new shopping venues, hotels, and new luxury high-rises, indeed, cannot exist without a large and growing class of low-wage service workers. This is, of course, not unique to San Diego. Key

Virtually every American city has undergone some form of urban revitalization, gentrification, and redevelopment over the past three decades, and with varying degrees of success. Get-tough crime laws and community-based policing, along with creative class and postmanufacturing urban economic development, are often seen as having transformed many inner cities for the better, despite concerns about gentrification, displacement, and fostering greater racial/economic inequality. Gentrification and displacement in New York, for instance, has become even more driven by developers and corporate interests, while antigentrification social movements are increasingly marginalized within the political sphere (Hackworth 2006). Meanwhile, in Los Angeles gentrification is often seen as either ruining the city or saving it (Simpson and Tavana 2015). Looking at San Diego, the general consensus appears to be that the city's urban revitalization efforts are a resounding success. Indeed, it is hard to argue with the windfall of taxes, new housing developments, expansion of the convention and visitor industries, and elimination of many of the seedier, run-down buildings and businesses that once populated the urban core in the 1960s and 1970s. But does this mean that this is a success? The answer depends on how we measure success, and as I argue throughout this book, taking a far more comprehensive look at urban revitalization and the impact on communities provides a more complex and less encouraging picture. It also allows us to see the deep, complex, and often intractable issues of poverty and the growing ranks of the working poor from new vantage points, and in the end, it offers us an opportunity to consider new policy options.

This book focuses on three distinct and overlapping topical areas: urban economic development and policy, changes in inner-city labor markets and the workplace, and challenges within poor inner-city communities with respect to such critical issues as social and financial services, and economic mobility. As such, each of the three sections of the book looks at these different aspects of San Diego's inner-city economy. Overall, what San Diego's experience shows us is that expanding low-wage service work not only was a misguided economic development strategy, but it in fact contributed to already existing problems and pushed some even further. Looking more closely at the struggles for those in the low-wage service sector, I find that like other research, the jobs pay poorly and have few avenues for career mobility, and that the labor market is flooded with too many jobs that do not offer much in the way of economic improvement or pathways to it. The contributions of this volume are less optimistic than much of the contemporary research on urban economic problems. Unlike studies of the urban poor, however, I find the issues that traditionally affect those in poverty also affect those who constitute the large and growing population of working poor (people earning twice the federal poverty line). Also, unlike many recent studies of low-wage service work (Appelbaum, Bernhardt, and Murnane 2006; Carré and Tilly 2009; Doussard 2013), which suggest that some firms may have better job quality than others and that devising strategies to promote these or improving job quality overall is an important policy option, I find that the overall quality of most service jobs is so poor and increasingly polarized that only substantial restructuring of the entire industry and business model would have any substantial effect. Finally, when looking at the issues the urban poor and working poor face regarding economic empowerment and economic mobility, the complex set of barriers or "poverty traps" they face are so interwoven and "overdetermined," in a sense, that even the most progressive urban policy prescriptions are likely to fall short: these would include increasing wages, improving union coverage, providing more workforce development and job training, and so forth. In sum, what the case of San Diego's urban revitalization tells us is that as cities shift increasingly toward more polarized, service-sector-dominated urban economies, the portion of those at that bottom of the income spectrum has not only grown, but they now face far greater barriers to economic mobility than conventionally assumed. This is in part because the barriers are everywhere woven through the increasingly unequal economy. This booming "servant class" faces polarized labor markets, low-wage and low-benefit jobs with few career paths upward, predatory and exploitive financial services from consumer credit to cars, dysfunctional public transit, expensive and risky educational and training programs (through things like for-profit colleges and technical schools), and so forth. Thus, in my conclusion and policy recommendations I argue for a more critical urban policy: one I contend must not just address pressing issues like the labor market, economic development, and so forth, but must fundamentally challenge the market forces that are driving these forms of urban inequality forward. As many other Rust Belt and Sunbelt cities look toward their inner cities for retail, tourism, and other service-sector-driven growth, San Diego provides a very cautionary case.

SAN DIEGO'S PUZZLE

Global forces—migration, the movement of capital, technological change, the globalization of housing markets—as well as endogenous forces like demographic change or industrial restructuring shape cities. Detroit is a notable example of how rapid industrial restructuring can affect a city, and other Rust Belt cities have faced dramatic economic transformation, especially during the past thirty years. Since the 1950s the study of "urban problems," such as chronic urban unemployment or housing discrimination, centered in these older midwestern or East Coast cities, and occasionally included Los Angeles. We know far less about how these concerns play out in the rapidly growing urban areas of the South and Southwest, in Sunbelt cities.

These cities have grown in somewhat different patterns than those on the East Coast or in the Rust Belt. They have slightly different economies and different geographies, which makes issues like concentrated poverty or challenges for the working poor unlikely to fit the pattern of the well-studied urban centers like Chicago, Detroit, or New York. Cities like Houston, Dallas, Austin, Phoenix, San Jose, and San Diego are also now large, globally connected, and significant metropolises, with newly emergent forms of urban inequality and stratification that are vital to understand as demographic, economic, and social shifts continue to transform the urban United States.

This book looks at San Diego, now the eighth largest city in the United States (by population). San Diego enjoys a public image of a sunny paradise: golden beaches, surf, and SeaWorld. San Diego is also, in many ways, at the crossroads of many critically important and intersecting global processes. It is part of the most heavily crossed land border in the world (San Diego–Tijuana), it is a central node in the transborder shipping and logistics boom in crossborder commerce with Mexico, and, like many California and Sunbelt cities, it has a very diverse, growing population, particularly with the ongoing influx of immigrants from Latin America. These factors make San Diego somewhat of a unique urban area to view how different economic and social forces are playing out for the poor and working poor in San Diego's inner city. San Diego is also a unique place to examine the issues of inner-city poverty and growing concern for greater numbers of working poor because it undertook one of the largest inner-city urban revitalization programs in the country. The entire downtown, contiguous with an entire zip code, and increasingly adjacent neighborhoods, experienced a more-than-thirty-year extended effort at redevelopment and economic development, using a range of federal, state, and local programs as well as attracting billions of dollars in private investment.

This effort took place in the center of the poorest urban communities: the urban core of the downtown and communities adjacent to it (see appendix Map 1). As such, this provides an opportunity to evaluate how this urban revitalization effort affected those in poverty or working and poor in the inner city, and how we might understand these issues in relation to broader debates about economic opportunity and inequality for lower-income urban populations more broadly. This is particularly germane to policy debates as the vast majority of public funding for San Diego's downtown revitalization was through redevelopment, which has as its stated purpose the alleviation of poverty, blight, and joblessness.

In my preliminary research I looked at the statistics for poverty and the working poor (defined as 200 percent the federal poverty level), for the downtown area and similarly poor adjacent neighborhoods that would be affected by the revitalization effort, both before and after the transformation of the area. The results are striking. After billions of dollars in public and private investment and thousands of new jobs created, the portion of those in poverty increased in the downtown area and remained relatively constant in neighboring inner-city communities, and the portion of working poor remained very high, rising in one area, but dropping slightly in others. Also, households with public assistance income dropped dramatically, while unemployment dropped slightly, but incomes overall remained stagnant or declined slightly (see appendix, Table A.1).

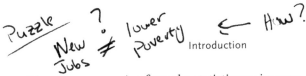

The picture emerging from the statistics on income, poverty, and related issues is that not much progress was made, and in fact in some areas poverty and the portion of those working and poor actually increased. This is despite a drop in unemployment and far fewer people on what is traditionally known as welfare: cash assistance.

The statistical picture in the study area (downtown San Diego and the adjacent low-income zip codes) that emerged was one of more people working, very few people on welfare, and in some cases unemployment rates reaching as low as the city's unemployment rate overall, but yet persistent poverty and stunning numbers of those working and poor (as much as 72 percent of households in one zip code). The deeper questions became: What was really going on in these communities? Why did thousands of new jobs in the poorest parts of the urban core not have much impact overall? How is it possible that poverty or the portion of working poor could actually *increase* in some of San Diego's poorest communities, despite thirty-year lows in unemployment and billions of dollars in investment, mostly by the private sector? Sorting out these puzzling questions became the center of this research project of more than a decade.

As I looked more closely at the labor market, changes in industry structure, and the economy of San Diego, the most straightforward answer to these questions is that urban revitalization in San Diego simply did not target inner-city poverty or the growing ranks of working poor directly, but like other studies of urban revitalization have shown (Hackworth 2006), the city embraced a neoliberal approach to urban revitalization, encouraging economic growth and development in the hopes that it would improve conditions more generally. That is to say, it was presumed that the effects of economic growth would "trickle down" to help even the poorest and economically disenfranchised. What occurred instead was the creation of thousands of low-wage service-sector jobs, concentrated primarily in the hotel/tourism and retail industries and a few others. The dramatic growth in this segment of the working poor I refer to as the servant class: those who work in occupations that provide a service to others, but for whom the wages are below what is a self-sufficiency wage for the city. The effects of these and other changes I consider as part of the broader, shifting political economy of San Diego's post-Fordist, service-dominated, urban economy.

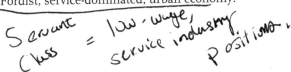

San Diego was indeed not explicitly "neoliberal" in its approach at the outset. The preliminary 1970s revitalization was aimed at bringing new retail and commercial enterprises back to the downtown and to redevelop vacant/blighted spaces. The landmark in this early effort was the Horton Plaza retail center; a suburban-style mall packed into an enclosed space over just four city blocks. As the effort in San Diego grew through the 1980s and 1990s, however, it more explicitly focused on using redevelopment authority and financing to attract and leverage commercial development.

RETHINKING POVERTY, OPPORTUNITY, AND INEQUALITY

Looking deeper into the communities, workers, firms, and families that make up San Diego's poorest inner-city areas, it became clear that the conventional understandings of urban poverty and economic opportunity, many of which have been resoundingly critiqued for years now, are not only inaccurate, but many of the assumptions and understandings of scholarly work on the urban poor do not fit the San Diego case very well either. For instance, in contrast to findings elsewhere that a dearth of jobs is the critical factor in isolated urban neighborhoods, thousands of new jobs have been created in San Diego's urban core. Every day there are hundreds of entry-level positions that require no specialized skills or education that go unfilled in Central San Diego (the term I use for the area encompassed by three zip codes in San Diego's inner-city area; see appendix, Map 1). In contrast to the notion that entry-level positions for lower skilled or disadvantaged urban workers can lead to a career ladder and greater rewards the more experience one gains, among the thousands of new jobs created in San Diego's urban core, far too many are in industries or firms that on average simply do not have strong career ladders. In contrast to assertions that the urban poor are financially illiterate or dependent on cash assistance through welfare programs, residents in the poorest communities have extremely low rates of public assistance income, and they have a great deal of financial savvy. One of the problems, however, is that they live in conditions of limited resources, and a lack of retail banks means that building assets and gaining a level of economic stability that would reap significant rewards in the long term is out of reach for most residents. These observations point to a structural approach to explaining persistent urban poverty, the working poor, and inequality. In contrast to the widely held culture of poverty arguments in the United States, which assert that individual attributes are to blame for these problems, structural approaches suggest that it is embedded structural barriers in the economy that are societal in nature. This does not mean, however, that my approach looks at simply structural factors; we have decades of research detailing these for a range of cities and circumstances, and the approach is too narrow to encapsulate the complexity of these issues.

Debates about urban poverty, growing inequality, and the working poor are typically constrained along a narrow explanatory continuum. At one end of the spectrum are structural explanations that view poverty as a product of structural forces within the economy that constrain and disable people's ability to get ahead economically, lack of job opportunities, failing educational systems, poverty-wage jobs, and so forth. At the other end of the spectrum are individual-level explanations that attribute poverty to individual shortcomings, such as culture or lack of human capital attainment. This oversimplification of human agency and social structure fails to grasp the interaction of individual attributes and decisions with social and economic structures and forces. Moreover, it continues to focus on the individual level of economic and social stratification, when approaches should move more broadly onto the actual structures and institutions of the urban economy.

My approach is to look empirically at the various institutions that are critical for the urban poor and working poor, and to examine them from a variety of different perspectives. This approach provides a complex view of the inner-city economy, and in order to understand the persistence of poverty and the working poor over time, it requires considering the behavior of the poor and working poor in relation to the structural parameters within which decisions and actions take place, as well as the effects of those decisions on the individuals and the structural forces at work. This approach is in part drawn from the understanding that poverty and forms of inequality can be recursive, such as the cycle of poverty research suggests (Bradshaw 2007). This book elaborates and extends the complex, cyclical approaches to poverty and relates them to more specific economic institutions in the inner city of San Diego and makes an effort to understand the growth and persistence of not just the poor, but the working poor who have higher incomes and theoretically should have broken through their low incomes into greater economic mobility. This latter issue is particularly important as there has been significant growth of the working poor in the United States but very little innovative policy debates about how to address the problem.

The idea that the poor start from a position of reduced resources and that this is in itself an impediment to getting ahead in life is not new. Gunnar Myrdal's classic work described American poverty as a product of "interlocking, circular, interdependence within a process of cumulative causation" (1944, 23). We can see how this process occurs more concretely at both the individual and spatial levels (of, say, a community, neighborhood, or larger area). Consider the following causal chain of events: a lack of employment or adequate wages can lead to inadequate savings, which means that there are fewer opportunities to invest in training and education or other forms of human capital. This in turn can lead to a continued lack of an ability to invest in businesses or in starting a business or in housing or savings or other assets, which in turn can lead to a lack of economic activity locally and further contribute to an erosion of markets and eventual divestment and overall economic decline. Within the cyclical approach we find other related theoretical constructs like path dependency and low-level equilibrium traps. These are all ways that provide different avenues to explain the reproduction of poverty and inequality. These constructs can be useful to analyze certain aspects of urban poverty, and I draw on them later in my discussion of different aspects of the overlapping forms of cumulative disadvantage that lower-income residents in San Diego face.

There is also the related issue of policy and urban and community development strategies that have a long history but often limited success, and which are deeply rooted in particular ideologies. While inner-city communities have been adversely affected by suburban migration, de-industrialization, and other forces of industrial restructuring and racial/class segregation and isolation, the role of public policy and the scholarship on poverty and the urban poor is notable for its inability to adequately address the underlying forces related to urban inequality. As Alice O'Connor notes, the history of federal policy works at cross-purposes with regard to addressing poverty. Local and place-based interventions or programs are aimed at addressing economically disadvantaged communities on the one hand, while large-scale public policies work in the opposite direction (O'Connor 2001, 79). Nowhere is this clearer than in central cities, which were targeted for renewal and urban revitalization in the postwar era. Inner-city revitalization was targeted with significant funds, while at the same time subsidies for home mortgages, commercial development, and highways drew more and more industry and relatively more affluent residents to the suburbs (79). Similarly, the effort to spur home ownership by pushing new tax credits and grants, as well as more loans from Fannie Mae and Freddie Mac, worked to provide low-income residents with an opportunity to purchase homes, and thereby secure vital assets that might not have otherwise been available to them. At the same time, banking and lending deregulation, particularly regarding the oversight of home loan lenders, resulted in waves of low-income individuals, most likely people of color, being devastated by fraudulent lending, misinformation, and bad loan products. More recently, community-based programs and grants have been undercut by broader economic policy that favors flexible, deregulated labor markets and has left communities with little recourse against declining wages, eroding public services, and the flight of banks and other institutions.

Historically, antipoverty efforts, federal policy, and what O'Connor (2001) calls "poverty knowledge" has become a widespread ideological field through which partisan politics operates, rather than actually addressing the real problems and concerns. A narrow focus on individual behavior, the use of rational choice models, and a preoccupation with welfare dependency reflect not sound efforts to address poverty, but the ideological dispositions of the researchers, policy-makers, and their broadly shared epistemology. Understanding poverty as a cyclical, recursive, and reproduced social problem, as well as the dramatic growth of the working poor and the role of urban revitalization and economic development, is critical to moving forward any productive approach to tackling these issues.

SITUATING SAN DIEGO

My focus in this book is on San Diego's inner-city revitalization, and the communities of poor and working poor that ostensibly were to benefit from a massive, multiyear urban revitalization effort. This was largely catalyzed through redevelopment powers under California Redevelopment Law, although there are other overlapping federal and local programs in these parts of the city. The reasons for focusing on this particular

set of communities and programs related to San Diego's inner-city revitalization are multiple. First, the issues of inner-city poverty, unemployment,
and racial/ethnic segregation remain serious problems in American cities (Goldsmith and Blakely 2010; Massey and Denton 1993; O'Connor,
Tilly, and Bobo 2003; Wilson 1996), but our knowledge of these issues
comes primarily from studies in northern, Rust Belt, or East Coast cities. With the boom of Sunbelt cities, their growing diversity, and clear
evidence of their own economic polarization, looking at San Diego's
urban core provides a new window into these important urban issues.
The second reason for looking at areas of San Diego's urban revitalization project as a research frame is the scale. With six redevelopment
project areas totaling more than 2,730 acres, and affecting more than
a hundred thousand residents in three zip codes that cover more than
15 square miles of San Diego's urban core, this is one of the largest
urban revitalization efforts on a number of dimensions. Additionally,
these areas that have undergone massive investment and revitalization,
the largest and most significant of which is the downtown area, are also
contiguous to the greatest concentrations of urban poor in the city. In
short, San Diego's use of public authority to transform its inner city over
a forty-year period provides an opportunity to assess the relative success,
how the urban poor have been affected, and to explore other economic
challenges that the poor and working poor of this city face. Lastly, while
San Diego's efforts are atypical in scope, they are not unique: other Sunbelt cities have ongoing or planned efforts to transform their older urban
cores, areas that also have some of the highest concentrations of inner-
city poverty and working poor.

How does San Diego's situation compare in terms of other Sunbelt
cities and other efforts at urban revitalization more broadly? San Diego
shares many characteristics in common with other Sunbelt cities. Economically, San Diego enjoyed much of the same economic booms during periods of population growth as other Sunbelt cities over the past
few decades, but the dependence of West Coast cities like San Diego
on defense and federal expenditures combined with recessions has
forced the city's economy into different directions. One of these was the
massive investment in tourism, convention business, and visitor services, and an effort to stay competitive with other cities across the United
States. This led San Diego, especially at the county level, to approach

economic development and planning from an industry-clusters approach. This meant pursuing and planning for specific industries like high-tech and light industrial manufacturing, tourism and visitor services, biotechnology, and so forth. All of these sectors are found in Sunbelt cities to some degree, but San Diego has particularly high concentrations of leisure and hospitality industries (BLS Industry Location Quotient Data 2013). Comparing industry and occupational employment citywide among large metropolitan areas overlooks the locally specific and spatially oriented dimensions of the urban economy. If we look more closely at the urban centers of other Sunbelt cities, then we can see the relative importance of San Diego as a case study on a more specific level.

As the urban core of San Diego is the location where this research was conducted, I look more closely here at other similar cities and their downtown/urban core revitalization efforts and low-wage service-sector employment. Table 1 shows the ten largest Sunbelt cities in the United States, ranging from Los Angeles at over 3.8 million people to San Francisco with 840,000. San Diego is a medium-sized Sunbelt city, but what is most striking is the relative similarity of servant class employment.

TABLE 1. Comparing Sunbelt Cities

	Population (millions)	Latino Population (percentage)	Servant-Class Jobs (percentage)	Inner-City Revitalization Effort?
Los Angeles	3.8	49	26	Underway
Houston	2.2	44	21	Planned
Phoenix	1.5	41	19	Ongoing
San Antonio	1.5	63	25	Planned
San Diego	1.35	29	25	Ongoing
Dallas	1.25	43	22	Underway
San Jose	1	33	18	Ongoing
Austin	.885	35	20	Ongoing
Jacksonville	.844	8	26	Ongoing
San Francisco	.840	15	24	Ongoing, and Planned

SOURCE: U.S. Decennial Census 2010. Servant class jobs are sub-self-sufficiency jobs that provide services based on BLS occupational data. Inner-city revitalization efforts determined by city planning documents, current district plans.

Despite the differences in size, location, or portion of Latinos (who are viewed as supplying much of the labor to Sunbelt cities for low-wage service work), the portion of overall employment that is in services but does not reach that city's self-sufficiency wage is remarkably similar. The portions of sub-self-sufficiency wage service work range from 18 percent in San Jose to 26 percent in Jacksonville and Los Angeles. This suggests that the industry and occupational matrix of each city, despite a great deal of diversity, still have around a quarter of the employment in low-wage service work. San Diego, therefore, is not unique at all in having a large low-wage service sector. Where the differences emerge is in the extent and concentration of the jobs in each city.

Table 1 also shows the extent of downtown revitalization in these cities. Each city has had over the course of many years, even decades, different attempts to revitalize their urban cores and the areas surrounding the downtown. Each of these cities has used different resources and approaches, and at very different scales (in terms of private investment and size, San Diego's downtown effort remains the largest to date). Los Angeles, Phoenix, and Dallas all have significant efforts underway, while San Antonio, Houston, and San Francisco have projects that are planned, but not fully underway yet. The remaining cities have ongoing revitalization efforts, relying on overlapping programs and different mixes of public and private ventures. Another commonality is that in terms of the spatial distribution of poverty and working poor, all of these cities have older, urban centers with the highest rates of poverty and working poor either surrounding them or nearby, making reinvestment and redevelopment in these areas an opportunity to address these issues.

The best comparisons for inner-city revitalization programs include those that have been long-standing and had significant numbers of new jobs created. San Jose has undergone downtown revitalization efforts similar to those in San Diego. San Jose's downtown, like San Diego's, became economically depressed in the 1970s as businesses and even the city hall relocated, some to outlying areas of the city, some outside the city altogether. Redevelopment and planned economic development with subsidies were implemented starting in the 1970s, similar to in San Diego. The difference between the two is scale. San Jose's downtown revitalization has leveraged 2 billion dollars in private investment compared to San Diego's nearly 15 billion. The other significant difference is the smaller portion of lower-wage service employment anticipated with the completion of the current and future planned projects in San Jose. Jacksonville also has a long-standing downtown redevelopment effort underway. That city's approach and strategic planning mirrors San Diego's in that it emphasizes the visitor services as a major component of inner-city economic development. The major difference is that retail and hospitality only serve as a minor portion of completed, supported, or planned development projects. This echoes similar industrial mixes in Sunbelt revitalization projects: they vary greatly depending on the city's development priorities, politics, economy, and so forth.

Phoenix also has a similar historical trajectory to San Diego in that both downtowns and adjacent neighborhoods saw movement out of the inner city during the 1960s and 1970s, and the periods of revitalization did not begin to really take place until the late 1990s and 2000s. Phoenix, like San Diego, invested significant amounts of public money into infrastructure and attracting and conducting new development, but the industrial mix of the two were quite different. As a result Phoenix's urban core remains more rooted in a mix of uses including biosciences, the Arizona State University campus, and a new convention center. The mix of high-tech and educational facilities makes Phoenix's urban core far more balanced in terms of employment and labor market outcomes. This is in part due to geography: Phoenix has the space and adequate parcels for infill development that San Diego lacks.

It should be clear that comparing urban-core revitalization strategies and outcomes is complex and fraught with difficulties. San Diego, San Jose, Jacksonville, and Phoenix are very different cities with different economies and politics. They do all have mixed-use revitalization strategies ongoing or in place for their downtown and urban core more broadly, and all of these have some level of service-sector employment embedded within them. The variation, however, is quite great. In Table 2, I chart out the estimates of low-wage service-sector growth in each of the inner-city areas that are undergoing plans for revitalization either through the city, with a nonprofit, or, in some cases, with a private nonprofit or development corporation. Based on the development type and proposed use of projects currently under consideration, I estimated the relative density of low-wage service-sector growth. If the estimated low-wage service employment is less than a third of projected jobs, then I ranked that as "low"; between a third to a half ranked as "moderate"; and "high" included any estimates that would see more than half of the jobs created being low-wage service jobs. San Diego, Houston, and San Jose all rank high on this list because of the large amount of planned or underway projects that are heavily concentrated in visitor services, retail, or other low-wage services.

We can see that while there is some degree of variation in how the inner cities of these Sunbelt metropolises are changing in terms of occupational and industry mix, it is clear that all of them have some level of low-wage service employment. The keys in variation appear to be the path-dependent nature of much of the urban revitalization plans combined with the political landscape surrounding development. In the case of San Diego there was clear push by certain industries to expand visitor services and retail. In the case of Phoenix there was political movement to get academic and high-tech employers downtown; while in San Jose an entirely different set of priorities is at work. With limited developable

TABLE 2. Comparisons of Inner-City Service-Sector Growth

City	Rate of Low-Wage Service-Sector Employment Growth in the Urban Core	Planned Expansion of Low-Wage Service Industries in the Urban Core?
Los Angeles	Low	Yes
Houston	High	Yes
Phoenix	Moderate	Yes
San Antonio	Moderate	Yes
San Diego	High	Yes
Dallas	Moderate	Undetermined
San Jose	High	Yes
Austin	Moderate	Yes, mostly built out
Jacksonville	Moderate	Yes
San Francisco	Moderate	Yes

SOURCE: Based on SIC industry codes for less-than-self-sufficiency wage industries and on planned and current employment. Estimated rates of low-wage service-sector employment growth are based on current square footage of planned development or projected development by industry type. High growth is more than 50 percent of total estimated employment growth, medium is indexed at 25–50 percent, and low growth indexed at less than 25 percent. Planned expansion of low-wage service industries is based on community and district plans for inner-city development combined with current development projects under approval.

parcels, and with political and planning priorities to have mixed uses in San Jose's urban core, the main efforts were focused on attracting employers in the information technology industry, and on the development of office space, as well as visitor services and retail. San Jose and San Francisco are two of the top "creative class" cities reflecting the recent push to make inner cities amenable to developing twenty-four-hour work/play spaces for higher-wage industries.

This demographic has been variously described as the "creative class" (Florida 2002), or as "smart labor" working in "innovation jobs" (Moretti 2012). This is the result not of federal antipoverty programs, charges Edward Glaeser (2012), but of urban economies attracting the right people with the right education to produce the right economic results. There are problems with this assertion that the new urban economy has supplanted the problems of Rust Belt cities, or that recalcitrant problems like poverty and inequality have been erased by tourism and service-driven urban revitalization. Part of this is simply a selective reading of how cities have been transformed: looking at the new shiny parts while neglecting the other aspects of urban economic restructuring. This is precisely the case that San Diego illustrates.

THE SERVANT CLASS EXPANDS

San Diego may appear on the surface, like many other rapidly growing Sunbelt cities, to be an urban area that has not only escaped the urban crisis of endemic inner-city poverty and joblessness but has accelerated far past it to become a new model for urban revitalization and postindustrial, service-sector driven employment. As Raymond's case makes clear, and what I will focus on in the rest of this book, is that this is an erroneous conclusion. In fact, there are two cities that have emerged in the contemporary urban economy. The first touts the high-wage, high-tech enclaves like the information technology, finance, and biotech sectors around the University of California, San Diego, campus in La Jolla; the other city is interwoven with the first, and it includes the communities in this study, places like Logan Heights and Chollas View where people like Raymond live and work. Those in high-wage occupations remain a small segment of the city economy, but they and others in households in the middle and upper incomes, consumers, and businesses are supported by large and growing ranks of low-income residents and workers.

I begin this book with Raymond's work and labor market experiences because he exemplifies the experience of so many of the expanding class of the new working poor and those "near poor" in American cities. They are part of a growing class of people for whom the "formal" economy is not working, but the off-the-books, cash-in-hand, informal economy is not a solution. Moreover, they are often, as Raymond describes, "stuck," with few options for economic or occupational mobility, and remain mired in an economy that is providing too few jobs, and too few jobs that provide wages, benefits, and opportunities to move up into a career. Raymond's predicament reflects his position in a growing servant class: a situation in which the barriers for full social and economic inclusion into society (which I view centrally as a function of economic opportunity and a level playing field of economic policies that treat people equally) have made it impossible to "get ahead."

How does Raymond's situation become a natural product of economic restructuring?

As a result of these new forces reshaping the inner city, a growing demand for low-wage and poverty-wage employment was expanding greatly at the same time that social safety net programs were being cut back. The result of these changes was greater economic security for vast parts of the inner city, precisely when it was being revitalized. Moreover, avenues for opportunity have changed because with fewer resources and shifts in the urban labor market, access to increased incomes or career mobility has become more challenging. This has led to a reproduction of a more highly stratified class structure, even as inequality by some measures (gini coefficient, racial segregation) have declined in San Diego, as in other Sunbelt cities. As a result, the urban poor and working poor in central San Diego have responded with a range of economic strategies, including working in the informal economy and taking on more debt and hence economic risk. These were not abstract market forces that produced the new urban inequalities; rather, they were a combination of market forces combined with policies undertaken over a period of thirty years or more; policies from the federal, state and local level that did not put new regulations on the private sector, but instead removed them. Capital was deregulated and promoted, even subsidized, while the poor, particularly immigrants and those on welfare, faced more and more restrictions. Moreover, what was transformed were not simply the inequality and class structure, but inequality of opportunity, as the costs of being poor grew, and opportunities in the labor market, via social safety nets, shrunk.

STUDYING URBAN TRANSFORMATION: DATA AND METHODS

This book began as a straightforward labor market study in low-income communities in central San Diego in 2002 and has expanded in the years since then. I began this project while I was a postdoctoral scholar at UCSD, and also working as a researcher for the Center on Policy Initiatives in San Diego. The central research questions I had at the outset were simple: what are the barriers to employment among the unemployed? and what are the skills deficits that low-wage residents had, preventing them from getting better jobs and earning more? It was clear almost immediately while I was conducting the first labor market surveys of the area that these questions were far more complex and difficult to address than anticipated, and were part of broader structural shifts in the local, regional, and national economy. Instead of a simple research report, the project turned into a decade-long study of urban transformation, poverty, labor market dynamics, and economic opportunity.

My main concern methodologically has been to be as empirical and analytically rigorous as possible. Studies of urban inequality and lower-income residents have typically drawn on large multicity surveys (Farley, Danziger, and Holzer 2000; O'Connor, Tilly, and Bobo 2003), while more qualitative studies have provided in-depth analyses of commu-nity change and illuminated many aspects of urban inequality, poverty, and the changing structures of opportunity for low wage workers (Anderson 2000; Dohan 2003; Venkatesh 2009). There are strengths and weaknesses to both qualitative and quantitative approaches, which is in part why I draw on both over the ten-year-plus period.

Methodologically, my approach to these issues draws on both ends of the research spectrum, combining survey data and analysis of census, employment, and labor market and occupational and industry data, with ethnographic, qualitative information. Each of these sources is discussed more in the appendix, including more specific information on the randomized sampling of residents over several years (N=421) in the study area zip codes. This approach became necessary, as the research questions I sought to answer are not easily assessed by any single perspective or data set. Indeed, some of the approaches here are methodologically innovative in that they involve new ways to approach some questions using data that has not been analyzed or combined in the way I have here. For instance, in chapter 2 I combine individual case studies with a quantitative analysis of several industries using Bureau of Labor Statistics Staffing Pattern Data to develop a quantitative measure of the change within career ladders among key service-sector industries over time. In chapter 6, which focuses on the informal economy, one of the central concerns I have is to establish the size and scope of informal work, and to estimate why people engage in such economic activity. This necessitated not only conducting a survey of residents in the study area zip codes, but also developing a regression model to predict the pathways into informal work, but again, this quantitative data is combined with important qualitative insights.

There is an additional issue related to methodology worth noting: *who* is in the study. While the ethnographic data and sampling frame are geographic, they are also broad in scope to gather information that usually is not obtained in studies of the urban poor: those earning incomes higher than the poverty line. As Katherine Newman and Victor Chen (2007) point out, most public policy debates on the urban poor focus on those in desperate poverty—at or below the federal poverty line. What is missing from the debate is the dramatic growth in what they refer to as the missing class—those who are between 100 and 200 percent of the poverty line. In many ways the missing class is invisible, both in academic and public policy debates, as well as our popular culture. This is in part because the missing class "does not live in neighborhoods mired in concentrated poverty; it lives in gentrifying enclaves that have seen both improvement and dispossession." "At times," they continue, "they feel like outsiders in their own communities, yet they readily admit that they now live in safer, more prosperous places" (Newman and Chen 2007, 204). This class "is not floundering in the labor market with no skills but have instead become repositories of work experience, even if those track records are newly minted" (204).

What Newman and Chen describe is indeed both a quantitative and qualitative shift in the nature of urban poverty and socioeconomic stratification. Following their insightful analysis, the sampling frame for this survey did not include an income limit. This ensured that people earning more than twice the poverty line—those who are in the "missing class"—were included. Indeed, one of the central goals of this study from a methodological point of view was *not* to focus solely on the poorest, but also include those up to and including lower-middle-income residents (those earning up to three times the federal poverty line, often those termed "the near poor") in order to better understand how the shift in the economy has strained people's economic standing far beyond just those at the poverty line or below.

OVERVIEW

As I have described, this project engages with three distinct and intersecting areas of research: urban policy and economic development, changes in the labor market and employment over the past thirty years, and conceptualizations and debates about the urban poor and working poor. To examine different aspects of the lives of the working poor and urban poor, I focused on three areas of research. The first part, examined in part I, entails looking at the broader political and economic context of San Diego's urban revitalization effort. What we find is that the inner city was transformed dramatically, reshaping the downtown through thousands of new jobs, development, and housing, but the effects of this were to flood the local labor market with thousands of new, low-wage, service-sector jobs. This reshaped the labor market, but with some very negative effects. Understanding the local labor market as an economic institution influencing people's lives is a vital part of piecing together the explanation for why the impact of San Diego's revitalization was so limited and in many ways was severely flawed.

In the second part of the book I move to another critically important economic institution: the workplace. By looking at two of the largest low-wage service-sector-employing industries in the inner city, hospitality and retail, we see how the quality of jobs has very limited impact in terms of lifting people out of the ranks of working poor, and can have adverse effects. One of these potentially negative impacts is the discouragement of workers from formal labor-force participation, and the growing incentive for people to seek work in the informal economy. As such, we can see how the erosion of job quality in the local labor market may actually encourage an expansion of work in the informal economy.

Finally, in the third part, I examine household and individual economic decision-making from a highly localized context. Often studies of the working poor are done at a national, state, or city level with survey data; more localized ones tend to be ethnographic. My approach has been to attempt to link together the very local-level processes to larger ones in order to construct an overall picture of what I refer to as structures of cumulative disadvantage. This is the basic idea from cycle of poverty research, stretching back to Gunnar Myrdal, that one cannot look at economic inequality and urban poverty and the growth of the working poor without seeing how different aspects of the local, regional, and broader economy interact to reproduce and reinforce the structures of social inequality.

PART I

Changing Urban Fortunes

Subsidizing Capital and Expanding Low-Wage Work

IN THIS CHAPTER I chart San Diego's development and revitalization of its urban core along the lines of other trends often labeled "the new urbanism," or urban entrepreneurialism. To put these shifts in municipal governance and inner-city revitalization in context, we can see connections to the broader political and ideological shifts at work since the 1970s.

Since the 1970s, growing inequality, declining economic mobility, and an erosion of standardized work and wages for most Americans has reshaped the postwar U.S. economy. The dominant shift throughout the 1980s and 1990s saw more neoliberal economic policies adopted at the federal level and below. These coincided or overlapped with urban devolution, reduced federal funding for urban renewal programs, a shift toward more conservative-favored efforts like enterprise zones, and the elimination of welfare as a system of income supports during the Clinton Administration. We can add to this list the shift in labor markets, inner-city abandonment/white flight, and a host of other rising problems in American cities. All of these changes resulted in growing income inequality and greater economic and labor market polarization overall, and they left many inner-city residents isolated and with high rates of joblessness. These forces, combined with a more punitive neoliberalism that combines "get tough laws" with high rates of incarceration, dramatically altered the landscape of many cities (Soss, Fonding, and Schram 2011; Wacquant 2009). During this same period, from 1970 to the present, urban revitalization, particularly in inner cities and downtowns, has been heralded as transforming many once-blighted areas to booming urban hubs.

This abbreviated account of these major trends reflects San Diego's trajectory as a changing urban economy. Within this broader context, the more specific history of urban policy and urban revitalization provides the context for San Diego's inner-city transformation.

URBAN REVITALIZATION?

Looking at recent scholarship, it seems American cities are undergoing something of a renaissance. Urban centers with decrepit downtowns are now homes to revitalized shopping and commercial areas, luxury lofts, and a broader "back to the city" movement. The comeback of cities has been discussed for more than a decade now. In 2000, after analyzing the preliminary 2000 decennial census data, Grogan and Proscio argued that "the American inner city [is] rebounding—not just here and there, not just cosmetically, but fundamentally. It is the result of a fragile but palpable change in both the economics and the politics of poor urban neighborhoods. Though not yet visible everywhere, the shift is discernible in enough places to unsettle longstanding assumptions about the future of older urban communities" (2000, 1). Changes in urban governance combined with new investment strategies and redevelopment transformed inner cities, but broader economic and political shifts took place as well. The new inner-city and urban-revitalization efforts have shifted dramatically toward a more cultural capitalism: emphasizing consumption and private-sector development while eschewing state-led development or targeted poverty-alleviation goals. These approaches have transformed many inner cities, adding entertainment and business-oriented facilities such as festival marketplaces and entertainment districts (Boyer 1992; Hannigan 1998), sports arenas (Chapin 2004; Noll and Zimbalist 1997), convention centers (Sanders 2002), and office complexes (Fainstein 2001). Public funding and focused public resources have been used for tourist development and for arts and cultural centers to attract both visitors and new "creative class" residents (Grodach 2012). Baltimore has a revitalized inner harbor and baseball stadium in Camden Yards; Los Angeles has an expansive redevelopment and enterprise zone; and other cities have seen urban gentrification dramatically transform much of the local and regional economy.

In San Diego, the approach to economic development has also been shaped by the trendy approach of creating industry clusters and chasing "creative class" jobs. The San Diego Association of Governments (SANDAG), which serves as the policy- and research-oriented arm of county governments, frames regional decision-making for the San Diego region. Much of the push from this decision-making process has been to consider San Diego's regional economy as a set of industrial clusters, an approach emerging in the 1990s as a way to think of regional economic strengths and how to combine industry and businesses to have a prosperous regional economy. Much of the research is centered on the business environment, locational theory, site-selection, and agglomerative effects of industry clusters. In San Diego tourism/visitor services are one of a number of clusters highlighted for development, as are the high-tech, biotech and other industries oriented toward the creative class. There are two fundamental problems with the approach, however. First, it does not address the issues of poverty, the working poor, or even labor market outcomes or housing; it is essentially aimed at getting the right "mix" of industries and businesses in a region. Second, by focusing in part on the creative class and IT/biotech industries, it does not address inner-city development per se as a place-based or focused economic development program. These types of industries do not meet the needs of the urban and working poor typically, and in San Diego they are located in the suburbs or fringes of the city, clustered outside of the poorer, inner-city neighborhoods.

These trends have been part of a longer historical shift. After more than fifty years of neglect and disinvestment, economically distressed urban neighborhoods have become the targets for reinvestment, but again, as I document in this book, for San Diego these are often the wrong types of investment in terms of labor market outcomes and addressing the problems of poverty and the working poor. By the 1980s the dominant urban development policy paradigm had shifted away from "smokestack chasing," in which cities competed for investment by offering lower costs (Strom 2002). By the 1990s and into the 2000s there was a greater emphasis not only on competing for corporate headquarters and service firms, providing tax abatements, and providing infrastructure improvements, but also making entire areas amenable to attracting the right workforce. This was part of a broader "back to the city" movement, led by developers and speculators as the returns to capital for building luxury lofts and leisure- and visitor-class amenities grew (Harvey 1989; Sassen

2001; Zukin 1995). As a result, cities have created appealing locations to market: enhancing natural and cultural resources, creating arts districts, providing new areas zoned specifically for recreation and recreational consumption (Clark 2004). As cities compete for the corporate headquarters of high-tech and biotech firms, they emphasize lifestyle and "creative-class" amenities. Thus, sports arenas, new museums, historic districts, and concert venues have become central aims in urban redevelopment. Moreover, city officials have become ever more aware of the economic importance of tourism and have put a great deal of energy into building and enlarging convention centers (Sanders 2002), building inner cities for the "visitor class" (Eisinger 2000), subsidizing new hotels, and attracting major retailers (Hannigan 1998; Judd 1999). These trends have become hallmarks of San Diego's transformation from a military base and small city to a city that is globally integrated with a downtown driven by service, tourism, and high-tech and convention business.

The most important urban revitalization program that San Diego, and most California cities, has implemented is redevelopment. In theory, California Redevelopment Law is very progressive, asserting that alleviating poverty is one of the central aims of redevelopment. The City of San Diego reiterates that

> Redevelopment Law was enacted to address deterioration and decay throughout California. Deteriorating areas become centers of poverty, overcrowding, crime, and disease for those who are trapped there, resulting in social and economic drains on the entire community. Redevelopment is one of the most effective ways to breathe new life into blighted areas plagued by a variety of social, physical, environmental, and economic conditions that act as barriers to new investment by private enterprise. (City of San Diego 2012)

In 2002 I had an in-depth discussion with a city staff member about the impact of redevelopment in central San Diego. When I asked how much the poverty rate had dropped in San Diego's inner city Redevelopment Project Areas since hundreds of millions of dollars had been spent to lure private investment, the staffer stated, "You'll see that sort of thing in the results, eventually, but it may take a while, poverty does not just go away over night, but you can already see the transformation [downtown]." When I pointed out that the latest census data showed the poverty rate had not moved much over the previous decade, despite the massive influx of new residents, high-rise condos, and public spending, he again stated that "change takes time." When I asked about programs targeted to low-income residents, he referred to a range of social service providers, including job training and ex-offender/reentry programs, but none of them were directly run by the state or any government agency. When I asked if the redevelopment, enterprise zones, or other programs beyond federal community development block grants (which do directly go to such programs) were addressing directly poverty or joblessness or specific populations in the inner city, he stated, "We don't do 'targeting' of specific populations. That's an org [local organization/nonprofit] function. We really target the whole area for urban revitalization." My reply was, "So how do we know that this broader effort will trickle down and help the most in need in the community?" He replied, "Again, we need to wait and see how we are doing in the long term." This view of urban revitalization is shared by the Centre City Development Corporation, a private nonprofit that leads up the central San Diego redevelopment efforts on behalf of the city of San Diego. A spokesperson at CCDC explained to me that "we have to wait and see all the buildings pencil out and then get filled before we see what types of jobs we have and how many there are."

These conversations, with a nonprofit representative and with a city staffer, both of whom are quite well meaning, serious about urban issues, and concerned about people living in San Diego's inner city, reflect the profound shift in both theory and practice of urban revitalization and economic development that has occurred over the past forty years. This shift has two main components, and these are part of the wider understandings of race, the urban poor, and the proper role of the social welfare state versus the marketplace. The first is that rather than having specific programs to target urban problems, the aim is more broad, to "target the whole area" of the inner city for economic development and revitalization. In other words, the state will not specify specific populations for assistance—the poor, blacks, Latinos, the homeless—but instead will encourage nonprofit and charitable organizations to do so, while it engages in "general development."

Place-based development vs. people-oriented development

← Does this ultimately just displace or (push) poor people into other places and reproduce poverty?

— What is the role of urban redevelopment programs in the reproduction of poverty (or elimination)?

Market-based, neoliberal approach to development in inner city

Here we see the market-as-panacea approach, embodied in the work of much libertarian and neoliberal thought that views the market as a "race neutral" social space wherein if people are simply left to pursue market-based exchanges, it will lead to the most stable and equitable society (Fukuyama 1992; Kuznicki 2009). This in turn has contributed further to the shift away from progressive policies of the social welfare state altogether in favor of regressive policies that promote the interest of capital and the private sector as a public good.

This further shift, promoting the private sector as a public good, is critically important because it signals a dramatic change in urban economic development practice. In contrast to the War on Poverty, which funded programs for urban development, the poor, job training, and other urban poverty and revitalization efforts, the new role of the state is aimed at subsidizing capital through redevelopment funding, enterprise zones, tax credits, and other forms of subsidies. Indeed, this is a national trend; the amount of corporate subsidies alone in the United States for creating jobs and other forms of economic development amounts to over $50 billion a year at the state and local level (LeRoy 2005).

In this chapter I detail the subsidization of capital through federal and local policy changes, look more closely at the ways that local economic development practice in San Diego has emphasized this approach, and then document how these changes have affected the broader class structure of cities, leading to greater polarization. I end my discussion of what I view as the remaking of the class structure through such policies, particularly the creation of a "servant class" in the inner city of San Diego—those working in the low-wage service sector as a result of the thousands of low-wage jobs that have been created in the process of revitalizing the inner city.

SAN DIEGO AND DOWNTOWN REVITALIZATION

San Diego's urban revitalization did not just emerge out of the context of deregulation and supply-side economic policies. Rather, San Diego's transformation and in particular its inner-city revitalization are a product of a long historical movement from a Fordist—that is, an economy based on manufacturing (and especially for the military) with relatively stable employment and wage structures—to one of a post-Fordist service industry–led economy with growing economic polarization and economic insecurity. San Diego has all the hallmarks of a younger, multiethnic, service-oriented city, with several globally integrated industrial clusters—notably international trade (the San Diego–Tijuana border crossing is the most heavily trafficked in the world) and growing information and biotech sectors, as well as a strong healthcare and education sector. Like many rapidly growing Sunbelt cities, however, this economic growth has been primarily in the suburbs and industrial parks of the city's periphery. The older urban core declined after the Second World War and remained on a steadily eroding path through the 1970s. The navy continued as a mainstay of much of the inner-city economy (notably the naval base and shipyard), but cuts in defense spending, the loss of some major defense contractors to overseas and out-of-state production, and the slow flight of smaller commercial enterprises resulted in a serious period of postwar decline. The downtown area, called the Centre City plan area, saw a downward spiral of declining property values, vacant buildings, expanding blight (defined as vacant, dilapidated, and unsafe structures), and a lack of employment opportunities. Crime, strip clubs, and vagrancy surrounded the municipal office buildings of the city, county, and state as well as some of the remaining private-sector employers. In 1975 CCDC (the Centre City Development Corporation) was established by the Redevelopment Agency of the city of San Diego as a private nonprofit organization to act as the redevelopment arm of the city of San Diego in the Centre City area.

The creation of a Redevelopment Project Area in the Centre City of San Diego addressed the need for urban revitalization, particularly because it has permitting and planning authority, but also because it can generate its own finances. The main financing comes through the creation of a tax increment finance (TIF) district. TIF districts allow the redevelopment agency of a municipality to collect the increase in property taxes due to the increased value of property within the district. Any increase in site value and/or private investment that generates an increase in tax revenues is the "tax increment." Tax increment financing thus dedicates tax increments within a certain defined district to finance the debt that is issued to pay for redevelopment. Thus, as a financing mechanism TIF creates funding for public or private projects by borrowing against the future increase in property-tax revenues. It is a risky proposition for cities and towns, as nearly one-half of all redevelopment project areas in California have been unable to generate adequate TIF returns in order to pay for projects and wind up failing (Dardia 1998). Redevelopment was absolutely critical to the CCDC project because without the capacity to use floating bonds to borrow from future revenues and generate tax increments, there would not have been any funding to catalyze the economic development in the area. In short, without this capacity, it is difficult to conceptualize how the area could have been invested in.

Despite the risks, redevelopment does offer advantages to catalyze economic growth. By using TIF and a broad set of powers from permitting and planning to eminent domain, redevelopment can foster new economic development, particularly expensive infill development, where the private sector may not have the capacity. With these powers, the CCDC could issue bonds and use different types of financing mechanisms for a range of plan area improvements from infrastructure to public services and thus provide a variety of incentives to leverage private investment in the project area.

The redevelopment project area has not gone bankrupt in San Diego, and in fact it has thus far had a history of success in terms of attracting new development and leveraging private investment. An award-winning example of redevelopment efforts is the Horton Plaza retail mall, located directly downtown, and its success is seen as catalyzing a growing interest by developers crowded out of other San Diego County municipalities and other parts of the city because of higher development costs and an ever-shrinking buildable land area. Horton Plaza has been followed by tremendous growth in retail, service, and tourist development combined with office developments in the 1980s and 1990s, including the construction of the convention center. During the recession of the 1990s the city of San Diego realized that it needed to rely even more on tourism as a revenue stream, and the Transient Occupancy Tax (TOT), paid by hotel guests, was seen as a major source of municipal income. As a result, by the 2000s a massive expansion of visitor services, including the expansion of the convention center, took place. Since the late 1990s the residential market had also begun to grow dramatically.

While the downtown area was undergoing a redevelopment-driven transformation, several other historical forces were influencing the restructuring of the city. First, the shift beginning in the 1970s of greater manufacturing and, more broadly speaking, economic competition globally, eliminated many jobs in manufacturing and other high-wage industries. This was combined with the concomitant rise in the service sector as well as the increasing push outward into San Diego County by economic development to seek cheaper areas of land and natural resource use. Instead of capital investment in manufacturing, higher-wage job sectors, or more stable, longer-term industries, San Diego's economy was increasingly driven by housing development and visitor services, and at the same time the city did not maintain adequate infrastructure spending to keep pace except for building more roads out of the urban core. Thus, as Hogan points out, "the economic growth of San Diego between 1972 and 1989 was based on a giant pyramid scheme in which surplus capital was invested in speculation on land use futures. Development . . . followed the rapidly proliferating maze of freeways, expanding in all directions to create suburbs" (2003, 48). This process was in part driven not just by the push of speculative land developers, but a neoliberal consensus surrounding federal regulations that fostered real estate speculation and hyper liquidity. Federal policies since the 1970s onward were aimed at encouraging the growth of real estate speculation, greater financial liquidity to invest in real estate, and new forms of financing real estate transactions. Additionally, tax shelters, deductions, and credits, combined with a growing pool of postrecession venture capital, accelerated the growing profit seeking within the real estate market. This was particularly strong in California where real estate had already been appreciating faster than in many parts of the country. Adding to this trend was the development of the secondary mortgage market. The introduction of new ways to securitize real estate debt, support and backing by Fannie Mae and Freddie Mac, and eagerness by investors to take advantage of emerging profits by investing in mortgage-backed securities and collateralized debt obligations all allowed a freer flow between investment capital and real estate finance.

With a flight from the inner city, fueled in part by deregulation, new incentives for land development, and investment, there was a greater push toward suburbanization. This push toward suburban sprawl, a failure to plan effectively, and the political clout of developers resulted in a devaluation and depopulation of many inner-city areas of economic activity, at the same time that millions of dollars in public funds were being used to redevelop it. This placed a greater strain on public finances due to ever more costly infrastructure and land development, but an intransigent political culture was unwilling to provide more public revenues to pay for such development (Erie, Kogan, and MacKenzie 2011; Hogan 2003). Thus, a reinforcing loop was engendered: to pay for more infrastructure due to city expansion, the inner city and other areas needed to be reinvested in, which meant paying for more infrastructure, and so on.

In fiscally constrained environments, but often with even more federal mandates, cities have been caught in a bind. In response, they have typically shifted even more closely toward a neoliberal form of governance, slashing funding for needed services and putting off painful cuts into the future, and in the case of San Diego, raiding the general fund and even defunding public employee pensions to ensure solvency (Erie, Kogan, and MacKenzie 2011). In addition to being encouraged to act more like businesses themselves, cities are urged to ally with the private sector to meet public needs, whether through privatization of services or promoting private-sector economic development. Thus, cities have been pushed to become revenue generators more than ever before, and by the late 1970s, municipalities started to use their submarket-rate debt-raising capacity to secure loans for middle-class homeowners, highly capitalized developers, and corporations (Hackworth 2007). As Hackworth points out, "the use of public debt for private gain became widespread enough for the federal government to intervene in the 1980s" (24). The Tax Equity and Responsibility Act of 1982 and the Tax Reform Act of 1986 were established in part to curb the most egregious uses of this privilege, but it is still entrenched in U.S. cities, particularly in special revenue districts. Thus, "public debt for private pursuits such as mortgages, sports stadiums, and miscellaneous commercial redevelopment projects . . . has become nothing less than an axiom of good governance" (27). It is not surprising then that San Diego's economic plans did not merge from "a rational planning process in which public officials take seriously their responsibilities for assessing the city's opportunities, prioritizing needs, and devising prudent and sustainable financing strategies" (Erie, Kogan, and MacKenzie 2011, 44). Instead of delivering a coherent assessment of city needs, San Diego's planning process has been co-opted by prominent business and civic leaders who can provide the costly resources necessary to sustain the costly efforts of turning blueprints into reality (Erie, Kogan, and MacKenzie 2011).

This transition toward greater fiscalization of land use and expansive urbanization has in turn placed greater strain on public finances—precisely those necessary for the redevelopment of urban areas and to support infrastructure in the aging parts of the city. At the same time, the TIF districts under the redevelopment agency were keeping tax increment, thereby reducing those parcels of land from the property tax coffers of the city as well. In other words, an increasingly competitive fiscal relationship between different parts of the city and between the city of San Diego and its neighbors evolved, giving developers more power because they were seen as a critical revenue and development source, and providing CCDC with greater authority because it was seen as a buffer against encroaching state regulation.

As a result, a vicious cycle developed. The city's economic incentives, particularly at CCDC, shifted from alleviating blight, creating jobs, addressing poverty, and building affordable housing to simply development for development's sake to maintain a growth in public revenues through new transient occupancy taxes (TOTs), which are paid for by hotel occupants, and the growth of TIF. This was needed because in order to attract more investment and development, new bonds and debt were floated to leverage private-sector development. As a result, the new debt required attracting more development to pay off the older debt . . . and so forth. In sum, fiscal concerns took the forefront of much of the apparent planning and permitting process, while the purported goals of redevelopment under California Redevelopment Law fell to the wayside. In the process, a massive push for new hotels, visitor services, a new baseball stadium, and other projects were pushed through, dramatically transforming the inner city.

FROM MANAGERIALISM TO MUNICIPAL CAPITALISM

These historical processes combined with the shift from urban managerialism, characteristic of urban governance in the 1960s to the municipal capitalism, or "entrepreneurialism" of the 1970s onward. These activities are, not surprisingly, in line with Harvey's (1989) analysis of the urbanization of capital through flexible accumulation, a means of providing more ways for capital to invest in urban areas to accumulate that were not rooted in the older Fordist economy of manufacturing and long-term sunk investments, but rather of speculative investments for short-term gain in areas like services and real estate given the increasing competitiveness for attracting capital in the global economy. Thus, municipal capitalism means that cities are now pursuing numerous new strategies as private- rather than public-sector actors. First, cities pursue innovative strategies to maintain or enhance the city's economic competitiveness in the global economy (in response to globalization). Second, cities use explicitly formulated, real, and reflexive strategies that are pursued in active, entrepreneurial fashion (referred to as operationalization of entrepreneurialism). And, third, cities market themselves as entrepreneurial and in the course of doing so they adopt an entrepreneurial discourse (thus establishing an entrepreneurial business climate). Many cities have also turned to partnerships with the private sector to obtain additional resources for redevelopment objectives (Frieden and Sagalyn 1991). To encourage private investment in ancillary development, cities are forced to invest greater public resources and authority in private-sector actors. This is precisely the direction the CCDC has taken for its development efforts, moving the decision-making and prioritization of economic development out of its own purview as a nonprofit corporation working for the city, to joint ventures with private developers.

Thus, as Clarke and Gaile describe, entrepreneurial cities rely on "market criteria . . . rather than political criteria for allocation and investment of public funds" (1998, 61–62), complex financing arrangements via public–private partnerships, and "contractual, contingent relations" between parties. They also note that entrepreneurial strategies are usually administered by quasi-public agencies, and decisions are arrived at via case-by-case negotiation rather than standardized decision-making. The entrepreneurial city is, therefore, distinguishable because it involves not only a reaction to globalization and the creation of a pro-business climate, but the use of specific, identifiable, and purposeful strategies (operationalized entrepreneurial activities) to promote economic development and the establishment of a new discourse centered on innovation and entrepreneurship (Clarke and Gaile 1998; Hall and Hubbard 1998). Using the distinguishing features laid out by Clarke and Gaile (1998) and Jessop and Sum (2000) as a framework, the city of San Diego can be said to have taken on the role of an entrepreneurial city in its choice of investments and its remaking of downtown into what has been termed a "place for play" (Fainstein and Stokes 1998). Investments in the Ballpark District, as well as an expansion of the convention center, waterfront redevelopment efforts, and the proposed expansion of the zoo, were undertaken to help ensure that downtown San Diego continues to compete in the increasingly competitive convention, tourism, and entertainment industries.

These shifts in public policy in terms of urban governance mean that rather than concern for public interests, the new growth politics and municipal capitalism meant that private-sector gain was tantamount to a public-sector good (Hall and Hubbard 1998; Roberts and Schein 1993). In other words, the best way to fight poverty and joblessness became not a public-sector project, or one with the targeted hiring of the locally unemployed and coordination with local job-training organizations or social service providers, or studying or evaluating the effects of redevelopment on the poor, but a private developer project where the benefits would ultimately "trickle down," to the neediest. As one local critic described it to me, "give big business what it wants, and hope that it all works out."

With all of these changes in the capacities of urban governance and the increased fiscal pressures put on the state and municipalities, we might expect redevelopment to focus increasingly on contributing to broader social goods, such as targeted poverty alleviation, job training, and so forth. This is not the case, however. The relationship of San Diego's downtown redevelopment with these broader trends is complementary, not conflicting. As many scholars argue, a neoliberal discourse—which endorses downtown economic development, fiscal conservatism, and retrenchment from redistributive social programs—has prevailed in New York and other cities since the late 1970s (Eisinger 1998; Petersen 1996). The result is cities pursuing largely their own fiscal and political ends, but deploying instruments such as redevelopment law—which is ostensibly aimed at blight, poverty alleviation, and affordable housing construction—to continue the growth politics of the city elite. As a result, this new municipal capitalism engages in a variety of activities to promote growth and infill development. Chapin (2002) suggests that these types of cities, such as San Diego, engage in several areas of economic activity, which makes the city or in this case redevelopment agency an enterprise driven largely by return on investment (for profit).

SUBSIDIZING CAPITAL: FROM CONVENTION CENTERS TO BALLPARKS

Looking at more recent redevelopment efforts in San Diego, we see that the shift from urban managerialism, with targeted programs for the poor and the most economically displaced, toward urban entrepreneurialism, where business growth is the main goal, has become fully realized. This can be seen in the continued flow of public- and private-sector money for development, but particularly in the funding of large-scale megaprojects requiring hundreds of millions of dollars of public investment and other concessions to private parties.

In San Diego, urban redevelopment and in particular the push for large, expensive projects became the proverbial goose laying golden eggs, generating massive revenues (as well as debt) but also creating potentially further revenue streams if the redevelopment paid off. The CCDC Redevelopment Project Area has seen a massive influx of private investment, more than $12 billion to date, but this has also been leveraged by $1.7 billion in public investment (CCDC 2012). The return, of course, is excellent in terms of fiscal accounts simply on a public/private investment ratio of 1:7.

None of this can happen without TIF financing. In addition to TIF financing, "gap" financing is also used. In order to maximize redevelopment efforts, it is preferred that redevelopment funds be used for closing any gap between what is possible for the developer to achieve and a project's total cost. All project proposals analyzed by CCDC include a financial proforma, identifying all costs anticipated for the project and demonstrating the developer's ability to achieve conventional financing prior to discussions regarding the need for assistance to close any existing gap. There is also the availability of direct financing assistance for projects, but this can only be provided to close any gap for the development of new low- and moderate-income housing projects. Other types of new development may be considered for indirect financial assistance, such as loan programs, land assemblage, or off-site improvements. Additionally, property owners throughout downtown are encouraged to work with CCDC to increase their property values through negotiated public–private partnerships, and gap financing can be provided in the form of rehabilitation loans to assist in accomplishing such projects. CCDC also finances public facilities, and can allocate funds for off-site public infrastructure needs necessary to make private projects work and accomplish redevelopment project objectives. Off-site improvements include street and sidewalk improvements, lighting, storm drains, and so forth. All of these improvements, as funded through TIF or bonds, represent the peak of municipal entrepreneurialism and a subsidization of capital.

The point here is that there is already a massive public subsidy nearing $2 billion in investment, much of it tied to bonds and future revenues, provided through TIF and gap financing. These revenues are not going into the broader tax pool or general fund of the city, but are kept in the redevelopment project area. Furthermore, the total subsidy to the private sector can be considered far beyond the $1.7 billion to date, as oversight and area improvements that support capital flows and investment are costly as well.

An additional dimension of these processes of urban revitalization is that the subsidies to capital are now made into industries that may be subject to significant volatility, particularly through national or global competition, and with limited consideration of the labor market or other impacts. Instead, growth for growth's sake and bringing in more municipal revenues had already become the priority. The three industries that have received significant subsidies and stand out are convention and visitors services and retail. Convention centers in the 1980s began a significant push for competitiveness, with new expansions and intensive marketing across U.S. cities, and the push to develop new professional sports stadiums also receives hundreds of millions of dollars in subsidies. These types of projects may or may not be in the fiduciary interests of their municipalities, depending in part on the terms of agreement for financing, or from the economic impact the proposed facility has in the long run. In the case of San Diego, a city with huge unfunded pension liabilities for city employees, significant deficits in public health and safety, including firefighting and other essential public services (Erie, Kogan, and MacKenzie 2011), and with poverty and the working poor expanding in many areas of the city, hundreds of millions of dollars have been found to support convention and visitors services as well as a new professional baseball stadium. In fact, the stadium development and proposed costs for a new round of convention center expansion combined total over a billion dollars (Erie, Kogan, and MacKenzie 2011).

San Diego's new convention center began as the brainchild of developer Douglas Manchester and was pushed by mayoral candidate Roger Hedgecock, being seen as a way to bring in more revenues and replace the old convention center, which needed significant repair and upgrading. Initially, developer costs were estimated at $95 million. Consultants considered the figure too low and would only provide 20 percent of the estimated convention space, and eventually the total cost ballooned to $164 million, to be funded by the port district (Erie, Kogan, and MacKenzie 2011). The convention center illustrates the close relationship between developers and their interests and the use of public resources under the banner of keeping San Diego competitive. Douglas Manchester already had long-term leases for lands the Port District held adjacent to the proposed convention center. A deal was struck between Manchester and the Port District to exchange the leased land to build the convention center, and Manchester would get a better parcel nearby to build more hotels. These hotels, of course, stood to be the primary beneficiaries of the convention center expansion. After opening in 1989, and with the recession of the early 1990s, convention center proponents argued for an urgent expansion to keep up with competition from other cities.

After a great initial start, the convention center had run a deficit of nearly $6 million by 1993. Continued deficits and pressures for expanding the convention center began almost as soon as it was completed. Plans to expand the convention center lumbered forward with political struggles over cost, financing, and how to bypass city residents' ire over funding such an expansion. By 1996 there were designs in place for construction, but no financing of the estimated $205 million cost, and eventually it was the Port District and bonds that allowed for the completion of the project. In 2009, there was concern once again that San Diego was falling behind as a convention destination. A new convention center expansion committee was assembled, and they produced an estimated cost for expansion of $750 million, with a cost to the city over thirty years of more than $50 million per annum. Recent estimates, with new pedestrian footbridges in place, put the convention center expansion at more than $780 million. A similar set of relationships between prominent developers and city officials fostered the development of the new base-ball stadium in the Centre City Planning Area. In addition to the flag-ship convention center, hundreds of millions of dollars have been spent on other projects, including Petco Park baseball stadium.

The new San Diego Padres baseball stadium, Petco Park, was opened in 2004. It was a product of a public–private partnership between the city of San Diego, acting with CCDC and the Port District, and JMI Realty, the real estate and development arm of the San Diego Padres baseball team. This partnership conjoined these entities into a number of agreements that codified the financing and responsibilities of different parties. Strik-ingly, a significant amount of land use and development rights was given away to JMI Realty. In particular, the company gained the ability to con-duct nearly unrestricted development in a twenty-six-block area border-ing the new baseball stadium and the East Village, the edge of the rede-velopment project area and the poorest part of downtown San Diego. Under the agreement, JMI would create new office buildings, retail out-lets, and affordable housing, as well as provide open space for use by the public. The city would provide upfront funding to help start the project, with JMI required to fill in more funding as the project was rolling.

In the final analysis, there was a $303.3 million investment by the public sector in the stadium, with the private developer committing $146.1 million. The ancillary development was modified later through negotiations with JMI, and it was able to avoid most of the requirements of the initial agreement (Erie, Kogan, and MacKenzie 2011). Together, the convention center and subsequent expansions as well as the new ballpark represent the classic "landmark" developments that cities have invested in, hoping to attract tourist dollars and raise revenues for municipal operations. These types of projects are driven not by debate about public need or pressing infrastructure deficits, but instead by a combination of elite politics and networks, and a neoliberal theory of social benefit. In other words, it is purported that the economic expan-sion and growth generated by these projects will eventually fulfill public needs through the generation of tax revenues and the creation of jobs (though there is no analysis of what types of wages and benefits will be paid by such projects).

We can summarize the policy and outcomes across different sec-tors of the urban economy as public and private monies benefit private entities first, and the public only indirectly. Developers are eager to look for public subsidies to support their private development. In the case of the convention center, the developer got access to prime land for hotel development. The city and Port District got new potential revenue streams. In a particularly conservative and challenging fiscal climate, the city of San Diego in particular saw convention center expansion as vital to continue to generate visitor revenue. The broader public would benefit from the use of public funds, notably bonds, because the potential future revenues would pay for themselves and add additional revenue to public accounts over time. In the case of Petco Park, despite much scrutiny and concerns that the project would not generate the type of revenues and benefits that were promised, private developers and the San Diego Padres received huge subsidies. The ancillary development around the ballpark has also occurred to some extent, but not in the way that it was originally envisioned, with the benefits to the inner-city communities still nebulous at best.

Comparing these cases, I argue, exemplifies the subsidization of private interests with the promise and faith that eventually public benefits will accrue. The central problem from the perspective of inner-city residents, beyond the immediate gentrification effects that raise housing costs, is that this industrial expansion is primarily in visitor services and recreation. This is a significant policy decision, and investment in projects that dramatically affected the labor market by expanding the low-wage service sector, creating thousands of low-wage jobs. The accommodation and food services industry (primarily hotels and restaurants) has the lowest median wage of all industries in San Diego, only $17,101 in 2011 (this figure is based on 2012 American Community Survey Data for San Diego). This public subsidization of low-wage job growth further expands low-wage occupational growth and the uneven development of the labor market and its stratification. This is precisely a trend that has already been in place in U.S. cities over the past thirty years, but this type of urban revitalization strategy merely sped it up, making the inner city more economically polarized in terms of employment, not less.

Are the jobs created by these massive public investments ones that will lift people and families out of poverty? Do they supply wages and benefits that will mean greater economic mobility and opportunities? Will they reduce poverty and unemployment in the inner city, as California

Redevelopment Law states is one of the principal aims of urban redevelopment? In the next section I look at the labor market impacts of the investment in the inner city, specifically what industries and wages have grown with this massive urban revitalization program, and how this new employment fits into the broader class structure of the urban and U.S. economy.

THE POOR, WORKING POOR, AND NEAR POOR

To put the wages of jobs created in context, particularly in relation to poverty and standards of living, it is useful to compare poverty with measures of the working poor and near poor as well as what is considered a self-sufficiency wage—a wage at which an individual can meet their basic economic needs in the city of San Diego. A self-sufficiency wage, which is out of reach for two-thirds of inner-city residents, means that some basic expenses simply cannot be met, on average. As Table 3 shows, even at double the federal poverty line (FPL), working in any of the lower-wage industries within the booming visitor-entertainment-sports downtown does not get someone to self-sufficiency.

TABLE 3. Comparative Income Levels from Poverty to Near Poor

Persons in Family	48 Contiguous States and D.C.	Working Poor 200% FPL	Self-Sufficiency Wage	Near Poor 300% FPL
1	$10,890	$21,780	$30,100	$32,670
2	$14,710	$29,420	Variable	$44,130
3	$18,530	$37,060	depending	$55,590
4	$22,350	$44,700	on the age	$67,050
5	$26,170	$52,340	of dependents	$78,510
6	$29,990	$59,980		$89,970
7	$33,810	$67,620		$101,430
8	$37,630	$75,260		$112,890
Additional person add	$3,820	$7,640		$11,460
Hourly wage for a single individual based on full-time, full-year employment	$5.64	$11.30	$14.75	$16.95

SOURCE: Federal poverty line in column 1 uses 2012 HHS figures. Self-sufficiency wage from http://www.selfsufficiencystandard.org (adjusted for inflation).

Table 3 also breaks down incomes on an hourly wage basis. It is not until $14.75 per hour that an individual reaches self-sufficiency in San Diego, and this is a general guideline based on a budget covering minimal basic needs. When unplanned expenses occur, or large expenses (such as a baby, medical bills, etc.), household budgets can be devastated fairly quickly. Even at the rate of $16.95, what I refer to as the "near poor," the income cushion available is still very limited in a high-cost city like San Diego. Take Rachel and Jim, married with a single child. Jim is a truck driver; he earns more than $46,000 per year, and Rachel works part time as a receptionist/secretary and spends the rest of the time taking care of her son. They earn approximately $60,000 per year combined. They are well above the median household income for central San Diego, but they have struggled economically for several years as inflation and housing costs keep eroding their income. "If you don't get a raise, you fall behind. When you fall behind, something's got to go." The problem for Rachel and Jim is that they are already stretched financially and are unsure what would be left to cut if either lost their job or had to take a pay cut. The most significant issue facing Jim and Rachel, however, is the same facing low-income residents of San Diego's inner city: the vast majority of employment created over the past ten to fifteen years has been in the low-wage end of the service sector.

Redevelopment and urban revitalization created thousands of new jobs, but these were mostly in the service sector, and the largest growth was in low-wage employment. The redevelopment of San Diego's inner city did bring thousands of new jobs, but these were primarily in the services and retail sectors. The visitor industry, serving firms in hotels, restaurants, and convention services, has created a lot of jobs, but these tend to be lower-wage jobs on average, and many do not support the standard of living needed in an expensive city like San Diego. Figure 1 shows the shift in employment over a thirty-year period since 1980, with most of the employment growth coming in services and retail.

The service sector, of course, is highly stratified. It reflects the most prominent economic polarization of the labor market, with high-wage service providers like law firms (the largest in the study area, for instance, had more than 350 employees and more than $33 million in sales in 2011), and lower-income service providers like some business services, cleaners, landscaping firms, and so forth. When looking at wages, the income

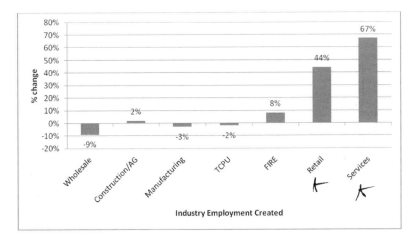

FIGURE 1. Industrial Shifts, Central San Diego, 1980–2010. *Source:* Author analysis of industry shifts based on Dun and Bradstreet data using Bureau of Labor Statistics SIC and NAICS codes.

polarization is very clear. While there is a good deal of employment in the high-wage jobs (above $40 per hour), most of the employment is in the lower-wage segment of the labor market (below $15 per hour) (Figure 2).

The wage distribution of the employment generated during redevelopment is clearly skewed toward the lower end of the wage scale, with 23,554 jobs, or 41 percent of all downtown employment, earning less than a self-sufficiency wage of $11.49 for a single adult, in 2011 dollars. Granted, a large percentage of workers are likely not to be single individuals or primary earners in their families or household, but the relationship to the self-sufficiency wage provides a guide to how much potentially unsustainable employment has been created. If we compare the median wage in the redevelopment area with the city ($24.04) and the county ($25.10), then 87 percent of the employment in the project area is below the median for both the city and the county. Furthermore, 60 percent of the jobs pay under $18.00 per hour, less than the median and less than the self-sufficiency wage for San Diego County for an adult and one dependent ($18.46–25.44, depending on the age of the dependent). This skewed wage distribution is not so much what we hear as an hourglass economy—middle-income jobs disappearing and growth at the top and

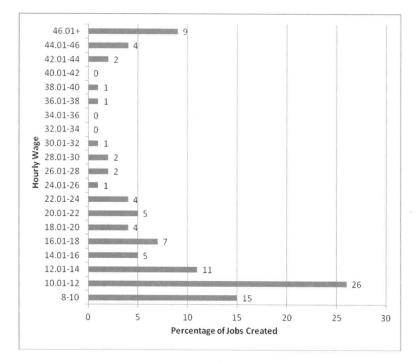

FIGURE 2. Distribution Percentage of Jobs at Different Wage Levels in Central San Diego. *Source:* BLS Industry Occupation Matrix, 2011; see appendix for data and methodology.

bottom of the wage scale; rather, this is a genie bottle distribution: the base is vast and growing, then there is a long but narrowing set of jobs through the rest of the wage distribution, until it reaches the top where it then expands again.

CONCLUSION

With new luxury high-rise condominium buildings, office towers, and retail stores, the inner city has been radically transformed in San Diego. While concerns of gentrification, a lack of affordable housing, and the transparency of CCDC operations have characterized much of the debate surrounding San Diego's urban redevelopment, my focus in this chapter has been to chart the transformation of the city's political economy in relation to broader shifts in state and regional economics. New regulations and fiscal imperatives encouraged redevelopment and tourism as a revenue stream. Pro-growth politics fostered this as well, and contributed to infrastructure stretched too thin to cover poorer communities, while visitor and tourist industries gained influence and grew exponentially in the inner city. Major industrial shifts turned San Diego's economy from a postwar military and industrial base to one built more on services and trade. As the shift-share analysis illustrates, while there has been a slight loss in manufacturing and transit and communications employment over the thirty-year period, there has been an explosion in services, real estate, finance, and retail industry employment.

In sum, the massive job growth in San Diego's urban core was driven by low-wage service-sector employment. Looking at the distribution of jobs and wages it is clear that these were not jobs that would provide self-sufficiency wages, nor did they require specialized education or training on average. Rather, the expansion of all this low-wage employment far outpaced any other labor market impact. Another conclusion to be drawn from this analysis is that San Diego's planning and economic development efforts as practiced through the arm of CCDC, a private nonprofit, made no effort to address the real aims of urban revitalization in terms of job quality, types of industrial and occupational mix, or outcomes. Rather it was political and fiscal factors that led to massive subsidies to developers and particular industries.

Key

o Revitalization

largely focused on development
private capital (e.g. hotels, business)
and promoted growth and
growth of low-wage positions

2

A Good Job Is Hard to Find

TAKE JENNIFER, KELVIN, MARCIA, AND MICHELLE, each hard working, in the labor force, but earning different wages and benefits: they illustrate the growing polarization of good versus bad jobs even in middle- and lower-income segments of the labor market. Jennifer, a truck driver with UPS, has good job stability, good benefits, and decent wages, in part due to her union membership. Then consider her neighbor, Kelvin, a pizza delivery driver. Some evenings he does well in tips, sometimes he is very poorly paid and simply works cleaning up the kitchen for an hourly wage. Marcia, an administrative assistant at a large nonprofit in San Diego, enjoys good working conditions—as she puts it, "helping people and working with a great office," and she has flexible enough work hours to take night classes that are leading to an associate's degree in human resource management. She hopes to use her degree and experience at the organization to move up into a higher administrative position. Despite the tight economy, her organization has seen some turnover, with openings above her promising to offer more pay and benefits once she has more experience and her degree completed. Contrast Marcia's opportunities with those of Michelle, who had a lot of work experience during her undergraduate years, who has a degree in English and was considering a master's degree in English with an aim of working in online communications or teaching or publishing, but who then decided to not pursue her MA as "there are a zillion people out there with English degrees already, even masters." Instead, Michelle remains working at a coffee shop where she has no real opportunities to move up; she remains mired in a low-paying hourly job, without benefits, and living at home, even though she has more work experience and education than Marcia does. The critical difference in career advancement for them is the quality of the job ladder that each firm offers. In short, the quality of one's job matters; it can have a very strong effect on one's occupational mobility over time, and ultimately one's economic opportunities in the long run.

Research on dual labor market theory has largely been with national-level data sets, or as specific case studies within industries. While both provide very useful information, less is known about labor-market segmentation and polarization when looking at more specific geographic areas, such as the inner city. One of the critical issues here is not just how polarized labor markets have become, but how they are socially constructed, and how policies to influence them may reflect ideological positions within economic or public policy (Peck 1996, 2001). This is particularly true of the efforts to portray labor markets as operating along the lines of some fundamental market-driven logic, or embodied by atomized workers as rational-calculative agents. Indeed, one of the central critiques of segmented and internal labor markets is that they reflect these underlying notions of market-driven economic models. In fact, even among insightful researchers like Michael J. Piore and Peter B. Doeringer (1971) they reproduce these very theoretical assumptions. Thus, in analyzing inner-city workers, they assumed that the segmented labor market provided an adequate explanation, when in fact the average American worker did not fit the standard model of neoclassical/competitive labor markets as much as they fit socially, culturally, and hence politically structured patterns—whites insulated from labor market pressure more than blacks because of inequalities based on race (Peck 1996).

JOB QUALITY AND SEGMENTED LABOR MARKETS

For decades, American society's discussion about creating jobs was fairly straightforward: the more the better, keep unemployment low. "Jobs, jobs, jobs" has been, and in many ways remains, the policy mantra from economists to politicians. For inner-city residents, this is one of the central arguments: that persistent poverty and low incomes are the result of a dearth of job opportunities, and that ultimately the only way to truly help urban poor is to provide more employment opportunities targeted to inner-city residents (Wilson 1996). Urban revitalization and targeted workforce development programs typically have focused on job creation and linking residents with jobs in inner cities. The problem with San Diego's urban revitalization, however, is not a lack of jobs, but job quality. As discussed in the previous chapter, the massive expansion of the low-wage segment of the labor market went far beyond what the needs were for entry-level positions. Rather than providing opportunities for the poor and working poor to move up the economic ladder, the over-abundance of low-wage and poor quality jobs merely created opportunities for prolonged employment in an ever-growing servant class.

The idea that job quality matters and that there are polarized or segmented job markets is not new. In 1969 studies of urban labor markets argued that the central problem facing inner-city residents who were living through high unemployment and high poverty rates was not the lack of jobs, but instead, a shortage of good jobs. Jobs for construction companies, hotels, and sweatshop manufacturers were available, but paid low wages, offered little opportunities for upward mobility within the firm or as a career, and had poor working conditions. Segmented labor market theorists showed that for many of these workers, blacks in particular, they remained in a secondary labor market, moving from bad job to bad job (Doeringer, Feldman, Gordon, Piore, and Reich 1969). This research dispelled the myth of a purely competitive labor market, showing how labor markets are segmented into different types of employment, good jobs in a primary sector and the bad jobs in the tertiary sector. Being trapped in a bad job and being unable to move into better jobs has been widely debated, and more recent studies show that nonstandard and contingent work provides further evidence that the portion of less desirable jobs has grown, though there are variations in how quality is defined (Appelbaum 1992; Barker and Christensen 1998; Carré 1992; Freeman 1999; Gonos 1998; Kalleberg, Reskin, and Hudson 2000; Polivka 1996; Tilly 1996). Nonstandard jobs or jobs that have less traditional work arrangements appear to have more sporadic scheduling, offer lower rates of benefits, and are more likely to pay low wages (Hudson 1999, 2001; Kalleberg et al. 1997; Kalleberg, Reskin, and Hudson 2000; Spalter-Roth 1997).

During the same period, since the early 1980s, there has been significant growth in immigration to the United States, with some evidence that the labor market is becoming even more polarized along the lines of immigration and citizenship status (Ehrenreich 2001; Hondagneu-Sotelo 2001; Massey 1995; Phillips and Massey 1999). Additionally, noncitizen and immigrant workers have great difficulty obtaining jobs in the primary labor market (Catanzarite 1998, 2000, 2002; Catanzarite and Aguilera 2002; Chiswick 1988; Chiswick and Sullivan 1995; Funkhouser and Trejo 1995).

JOBS AND JOB QUALITY

The idea of segmented labor markets has been around for quite some time, but what has typically been neglected in studies of job quality today is that the lack of good employment opportunities has hampered poorer urban communities for decades. By the time that significant urban revitalization began to transform inner cities during the 1990s in places like San Diego, decades of low-wage jobs had already taken a significant toll on poorer communities. Recessions in the 1970s, 1980s, and 1990s had each put the economically marginalized of San Diego's urban core on an economic roller coaster.

As the expansion of low-wage and service work has expanded throughout the past two decades in central San Diego, this merely exacerbated an already segmented labor market. This reflects the broader trend of a clear inequality developing in the labor market between good and bad jobs that has expanded with the decline of manufacturing employment in the United States. This is not a temporary condition: it is instead now a structural feature of the changing U.S. labor market, with precarious employment systems that encourage more market-mediated labor force mechanisms, the removal of institutional protections, and the decline of union power. These are not new, but systematic restructurings that have developed since the 1970s; they are not part of the business cycle or temporary conditions, but more stable and permanent features of an increasingly polarized labor market (Kalleberg 2011, 15). Cost pressures and employers' desire to shift fixed costs and the risk of employment to employees, driven in part by the decline of worker protections, has reduced the proportion of workers in the United States with health and pension benefits from their employers and eroded their capacity to bargain or maintain wage levels (125). Thus, the issue of eroding job quality has emerged at the same time that rapid employment expansion has taken place in previously distressed inner-city neighborhoods. To put it directly, a lot of jobs have been created for the poor and unemployed, but they are not very good jobs, and they do not necessarily lead to greater economic self-sufficiency. The same types of labor market polarization found in the late 1960s are still here today, and in many ways with greater veracity.

In the context of San Diego's urban revitalization, thousands of jobs have been created in the inner city since the 1970s. This job creation is touted as one of the greatest accomplishments (CCDC 2011) and is a critical part of the transformation of the inner city. Yet, the creation of jobs has encouraged greater economic polarization in many ways. As noted in the previous chapter, many jobs have been created, but these have accelerated the already growing "genie-bottle" economy through greater labor market polarization. In short, a lot of jobs were created, but mostly in the lower-wage service sector—in other words, these were "servant class" jobs.

DEFINING JOB QUALITY

"Job quality" remains a difficult thing to define precisely. It can include either very objective and clear criteria like wages, or more subjective criteria like flexibility of work schedules—something that can be measured but is done so subjectively depending on how we define "flexible." The simplest approach to defining job quality is to use wages as a proxy. Higher-wage jobs are seen as better jobs. This research explains where the wage distribution in the labor market is headed—are there more high wage or "good jobs" being generated or not? It does not tell us much about the multidimensionality of job quality, however. When including benefits like health care, pension plans, or working conditions, for instance, the picture becomes far more complex. This is challenging because multiple databases need to be synthesized in the analysis, but multidimensional approaches provide a more complex picture of what is going on in the U.S. labor market.

I approach job quality by looking at several different dimensions: wages, benefits, underemployment, earnings mobility, and occupational mobility. Wages are simply measured in terms of monthly income. Benefits refer to the availability of health care and pension plans. There are two dimensions to underemployment. The first refers to the skills mismatch between worker and occupation; that is to say, whether someone is doing a job they are overqualified for. The second dimension is the amount of work. This means that someone searching for full-time or long-term, permanent employment is only offered short-term or part-time employment. This is often the case for people who are working at temporary hiring agencies or who are trying to get full-time hours out of a position that only is able to provide enough for part time. Earnings mobility refers to people's ability to earn more over the course of their working years. Closely tied to earnings mobility is the issue of occupational mobility. This refers to the ability of people to move up a career ladder within their field. The extent to which people can move up or not determines occupational mobility.

Wages

Table 4 lists the largest occupations, wages, and Bureau of Labor Statistics (BLS) training levels. All the wages in this chapter are drawn from the BLS data, further compiled by the California Economic Development Department for the City/MSA region of San Diego. These figures show that the growth in low-wage employment also coincides with the growth of positions that also require little training or education. This raises the issue not only of wage quality, but the types of jobs that are emerging in a highly polarized labor market. Low-wage growth occurred principally in the area of the lower-wage service sector. This was due to the dramatic expansion of the inner city into a "lifestyle" and "tourist" destination emphasizing hotels, restaurants, bars, and retail. This dramatically increased the number of low-wage jobs in the service sector. This belies the view of cities like San Diego as harbingers of the "new economy" of high-wage, biotech, and information technology jobs. While there are a number of these sectors developing in the edges of the city, they still contain a number of low- and lower-middle-income jobs, and the total of high-wage jobs remains small. Table 4 shows the occupational growth during the period of redevelopment for which there are data available, 1980–2013. As the table indicates, the vast majority of job growth occurred in the lowest paid, service sector–based jobs, retail sales and hotels/restaurants in particular.

This runs counter to many public and even scholarly perceptions, despite the touting of San Diego as a new model of a city economy based on high-tech and high-wage services. For instance, in Richard Florida's

TABLE 4. Occupational Growth during Redevelopment, 1980–2013

Number of Jobs	Portion of Jobs (95%)	Occupation	Median Wage Rate
4,503	19%	Retail Salespersons	9.29
4,100	17%	Waiters and Waitresses	9.03
2,420	11%	Cashiers	9.29
1,100	5%	Maids and Housekeeping Cleaners	9.79
1,029	5%	Food Prep and Serving Workers	9.3
1,100	5%	Security Guards	11.57
747	4%	General and Operations Managers	53.86
745	4%	Cooks, Restaurant	12.05
339	2%	Bartenders	9.16
334	2%	Hotel, Motel, and Resort Desk Clerks	11.14
332	2%	Executive Secretaries and Admin Assistants	22.08
330	2%	Office Clerks, General	14.44
321	2%	Janitors and Cleaners	11.13
310	1%	Dishwashers	9.14
301	1%	First Line Sups/Mgrs of Retail Sales Workers	17.91
300	1%	Secretaries, General	17.53
300	1%	File Clerks	12.69
299	1%	Landscaping and Groundskeeping Workers	11.63
272	1%	First Line Sups/Mgrs of Food Prep/ Serving Workers	14.66
271	1%	Customer Service Representatives	17.19
270	1%	Bookkeeping, Accounting and Audit Clerks	18.46
220	1%	Maintenance and Repair Workers, General	16.24
199	1%	Receptionists and Information Clerks	13.59
187	1%	Taxi Drivers and Chauffeurs	10.6
181	1%	First Line Sups/Mgrs of Office and Admin Support	25.34
177	1%	Financial Services Sales	28.26
163	1%	Dining Room and Cafeteria Attendants and Bartenders	9.08
110	1%	Parking Lot Attendants	10.15

SOURCE: BLS Industry Occupation Matrix 2011; see appendix for data and methodology.

(2010) "Brainpower Map," which examines levels of human capital in metropolitan areas across the United States, he argues that human capital is the key driver of economic prosperity; this means the economic fortunes of American metros and cities are diverging and quite likely to diverge even more in the future. The problem, however, is that increasingly, job growth is occurring in the high and low ends of the skills spectrum. Thus, economic and social inequality is increasingly overlaid with a deepening economic geography of skill and of class. Yet, Florida, like others, often assumes that investment in skills leads to higher wages and higher benefits, and overall a more prosperous economy, both on aggregate and for individuals and families. This is the logic underlying Moretti's (2012) assertion that there are two approaches to helping poorer inner cities: either attract the high-tech/biotech jobs and let the economic activity trickle down, or attract the workers and hope they generate the jobs and let the economic activity trickle down. In San Diego, firms were attracted, luxury high-rise condos were built, and artists and a host of creative class residents were attracted, but wages actually fell for those in the servant class occupations.

Wages in servant class occupations actually declined on average over a decade-long period of dramatic urban revitalization and gentrification. How could this happen despite the finding that on average urban revitalization may increase overall wage rates? The reasons for the wage stagnation and decline are difficult to pin down. Conventional labor economics assumes that there is either an increase in supply of labor, or a decline in productivity, or a decline in economic competitiveness of industries, and so forth. In the case of San Diego none of these factors were clearly at work. There has been a slight increase in the supply of lesser skilled labor, but not nearly enough to suggest that the wages would decline as well. This is further reinforced by the fact that job openings for many of the lowest-paid servant class occupations go unfilled in San Diego's rebuilt downtown.

Underemployment

Underemployment based on educational attainment runs counter to the conventional wisdom regarding labor markets in the United States. The U.S. economy is typically seen as one in which the demand for high-skilled labor is growing; after all, employers report shortages of skilled workers in a variety of fields, and the United States maintains a growing H-1B visa program to bring in skilled workers from other countries. The issue, however, is more complicated when looking closely at labor markets on a more local or regional level.

Underemployment is chiefly thought about in two dimensions: education/skills and hours worked. For education/skills, underemployment occurs when someone is working a job for which they have more skills or education than the job requires. In other words, they are overqualified, but remain working in the position because they cannot get a better job that takes advantage of their skills or qualifications. The economic recession of 2008 onward has highlighted this problem acutely for college graduates, a cohort with not only record high levels of unemployment, but also underemployment. Yet, underemployment also occurs across a range of demographics. Older workers who are displaced by industry shifts or corporate consolidation can find themselves in less-skilled positions; sometimes technology takes the place of occupations, and often people get skills or training but cannot find a job in that particular field, so they take a job that does not require the skills or training they have invested in.

The other dimension of underemployment generally looked at is whether a worker is working an adequate number of hours during a typical workweek. This is often seen as part of the problem of contingent and temporary work: workers want more hours and full-time pay status, but firms are unwilling or incapable of hiring them for a full-time workweek. I look at both of these dimensions from the point of view of the labor market changes that have occurred with the rapid growth of jobs in the inner city, and through surveys of workers in central San Diego. Figure 3 shows the education and training levels established by the Bureau of Labor Statistics for the jobs created in central San Diego since 1980. A striking 62 percent of jobs only require on-the-job training (OJT), while another 14 percent require some experience and postsecondary education. Only 22 percent of the jobs created require a bachelor's degree or higher. This is primarily due to the expansion of the lower-wage segment of the service sector as San Diego's inner city has been geared toward visitor services, entertainment, and retail development.

Underemployment in central San Diego is spread across the low-wage population regardless of age, ethnicity, or education. It does, however,

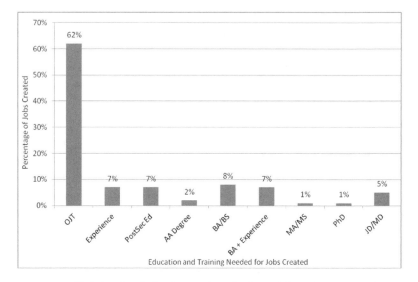

FIGURE 3. Training Levels for Occupations in Central San Diego, 2013. *Source:* Bureau of Labor Statistics training levels matched with occupations in the study area.

appear to decline with age. As Table 5 shows, those who are younger in the labor market report more underemployment (either by education or hours worked). Younger workers also appear to seek work actively while employed a quarter of the time, while older workers report less underemployment and are less likely to be actively seeking work.

Joseph, thirty-five, is an immigrant from East Africa. He arrived with his family more than a decade ago, with a degree in accounting. For several years he worked at a number of small immigrant businesses in central San Diego, and further north in the Mid-City neighborhoods. He kept books for the businesses, did their taxes, purchased tax software, and invested in a good laptop to do taxes for other members of the African diaspora in San Diego. On the surface, he appears reasonably successful, but he is frustrated by what he says is a series of challenges that are holding him back in the economy. The first is the perception that businesses and potential employers or clients have of his credentials from Africa. Prospective American clients or employers, he says, scoff at his degree from Ethiopia. The second problem he encounters is that he is only able to get work on a part-time basis, rotating often between

TABLE 5. Underemployment by Age and Those Seeking Work while Underemployed

Age	Underemployed (percent)	Actively Seeking Work (percent)
18–27	48	25
28–37	30	12
38–47	27	14
48–57	6	12
58–68	10	5

SOURCE: Central San Diego Survey 2002–10.

clients and temporary work. He has had several full-time jobs via temporary employment agencies, and many with good pay and benefits. The work, however, he finds mundane and boring, as most of it is very simple accounting—"working like a robot," as he describes it. Another problem with the temporary agencies is that the positions he gets placed in have typically been without much room for movement up a career ladder. He would rather work for himself and combine different jobs with the occasional temping as necessary. As a result, he has neither the hours nor the benefits that he would like, despite having the desire for a better-paying, full-time job.

Overall, the effects of underemployment are widespread. Large segments of the inner-city labor market have shifted toward occupations where very little education or training is required, while at the same time, for many groups, notably whites and Asians, the rates of education have increased. Meanwhile, large numbers of central city residents are not working enough hours to meet their employment needs. In a striking note on the issue of job quality, the high rates of underemployment due to being overqualified for one's job is hugely significant. Given that central San Diego has lower rates of educational attainment than most of the city, the rates of underemployment due to educational or skills gaps is striking, illustrating how few skills the new urban labor market is demanding of lower-income resident workers.

Career Ladders and Occupational Mobility

Career ladders, critical for entry-level workers, are pathways through a firm or industry where entry-level workers can move up to better, higher-paying positions. The tendency among firms is that these career ladders narrow as one rises up them. That is, there are a lot of entry- or lower-level positions, but fewer at the top. Employers and employees typically declare the value for career ladders in a firm. Their presence allows workers to have some sense that there is opportunity both occupationally and financially within a firm. Having the opportunity to improve one's position and earnings without leaving a firm or industry is typically valued by workers. There is little incentive to obtain greater job-based expertise and put in more effort for a promotion if there are no positions available within a business. Employers often value career ladders because they want to offer employees incentives for job performance and opportunity for people to move up in a career without the risk of losing valuable employees, especially if the firm has invested a lot in training that employee.

Despite their value, however, career ladders are not always a useful mechanism for occupational or economic mobility. Career ladders have been found to be limited in a range of growing industries, and with limited national or even local policies to promote or improve them (Fitzgerald 2006; Osterman 2008). A good deal of research shows that economic mobility is more likely tied to workers who change jobs or industries, and in some cases this is particularly true for entry-level or low-wage workers (Fitzgerald 2006). A deemphasis on the importance of career ladders has grown in part with the shift from an economy with relatively more labor market stability (career-long jobs), to one with more labor market flexibility where economic mobility is tied increasingly to job insecurity, a constant search for different and better jobs, and less reliance on a single firm or industry for a stable career with advancement (Farber 1998; Kalleberg 2011). On the other hand, there is continued evidence that career ladders can have an important impact on workers, particularly in providing an avenue up from entry-level and low-wage positions (Holzer 2007; Holzer et al. 2011). In fact, there is strong evidence that effective job advancement strategies can occur if low-wage workers are hired by higher-wage industries, and if they receive targeted training and those industries have career ladders. The essential idea here is not new: bring entry-level workers into a high-wage industry, train them, and offer them positions to move into as they gain skills, experience, or education.

Even in low-wage service-sector industries this is possible. While some employers may respond to competitive pressure and new technologies by reducing worker compensation and replacing semiskilled workers with even lower-skilled ones or reducing services or implementing labor-saving devices, other firms in the same industry may respond by increasing training opportunities and providing career ladders so that unskilled workers can become more productive over time (Appelbaum, Bernhardt, and Murnane 2006). For instance, WalMart is often criticized for the former approach, while Costco is often applauded for the latter. The important point here is that career ladders can play an important role in economic and occupational mobility, especially for entry-level and lesser-skilled workers. For those with less access to training, education, or transportation to address a wider range of jobs either based on training or geography, having jobs locally that offer entry-level workers a career ladder is an important part of economic development in inner cities.

Firm size matters to the extent that larger firms tend to have more career ladders than smaller firms. For very small firms, this is in some ways unavoidable as there simply aren't enough jobs to constitute a range of upward jobs paths in the first place. As an example, working for a corner grocery store that has three employees—an owner, a cashier, and a stock clerk/cashier position, respectively—does not offer much room for advancement. Working at a large health care provider, such as a hospital, or at a large social service organization, however, does offer a lot of different occupations with their own career ladders. One of the key questions becomes whether lower-wage workers are clustered in smaller firms with flatter organizations in which they are less likely to move up, and thus they are required to switch firms if they want to make gains in career or in terms of income mobility. The portion of people working in small firms is relatively high in central San Diego. With half of residents working in firms that have ten employees or fewer, and 72 percent of residents working in firms that employ twenty-five people or fewer, the prospect of significant career ladders being available is far less than if they were working at larger firms. The prospect is particularly daunting for Latinos in this regard, as they tend to work in smaller firms, many of them small businesses that operate in the niche economy. Latinos have a 75 percent chance of working in a firm with fewer than ten employees in central San Diego. This means that upward mobility within a firm will be far less likely.

Some specific cases will illustrate this issue more fully. At a small retail store, there are eight employees; positions include manager/owner and cashier/stock clerk. This is a family-run firm with almost ten years in business. The payroll tends to vary depending on the economy, with more help being hired during the holidays. In the case of promotion within the firm and the development of new skills, higher wages, or better benefits, the organization is essentially flat. The owner describes the pay scale in terms of "topping out" at about twelve dollars per hour. This is the rate at which employees become too expensive to keep on. Cashiers typically earn about nine to ten dollars an hour, so gaining more responsibility at the store over time and gaining greater income can mean a boost in pay, but these types of wages still do not meet self-sufficiency. This makes it nearly impossible for someone in this type of occupation to raise a family as the sole earner, and challenging even with a second earner, unless that person has a significantly higher income.

Table 6 illustrates the difficulty of moving up through career ladders in different types of businesses in central San Diego. The firms surveyed here represent a range of businesses in different industries. Listed are the total number of positions, the number of positions that are entry level (where no previous experience or education is required), as well as positions that require additional education and/or training and those that require a college degree or higher. These are businesses that were selected randomly from those firms that are likely to have entry-level jobs for lesser-skilled workers. My aim here is to illustrate the difficulty in moving up in a broad range of businesses. These may have entry-level openings, but the career ladder either ends fairly abruptly (these tend to be flat organizations, particularly in small firms) or they have very steep career ladders. A steep pathway means that a large jump is required in the education or training attributes of an employee in order to move up in a career ladder.

As the table indicates, hotels have a large portion of entry-level positions. These tend to flatten out as someone gains more experience. This is not to say that someone cannot start out as a janitor in a hotel and eventually become an executive. This does happen, but it does not happen very often due to the fact that the career ladders narrow dramatically as one moves up in an organization. Hotels and motels, for instance, have 56 percent of their jobs in building and ground cleaning and maintenance and in food preparation and service, while office and administrative support occupations occupy 19 percent of jobs in the industry, and management, business, and financial occupations just 5 percent of the industry.

Restaurants, similarly, have few ladders for making a career path toward a self-sufficiency wage. Most restaurants, even full-service ones,

TABLE 6. Career Ladders at a Sampling of Firms in Central San Diego

Ratio of Entry-Level Positions to Non-Entry-Level Positions	Industry	Total Positions	Entry-Level Positions	Positions That Require Additional Education/ Training	Positions That Require a College Degree
0.92	Retail store, large national chain	26	24	6	5
0.90	Cleaning service	10	9	0	0
0.86	Retail store, medium size	14	12	2	1
0.75	Printing/copying services	16	12	2	1
0.75	Fast food restaurant	8	6	2	1
0.67	Retail store, small	3	2	1	0
0.50	Restaurant, full service	12	6	4	1
0.43	Hotel	82	35	9	10
0.38	Small manufacturer, machine parts	8	3	0	2
0.25	Auto repair, small, local	4	1	3	0
0.20	Social service organization, large	100	20	72	40
0.17	Medical office	6	1	5	5

SOURCE: Employer survey, central San Diego.

provide a limited route for economic mobility if staying entirely within the firm. For instance, workers starting out in the kitchen move through the following occupations: dishwasher, prep cook, fry cook, grill cook, buffet cook, line cook, sous chef, chef, kitchen manager. A sous chef and a chef or kitchen manager may earn between forty-five thousand (sous chef) up to fifty thousand dollars or more for the top two occupations. The challenge is that these jobs are only available for one person, and there is a lengthy queue to move up within the firm. Additionally, these positions usually require specialized training or education. This may or may not provide an incentive for the employees in the restaurant. For instance, working as a prep cook may pay $9.61 on average, but moving up to a line cook, with more hours, stress, and work, means a boost in pay to only $10.20. It is not until reaching the top position of restaurant chef that wages really improve, surpassing $20.00 an hour on average.

Another issue raised by this sampling of career ladders in local firms is that the size of firms matters. Smaller firms have fewer positions, and while there may be a number of good entry-level positions available, far fewer upper-level positions may exist. In fact, in very small firms, the top position may simply be a general manager spot occupied by an owner, or in some cases there are positions above entry level, but they are few, competition for them is strong, and they require higher rates of education or skills.

The effect of having a lot of competition for few positions is one of growing labor-market polarization for those who may not have the same types of educational credentials, or for whom obtaining them may not be reasonable. This is typically a situation that leads to the labor queue "leapfrogging" of employees within lower-wage industries. Many immigrant Latina women, for instance, describe how they have worked for five or more years at a business, then a college student is hired, and the student is promoted to a managerial position very quickly, sometimes within a year or as soon as they complete their degree. In such cases, the credential is deemed to usurp experience and time with a firm. All of these barriers often mean that workers hit a wall that is established in the firm through credentials that are too difficult to obtain, too much competition for too few spots higher up in the career ladders of the organization, or a combination of factors.

Earnings Mobility

Earnings mobility is another critically important dimension of job quality and labor market outcomes. In central San Diego earnings mobility has slowed over the past decade, and has declined along with the rest of the city since 2007 (when looking at the American Community Survey data for San Diego). This is matched by greater income inequality, where the majority 65 percent of lower-wage workers have been earning less in real wages since 2000. In sum, central San Diego has seen dropping unemployment and lots of job creation, but lower earnings in the lower-wage sectors of the labor market. This reflects a broader problem of lower-wage mobility over time.

Wage mobility refers to the ability of people to earn more in a specific industry over time, either through wage increases or moving up within a career ladder to a higher-paying position. My residential survey did not identify people personally and thus did not gather data longitudinally, which is the only way to fully understand earnings mobility over time. However, I did ask residents about their earnings histories. This included several questions. First, if they had pay increases during the previous year; second, if they were seeking to earn more in the future; third, if they were seeking to increase their earnings, how they were planning to do that. Finally, in relation to the issue of career ladders, I asked people if they were going to earn more staying in their current job, or if they had to change jobs to a different firm or industry altogether to earn more.

Most residents (Table 7) report having a pay increase during the previous year (65 percent), but this still does not get them above economic self-sufficiency on average. For the majority of lower-wage workers in central San Diego, earnings mobility varies, but most have plans to increase earnings (34 percent). As a result, a significant portion of workers aims to increase earnings. The two most widespread efforts involve finding a new job (29 percent) and getting more skills through either training or education (18 percent). A significant portion (17 percent) also seeks a second job, or plans to work informally (9 percent).

Strategizing new ways to bring in extra or supplemental income is widespread across the low-wage labor market. I detail the combination of informal and formal work more in chapter 6, but a good example of this type of strategizing by combining multiple forms of employment is provided by Marcia, thirty-four, mother of two and recently divorced.

TABLE 7. Plans to Increase Earnings among Residents in Central San Diego

None	Pay Raise	Get a Second Job	Get a New Job	Work Informally	More Skills Training	Promotion
11%	8%	17%	29%	9%	18%	8%

SOURCE: Central San Diego Survey 2002–10.

She works between thirty and forty hours a week as a home health aide, and she earns about $22,000 dollars per year, just above the poverty line for a family of three but well below self-sufficiency. With some child support from her ex-husband, she is able to be self-sufficient, but she still wants to earn more. She has taken on some informal housecleaning work on the side but continues to look for a better job. Her ultimate goal is to get specialized training in a program like one that leads to becoming a dental hygienist, which pays around $69,000 in San Diego, a spectacular pay increase, but she would need to complete a degree program, and the time and resources to do so are not available at present. In the interim, she is looking for temp work in addition to her regular home health aide work.

Similarly, Richard, a young, white recent college graduate with an associate's degree in logistics management, has been shuffling from job to job in search of better wages. He started as a shipping clerk at an office supply store after he got his degree, then worked briefly for a trucking company as a logistics operator, then moved on to managing shipments for a delivery company, and interviewed for a job at UPS. "Basically I have worked in every part of the industry, but you can't earn much more than what the industry pays, unless I went into management, but that takes a long time," he says. When I asked about his salary throughout this multijob, multiyear employment record, it reflects some ups and downs but basically remains locked at about $35,000 a year despite a decade in the industry. He describes his efforts with frustration: "I have looked for jobs, tried to get more skills and experience, you know I have more skills and experience, but I haven't been able to move up, mostly it is sideways." The issue here is beyond career ladders; it is also a question of how industry wages may be stagnant or occupations may not have much income growth. For people working in logistics, some occupations have seen good wage growth (there is a shortage of truck drivers, which has boosted wages), but for many occupations in trucking and logistics, real wages are flat or have declined.

Of those that want to get a new job, nearly half (45 percent) wanted to get into a business where they could work for themselves. For those who want more skills training, the vast majority wants these skills to move out of their current job into a better one (75 percent). In short, most people realize that they will be very limited in terms of income generation unless they leave their current occupation. Whether these jobs are entry-level positions on a ladder to higher incomes appears not to be the perception of most workers. They see the limitations of working in fast food, full-service restaurants, landscaping, janitorial companies, warehouses, and even some of the remaining manufacturing facilities.

Benefits

The growing inequalities among the urban working poor are to be found not just in wage differentials, but in overall compensation, which includes benefits, notably health insurance and retirement plans. Health insurance is an obvious need, and the crisis of coverage in the United States continues to grow. Access to health care has traditionally been through employers in American society, but with escalating health care costs and many of these rising costs being transferred to employees, more and more people are losing coverage. This trend was dramatically sped up in California between 2009 and 2012 when 1.2 million Californians lost employer health benefits (Terhune 2012). Additionally, other benefits like retirement plans, especially defined benefit programs typically associated with union contracts, have been declining over the past two decades and shifting more toward defined contribution plans (Wiatrowski 2011).

Table 8 looks at benefits coverage in central San Diego and compares it to national estimates. The central San Diego sample is limited to those who make low wages to compare with the other estimates (low wage as defined as 200 percent FPL or lower). This is the vast majority (96 percent) of survey respondents. Residents in San Diego's urban core not only have poorer job quality based on the aforementioned data, but when looking at overall benefits, the differences between low-wage workers and those earning more is even more stark. Despite some improvements over national surveys (health coverage for families, paid vacation days, and paid holidays are higher for central San Diego workers), other

TABLE 8. Benefits Coverage, Central San Diego and National Estimates Compared

Benefit	Central San Diego Low-Wage (200% FPL or lower)	National Estimates Low-Wage	Mid Income	High Wage
Health coverage, employer contribution, individual	41%	42%	87%	94%
Health coverage, employer contribution, individual and family	36%	34%	78%	87%
Paid time off for illness	32%	39%	74%	90%
Paid vacation days	57%	51%	89%	88%
Paid holidays	60%	46%	86%	89%
Pension (defined benefit)	9%	16%	39%	48%
Any retirement plan with employer contribution	26%	32%	72%	87%
Job training/education	36%	45%	64%	81%

SOURCE: Central San Diego Survey 2002–10; Buffie 2015.

indicators are behind national estimates of low-wage worker benefits. Notably, there is less paid time off for illness, individual health coverage, and extremely low rates of pension coverage. Only 9 percent of workers in central San Diego report the presence of defined benefit pension coverage, and just above a quarter (26 percent) have some type of pension program with an employer contribution. Low-wage workers in central San Diego also have very few options for employer-sponsored education and training: 36 percent. This is a figure far lower than national estimates.

The reasons for these low rates of benefit provision are complex, and a much larger sample of employed residents would be required to statistically discern the reasons for such differences. There is good qualitative evidence, however, to suggest why some of these benefits coverage rates are so low. First, part-time workers and those in intermittent employment (people moving from job to job) may have difficulty getting good benefit coverage; rates for these types of workers have far lower rates of coverage than full-time and more career-track workers. Additionally, immigrant workers have lower rates of benefits despite working in a range of industries (Kaiser Family Foundation 2011). With approximately two-thirds of central San Diegans Latino, and many working part time, rates of coverage are likely to be lower.

The extremely low rates of pension coverage, job training/education, and health care do present very serious problems. Without adequate health coverage, workers are either forced to go without coverage or to seek a public program. Incomes often cut families off of public programs at certain levels, however, and therefore this low rate of employer-provided health care coverage is likely to lead to a higher rate of uninsured among the lower-income workers. As the California Healthcare Foundation found in its 2012 annual survey of the working uninsured in the state, 79 percent were employed in the private sector, 54 percent worked full time, all year, and 29 percent had family incomes up to $50,000 dollars (California Healthcare Foundation 2012). Pension coverage is also a serious challenge: the poor and working poor face greater economic insecurity as they age if they remain in low-income households and low-wage jobs. A lack of employer-sponsored education or training is also a severe problem. With lower-skilled and lower-wage workers seeking to increase their earnings and gain some level of occupational mobility, any opportunities in the workplace for training and education are typically a boon for workers. Yet, lower-income workers have extremely low rates of workplace education and training, unlike higher-income earners, who are two to nearly three times more likely to have such programs.

The effects of job quality are significant. While welfare reform sought to "reward work," the occupational growth in central San Diego has generally been less than fully rewarding when looking at the issue of job quality. As a result, we have not only further polarization of the labor market, and perhaps greater segmentation as well, but we also have further impacts beyond just job quality. The case studies below illustrate the difficulties faced by workers seeking employment in the inner-city labor market, as well as cases where some succeed at moving up occupationally.

THE EFFECTS OF POOR JOB QUALITY: THE "STUCK" WORKER

The majority of workers in this study were "stuck" in a low-wage career with little mobility either in terms of income or occupation. The reasons for being in this situation are numerous, complex, and often interacting. Understanding these barriers to moving either out of the labor force to gain more skills or up within their own industry or occupation is critical to policymaking aimed at improving economic opportunity.

In nearly every case, however, workers who experience limited economic mobility face multiple, often mutually reinforcing barriers. A problem with a car or other means of transportation can make the employee seem unreliable. In some cases, a change in day care providers or elder care needs, or simply family rearrangements meant changing work schedules and asking for increased time off. These types of intermittent disruptions of a regular work schedule should not disrupt one's potential career trajectory, but for many low-wage and entry-level positions, these types of issues make a worker more likely to be passed over for raises or promotions.

None of this analysis removes responsibility from workers themselves, and indeed many do make poor choices—flying off the handle, hitting a coworker, and getting fired, and then drinking and getting incarcerated ruin a person's labor market trajectory. Any experience or work reference cultivated over those two years of working at a low-wage warehouse job are wrecked by a bad set of decisions in as few as eight hours. This, indeed, can happen to anyone, but the critical point is what happens to that person once those bad choices are made—are there supportive services to get that individual back on track, or is the prison system and rehabilitation just a revolving door for people to continue to make poor choices? Is there an apprenticeship program, or an effective workforce investment board, or a job-training program like job corps? Are these programs effective for urban workers? What of the marginalized or displaced worker at the edge of a segmented labor market?

THE ROLLER COASTER

Ellie's story is all too familiar. I have heard it a dozen times; the content of the story rarely changes, but the significance can vary widely from person to person. Her story is one of someone on a low-wage career roller coaster. Her work history is not a neat, linear progression from entry-level positions to middle-career jobs, and eventually a high-paying job through more skills attainment, work experience, and education. Instead, Ellie has been moving up and down in the labor market from entry-level positions to assistant manager positions in the retail and social service sectors, but she has never been able to get a steady salaried job. The reasons for this she describes as a combination of bad luck, too many qualified candidates for the jobs that she has tried to move into, and a limited capacity to get the right types of qualifications that would mean a more steady income from a salaried position.

She describes her work experience as a roller coaster because she has run into barriers for promotion at different organizations, including outside candidates recruited for management positions and lots of college educated applicants applying for them as well, and she has yet to complete her associate's degree. She has also switched jobs many times, making some employers skeptical of her commitment level. She explains that she has moved around a lot in part because she has always been seeking a better job, and that some employers who were not doing well would cut back hours and failed to give pay increases over time for good work and productivity. In one case, she started at a retail location downtown, and then moved to a mall location when a management trainee position opened up, but then found herself out of a job entirely when that store was closed. She started climbing a career ladder in another retail firm until she realized that after two years and with nearly a decade of experience in the industry, she was not going to get anywhere. She left and took a part-time job in a social services organization and started a business management program, working toward a two-year degree.

The investment in studying at a local community college has yet to pay off. The program she was in for an associate's degree in business management did not have the type of scheduling flexibility to mesh with her family obligations (she has an eight-year-old and a husband who works full time as well), so she has been taking courses sporadically over a five-year period. She only has a couple of courses left, but the cost and time commitment has kept her from completing them. The other issue she has encountered is that she has been reluctant to complete the program because the recession hit, making the labor market very bad for even those with an associate's degree, and concern that if she went on the job market and took a new job in the uncertain economic environment, she might wind up back on the roller coaster of climbing up and sliding down career ladders. For the moment then, she remains working part time, chipping away at courses, and spending more time with her family.

Young Latino and African American men describe a similar process on the labor market. With these two demographics having the highest dropout rate in the city, and with many low-wage entry-level positions beckoning students who are disengaged from school, the experience of younger minority workers is exemplary of the types of up-and-down swings that can occur for inner-city residents in a poor job market. Many young Latino men who got jobs in the service industry or construction wound up unemployed during the recession. Some worked odd jobs and continued to look for work, and their labor force participation tends to be sporadic in many cases until the economy generates greater employment demand. Part of the problem, it seems, is that with the highest rates of unemployment among eighteen- to twenty-four-year-olds in U.S. history, there is a glut of young, better-educated labor on the market. As a result, many young Latinos worked in the service sector as low-wage workers—as dishwashers, janitors, or prep cooks, or in fast food—and then moved into construction to earn double or triple the wages, then wound up unemployed when the housing market collapsed in southern California. Their fortunes, in short, were tied closely to the fortunes of housing, remodeling, and the overleveraged economy. Now, many of them are back competing for low-wage service-sector jobs, starting out again at the very bottom of a poor career ladder.

Young African American men have faced similar challenges in the labor market, but with a difference in terms of barriers to career mobility, notably education. Younger African Americans I spoke to about their work histories illustrate how they have worked hard to attain greater skills, often getting their GEDs or high school diplomas, but that they perceived this was still inadequate to get a "good job." Reflecting national trends, a growing number of young African American men are not completing high school, making them even more disadvantaged in the labor market (Offner and Holzer 2002). Compounding this is that many young black men are getting left behind by the labor market not just through the demand for greater skills among workers, but also due to employer discrimination based on perceptions of criminal or deviant behavior among young black men (Mincy 2006). As a result, many young African American men describe a highly irregular form of labor force participation, often characterized by short-term efforts at finding one's way in a job, until, as precocious twenty-four-year-old Andre described it, "I woke and realized that I was not going anywhere," and then quit.

His job was in the shipping and receiving department of a local manufacturer. He packaged orders and got them ready to send out, working full time for $11.50 an hour, including some benefits, but he realized that nobody in the company beyond entry-level positions was black, so he felt he needed to move on to get a better job. He took a pay cut and worked at a small retail store, then a large hardware store. He left the labor force for a year, doing odd jobs. He tried staying with his uncle while he took a new job at a shipping department in the Otay Mesa area, but he was then let go, for reasons he still does not understand. He returned to central San Diego and now is unsure what to do. His latest job offer in 2012 was for $8.50 with no benefits. For several years Andre has tried to stay in a firm long enough to see some adequate pay increases, but they have never come. In other words, his labor market experience tells him that hard work and effort is not always rewarded, and his perception of employer discrimination does not help. When labor economists refer to the "discouraged worker" effect, they often do not realize the extent to which bad labor market experiences can affect someone's likelihood of remaining in the formal labor market. After several years of ups and downs and with little job stability, what is the incentive for Andre to continue down this route?

THE UPWARD BOUND

Poor jobs with few avenues for income raises or career mobility do not make up all of inner-city employment. Some workers do move up, and some do rise very high within organizations or in terms of income. Who were the upward bound in central San Diego? For workers who are doing well in the labor market, they share four characteristics. First, they worked in an industry that had a career ladder, and after a significant amount of time, they were able to move up. These were most likely people working in large firms, typically manufacturing, transportation, or utilities. In fact, the hallmark of these people is that they almost universally worked in a "good job," one where wage growth, firm stability, and career ladders appear to be holding firm over a long period of time. These include shipyard workers, power company workers, and people working in logistics and freight. Additionally, some health care workers, primarily those in administrative positions, were able to move up over time.

The characteristic of upwardly mobile workers in central San Diego is often risk taking, but risks, of course, imply potential costs, and the urban poor and working poor may reasonably be expected to be somewhat risk averse. People who had to take the risk of leaving the labor market to obtain more human capital and then return later at a better job sometimes were rewarded. This was predominantly the path up for younger and single workers. A social worker who started out as an administrative assistant but then got her degree in social work made an important career shift, but only after investing significant time and money into upgrading her education and skills. Several construction workers I met during 2009–10 who were looking for work decided to get some experience in different fields. One became quite successful in sales for a construction safety equipment company, and another took welding courses to become a certified Arc and TIG welder. This allowed him to apply for a broader variety of jobs, including not just construction but also welding positions. He quickly got a job as a stick/TIG welder at thirty-five dollars an hour, including benefits. These workers exemplify the type of highly flexible navigators of labor markets that many economists, particularly conservatives, view as necessary for income and job security. Finally, there are those who worked in the public sector or a job with a union. These types of positions typically pay higher wages and benefits than in the private sector, and provide a greater means of economic security.

DISCOURAGED AND DISINCENTIVIZED WORKERS

Discouraged workers are those who stop seeking employment after long-term unemployment. Marginally attached workers are typically defined as those who would like work and have looked for work at least once during the previous year. We know from a raft of research that urban neighborhoods with chronically high levels of unemployment have high rates of discouraged workers. This is certainly the case with the research on the urban poor and in areas of high racial segregation/isolation. In the case of San Diego, however, the issue of job quality is a factor in discouraging inner-city workers.

It is generally assumed that discouraged workers drop out of the job search because they have no luck in getting a job. In the case of San

Diego's inner city, there are jobs, but they offer so little that job seekers give up looking. These potential job seekers are discouraged not simply because their reservation wage (the minimum wage they would need to take a job) is too high, but because the job itself they view as a dead end, not worth the effort, and in some cases ones that discriminate against certain ethnic minorities. Research shows that poor job and career options lead to higher rates of crime at the individual levels. Higher quality jobs with better hours and pay lead to more viable work careers (Allan and Steffenmeiser 1989). If lower-skilled workers have higher rates of human capital, social networks, or other factors, this may be a further boost and lead to less discouragement among job seekers (Uggen and Staff 2001), but in central San Diego the discouragement appears to be in part due to three factors: first, the scale of low-wage service-sector work available; second, clear perceptions of discrimination by job seekers; and lastly, the presence of alternatives to formal labor force participation (notably informal and illegal work).

There are no data within these communities to directly speak to these factors in relation to discouraged workers, but there are cases that illustrate the processes and how they unfold. And there is a particular gendered dimension to the issue of long-term discouraged workers; most, in my experience, are men. Women may enter or exit the labor force for a variety of reasons, but they do not have the same level of discouragement in relation to job quality and perceived discrimination as men do.

In an earlier part of this project I spoke to a number of men who were unemployed and looking into job-training programs through a local nonprofit. The program was aimed at getting them into a job through specialized training and any needed additional support, such as résumé writing, interviewing, and so forth. All of them had been out of the labor force for several years; they were all African American and in their late twenties to mid-thirties. When asked about why they don't take any of the hundreds of fast food, cashier, or other service-sector jobs that are on offer in the revitalized downtown, I heard the same refrain, over and over. There were three reasons that these men did not apply for these jobs. First, the jobs were simply "not worth it." The wages were too low, the benefits limited, and they already knew from their own experience or the experience of family or friends that there were few long-term rewards to be gained. Echoing sentiments of other studies of fast food workers

(Newman 2009), these men viewed the career path as very limited, knew that they would ultimately have to find something else if they were to be economically independent, and expressed dismay at the personal costs of doing low-wage service work. One man expressed his frustration with fast food and restaurants in general, clearly dissecting the lack of career ladders:

> So you start at the front [of the restaurant] taking people's orders. They yell at you and tell you that you got their order wrong. Then you work hard and move up to putting the food in bags, or running the fryer, or if you are really lucky maybe the drive-through window, or if you work really hard in seven or ten years maybe you become supervisor of something and they bump you up to like 9 dollars an hour. Shit, I can't even get my own place on that. I'd still have to be working something on the side anyway.

This reflection hits on the insufficiency of the wages, meaning that more than one job would have to be maintained in order to reach self-sufficiency.

Another man reflected on how the levels of disrespect and discrimination drove him out of the food service industry. He worked at a couple restaurants until he gave up because of what he felt was persistent "personality" mismatch between him and the jobs:

> I did two years, at two different places. Each place, I was the only black guy. I was the only black person, and everyone knew it, and everyone worked with me like I wasn't right for the job, always correcting me, what I should say to customers. It isn't like I can't speak politely to people, it was them [other employees and management] always treating me like I was just good for sweeping the floor or washing dishes. I don't mind taking a bad job, or being disrespected, but I don't have to stay at a place that treats me like I'm an idiot all day. That's not worth it.

I asked him if he would have stayed at the job longer if he was paid more. His reply is instructive:

> It would have to be a lot more. I mean, how much would you need to go to a place every day and work and everyone just tried to make you feel stupid?

All day. Even for more cash that's hard, and that happens a lot. There are a lot of guys out there who have too much self-respect. They won't go near a fast food restaurant, or take a janitor job. You know, think of some guy like I know, rolls around in his Camaro, livin' in his mama's apartment, but acting tough and street and he's gonna take a job flipping burgers? I know what you are thinking: that's the problem, people have to start somewhere, work hard, but you know there is a problem when the only hard work around is doin' that [fast food].

This is a direct critique of the level of low-quality jobs and an implication for aspirations of better employment opportunities. Some of these men have had several years of work experience, some of it sporadic due to periods of being out of the workforce and/or problems with the criminal justice system.

The same issues face Latinos as well, but with different circumstances and personal decision-making. For Latino men who have spent a long time out of the formal labor force without plans to return, the reasons echo those of African American men. In particular, the concern over job quality has encouraged Latino men to look elsewhere for work, most notably in the informal economy for construction work. As many Latino men I've spoken to stated, they would prefer to move into construction, even if the jobs are informal, cash-in-hand work because they pay much more and they view the skills as valuable. As one man described, "Washing dishes gets you little money, long hours, and nowhere. That's not a career, its just survival. All the guys I know want something in construction because you can earn a lot more and you get skills. Even if you don't have skills, you can learn on the job; guys will teach you. The problem is there aren't enough jobs." What he referenced further in our conversation is that there were not enough jobs that were in construction, for example, good jobs that had opportunities for entry-level workers to move up through skills acquisition and with increased earnings potential. As a result, he and other Latino men describe how they often work informally instead of seeking a job through formal channels because the wages and skills acquisition is higher in these jobs. When the housing boom ended, this severely hit the building trades, but these jobs still remain far more desirable than low-wage service-sector jobs, so much so that the Latinos seeking jobs in the field prefer to take off-the-books or odd jobs, or even do temp work until they can get a construction job, rather than work in a low-paying service-sector job. They may be working for less money, have no benefits, and/or be working illegally, but this is viewed as preferable to the jobs they could find in the formal labor market.

Finally, it is also clear that the rise of contingent, part-time, and substandard hourly jobs has eroded lower-skilled workers' confidence in the labor market. Within the retail sector, for instance, I find it hard to locate a worker who is satisfied with the scheduling and hours at their workplace. Schedules change and shift very quickly, and there are not enough hours to earn enough some weeks. These problems are well understood by residents of the inner city, and they are widely discussed and disparaged. I detail these issues more in depth in the later chapter on the retail industry itself, but the salient point here is that job quality has a detrimental effect on labor market attachment and labor force participation.

Another negative effect of the exponential expansion of the low-wage service-sector job market was to disincentivize many inner-city residents from considering increased education or training. This sounds counterintuitive; more low-wage jobs would presumably encourage workers to seek more education and training to move into a better job. The problem, however, is that there was already an oversupply of low-wage jobs in San Diego. In 2000 there were already a hundred thousand more jobs in San Diego County that did not require any education or training beyond high school than there were working-age residents who had only a high school education or lower. As a result, thousands of San Diegans are employed in positions that do not require the college education they have. This in part explains why there are workers with college coursework or degrees working in entry-level positions that often require no specialized training or education. There are not enough jobs demanding the higher rates of education in the county. In San Diego's inner city, these same labor market effects can be seen among even some of the lowest-paid service-sector jobs: many are filled with people with college degrees. In short, there is a growing underemployment problem. This in turn is related to the queuing up of workers for positions even if they are overqualified for them. As a result, there is a very real perception on the part of less-skilled workers in central San Diego that the labor market is too competitive with so many low-skill-demanding jobs, and they must compete against more highly educated workers. Why should a retail sales clerk seek to earn a college degree when the jobs that she or he will likely be applying for upon graduation are the same low-wage retail jobs that they have now?

Workers' knowledge of the low-wage labor market and career ladders should not be underestimated. Many of those I have interviewed have spent years or decades working in servant class jobs. They have experienced the limitations of career ladders directly, they realize that they are often passed over for promotion because there is always a line of college graduates ready to take higher administrative or managerial positions, and they understand that getting additional education and training carries with it great risks. I discuss these factors in more depth in chapter 8. The point here is that thousands of low-wage jobs did not incentivize people to upgrade skills; it merely resigned them to struggling in servant class occupations.

CONCLUSION

The issue of job quality and in particular polarized labor markets split between good and bad jobs has been studied widely. With the rise of contingent work and the push for more labor market flexibility, as well as the erosion of job quality overall, providing jobs with greater wages, benefits, and career ladders is vital for addressing the issues of inner-city poverty and growing numbers of working poor. The city of San Diego had opportunity to accomplish this and push for a balanced, thoughtful approach to inner-city revitalization. Such an approach would push a more balanced set of industries for job creation; link them more closely with labor market institutions, intermediaries, and other organizations to connect workers to jobs; and collaborate with educational and training resources to provide skills needed to move up in career ladders. As I discussed previously, this did not happen. Instead, the aim was to promote development as much as possible, with some targeted industries in particular, such as the hospitality industry. There was no consideration for the labor market impacts of this approach.

The results of this effort were what we can expect with low-wage service-sector job growth. Reflecting the voluminous research on the topic, poor job quality means relatively low wages, inadequate benefits, and very limited career ladders. Additionally, the scale of job growth in low-wage service work was particularly large. The scale of labor market transformation had its own effects. We find that some workers may move up economically, but far too many get stuck, moving horizontally, or in some cases drop out of the labor force altogether. In short, the type of inner-city labor market that was found to be lacking good quality jobs is precisely what has been reintroduced today, but under the auspices of urban revitalization! The effects of this on a more individual level are significant and in some cases very unexpected.

Two findings stand out from this analysis of the labor market in San Diego's revitalized inner city. The first is that the scale of low-wage job growth has discouraged many people from seeking additional training or education. A job market overwhelmingly tilted toward low-wage service-sector jobs with lots of competition for a few good jobs does not encourage lower-skilled workers to seek more education and take their chances in the competition for the better job. Second, the lack of job quality has discouraged labor force participation, or more active participation. Many residents give up looking for work because their reservation wage is higher than what is being offered. They may wind up working in the informal economy or illegally, or working part time and combining this with some other forms of income. Whatever the particular strategy, because the job quality is so low, these workers do not benefit much from the revitalized inner-city labor market. Finally, there is the issue of those left behind. This demographic includes those people for whom the new low-wage service-sector jobs offer nothing, because of discrimination or perceptions of discrimination, or because of chronic long-term unemployment. Ex-offenders fall into this category, especially if they are black, Latino, or male. In the end, the most disadvantaged in the labor market have been discouraged from applying for jobs, and as a result, many with low rates of labor force attachment continue to remain unemployed or sporadically employed. Thus, job quality matters for inner-city residents; in many cases, the surfeit of bad jobs is worse than no job at all.

Ultimately, the issue of job quality has become a more pronounced debate within public policy circles, not just among labor economists. What can be done and is being proposed, however, is still a set of nascent policies (see Kalleberg 2011; Osterman and Shulman 2011). How the labor market has already been structured, however, has had a dramatic impact on the lives of the working poor, precisely during an era of massive urban revitalization that was ostensibly aimed at helping them. The new urban labor market of San Diego's inner city has instead reinforced labor market polarization and erected a scaffolding of potential barriers to economic opportunity and occupational mobility. It should not be surprising, then, that as I document in the next two chapters, a burgeoning informal economy has emerged not just for income generation, but also for goods and services through what I call "DIY," or "do it yourself," safety nets. There is no question that the lack of both public-sector provisions and the collapse of good jobs with career ladders have contributed to the expansion of both of these informal sectors of the urban economy and communities.

PART II

Working in the Servant Class

3

Working in the
Hospitality Industry

FOR THOSE WORKING in low-wage service work, the hospitality industry, which includes restaurants and hotels, provides thousands of entry-level positions for San Diegans. Overall, the hospitality industry is characterized as a low-wage industry that is labor intensive and employs large numbers of low-income workers, immigrants, and people of color (Bernhardt, Dresser, and Hatton 2003). Research on the industry points to how restructuring has led to a decline in job quality, but it also shows that there is some degree of variation depending on other factors such as managerial priorities, firm size, and unionization (Bernhardt, Dresser, and Hatton 2003). Like other low-wage service industries, new forms of labor flexibility have transferred pressures and greater job-related risk onto hourly workers in hotels (Lambert 2008), while there is some evidence that despite the restructuring of the industry and greater demands for employee flexibility, management practices that emphasize a meritocratic career ladder, including job security, training, and opportunities for advancement, can abate some of these conditions (McPhail and Fisher 2008). The picture, therefore, is fairly mixed, and unfortunately the research on the industry from a perspective of workers and job quality is quite limited. Yet, this is also one of the largest employment sectors in the inner city and one of the key industries promoted through urban revitalization. The industry was promoted and planned as one of the central industry clusters to revitalize San Diego and touted as a job creating engine. As such, in this chapter I look more closely at industry employment, particularly regarding job quality and occupational mobility.

Travel and hotel related economic activity in San Diego generates more than 27 million visitors and 6 billion dollars spent annually (SDCC 2010). With travel and hospitality employing more than thirty-three thousand people in the county, the majority of those employees in the city of San Diego, the industry is very important to the urban economy. While many visitors spend their time at attractions like Sea World and Legoland, the urban core has seen a significant focus on hospitality and visitor services development as well.

The hospitality industry has been central to the redevelopment of San Diego's urban core. Planning, investment, and the direct promotion of the hotel and related visitor services industries were and continue to be central to the development of the inner city. As I discuss in this chapter, the emphasis on hotel developments generally focuses on generating tax revenues, creating jobs, and bringing visitors to the city, thereby creating more indirect economic benefits. From an economic development perspective, however, this approach on fiscal returns and broad indicators of economic growth is too narrow. Such an approach simplistically emphasizes these positive elements without looking at whether or not this is the best approach for inner-city revitalization; whether or not the push for this industry provides the best way to revitalize the urban core in terms of job creation, reducing poverty and providing economic opportunity.

The data I draw on for this chapter include interviews with employees and managers at downtown hotels. These are all businesses that were built or established during the period of the redevelopment of the urban core. I also draw on wage data for the industry and based on interviews with management I develop estimates of staffing patterns as representative of career ladders in the industry.

My analysis here is mostly within higher end "class A" hotels, but I also include interviews with employees of lower, class B and C hotels—those that are not full service and have fewer amenities. Class A hotels are more luxury and well-known national chains that have been the largest segment of the industry to expand during San Diego's inner-city redevelopment. This class of hotel caters largely to the visitor, convention, and business-class customer, and is reflective of broader trends within the industry in terms of human resources and management practices.

HOTELS AND REDEVELOPING THE INNER CITY

Hotel development has been central to San Diego's inner-city revitalization for a number of reasons. In the past thirty-four years of downtown redevelopment more than nine thousand hotel rooms have been added to the area, and more than two thousand hotel jobs created during the same period. Lobbying by convention center and visitor services allies is one critical factor. Gaining revenues for public accounts is another. Hotels bring in sales taxes, but also the Transient Occupancy Tax (TOT), which is a particularly appealing form of public revenue generation in tax-averse cities like San Diego because it is a high tax (10.5 percent) levied on visitors (unless local residents pay for a hotel room). Since the larger hotels offer room service and incorporate large restaurants and sell prepared food mainly to non-city residents, these businesses also generate significant sales tax revenues. Hotels also have very high real property tax assessments, providing a third source of general fund revenue. These fiscal considerations are not lost on the approving bodies and public discussions of economic development when hotels are concerned.

During the dozen meetings I have attended when hotel projects were discussed in public meetings at CCDC or the City Council, I learned that fiscal returns are paramount. In numerous hotel planning and approval meetings the central concerns, as for any project, are how much property tax revenue will be generated, how much TOT will be generated, and whether the aesthetics of the building fit within the planning guidelines and meet people's personal aesthetic tastes. For instance, in one meeting on the approval of a new hotel project, two-thirds of the discussion concerned whether or not, to quote one of the CCDC board members, "the upper tower articulation was conducive to the broader architectural design schema for similarly sized buildings." In short, the vast majority of the discussion centered on what the roof should look like.

This is not just an isolated case, but rather the typical discussion regarding large inner-city developments, particularly hotels, within the CCDC planning and approval process. In essence, urban revitalization and redevelopment is reduced to architectural and fiscal concerns, while all of the "downstream" impacts such as job creation, poverty alleviation, and so forth are assumed to be accomplished indirectly, eventually, by someone, although this is never evaluated, no programs are in place to ensure this is accomplished, and most importantly, these issues are never part of the discussion and decision-making criteria in the economic development process. Thus, redevelopment, which has as its guiding principles laudable aims such as the elimination of blight, poverty alleviation, and creation of jobs, becomes a tool through which economic development can be catalyzed in a variety of industries, but in the case of hotels, the question as to how a particular development is meeting these aims is nebulous. Many hotel projects occur on parcels that do not necessarily meet blighted conditions; in some cases eminent domain has been used to appropriate other businesses in the interest of redevelopment to allow a hotel project to go forward. But how does a hotel meet the aims of redevelopment, poverty alleviation, a reduction in unemployment, and so forth? Projects, as we can see from the planning and approval process, do not directly address these concerns; instead, development is the main concern, and relatedly the possible positive fiscal impact the project will have on the city and redevelopment agency.

More importantly, hotel and related visitor services have been an economic development priority: the industry and its related services are part of the economic development program for revitalizing the inner city. Consistently, hotel development has been viewed as essential to the planned development for visitor services. The expansion of the convention center, the building of the new ballpark for the San Diego Padres, and expansion of the convention center are expected to provide an economic boost to the city and region, providing more than $13 million in new tax revenue, generating nearly 4,000 construction jobs and an additional 6,885 permanent jobs, and producing millions of dollars in additional revenue for the region's economy, according to the Mayor's Citizens Task Force on the convention center expansion (Port of San Diego 2012).

This continued push for expansion of the convention center and related visitor services is in part a product of the need to stay competitive within the meeting and convention market. As more and more cities have pushed convention and visitors industries as a form of economic development, San Diego has had to continue to push for expansions and public resources to keep pace with other cities. This chasing of important tourist and business and meeting travelers has made the hospitality industry a cornerstone of the economic development plan for San

Diego's downtown, and this in turn has been functionally dependent on the large low-wage workforce that is employed in that industry.

INDUSTRY RESTRUCTURING

As San Diego was going through a push to improve convention and visitor amenities in the downtown area, the hotel industry was also going through a series of restructurings. In this next section I look at how the industry has changed over the years in terms of employment, and examine more closely the issues of job quality and career opportunities in the hotel sector.

The hospitality industry saw dramatic growth over the past few decades, with employment nearly tripling between 1970 and 2000. Two trends have characterized the industry over the past twenty to thirty years: consolidation and restructuring. Hotels merged to increase market share and spread their risk across different markets. By the 1990s, the industry was dominated by a handful of large corporate-owned hotel companies that began to drive industry practices (Bernhardt, Dresser, and Hatton 2003). These changes, particularly with the drive to profitability in an increasingly competitive environment, further driven by shareholder and investor pressures on the publicly held companies, pushed for greater performance and profitability. These pressures led to changes in management to cut costs, increase revenues, retain or expand market share, and make each hotel perform to a set of metrics set out by corporate offices.

Recent net profit margins attest to the competitiveness of the industry. Over the past decade, net national hotel profits have ranged from 5 to 9 percent, with submarkets sometimes performing better or worse (CSI Market 2014). Operating margins often run between 6 and 14 percent, and managers at local hotels often reference these constraints when considering wage or benefits increases. Increased labor costs reduce the operating margins, which are critical to maintain not just net operating expenses, but also long-term debt service, something that the vast majority of hotels in the region share. Trying to expand labor costs erodes these profit margins and in the view of the management makes a hotel less competitive in terms of pricing. With the business for conventions and other travel-related visitor services truly global, pressures to keep average daily rates of hotels as low and therefore as attractive as possible

remain constant with local hotel operators and larger chains that operate in San Diego. Of course these pressures also translate into efforts
to increase labor productivity across the industry as well as ensure that
labor costs and staffing are kept as low and flexible as possible.

The U.S. hotel industry is a cyclical business that varies with response
to the business cycles of the economy. Since 1990 the industry has seen
a long run of profitability. Consistently, between 1991 and 2007 RevPAR
(revenue per available room, an indicator of hotel performance) increased
by an average of 12.4 percent each year, with a brief drop in RevPAR in
2008 of 1.6 percent (down from the previous year when there were
record profits). The recession hurt profitability for several years, but the
hotel industry responded to the recent recession by cutting labor costs to
maintain a profit. As travel began to shrink in late 2008, hotel companies reduced staff by the thousands nationally and reduced hours and
overtime for remaining employees. As a result, profitability was restored
even with the reduced travel and hotel occupancy, because expense re-
ductions have been so dramatic that even "a slight improvement in revenue per available room growth should lead to outsized profit gains"
(Goldman Sachs 2009).

Lean Staffing and Flexible Workforces

The hotel industry has undergone major restructuring in its staffing
practices and training over the past two decades. These changes are in
part a product of the broader push for greater efficiencies and flexible
staffing capabilities within labor-intensive industries ranging from manufacturing to services. In hotels, the introduction of new techniques for
personnel management is aimed at making the industry more flexible in
terms of staffing competencies. This means that employees are cross-
trained in a range of activities so that they are more capable of "filling
in" if there are critical staffing shortages at any given time. In another
dimension, more intensive training is used to improve customer service
and efficiency.

This push toward reducing labor costs to ensure profitability is part
of the broader trend since the 1980s to reduce costs through labor flexibility. Since the late 1980s, hotel companies steadily reduced the number of workers employed to provide service to guests. In 1988 nearly

seventy-one workers were employed to service a hundred occupied guest-rooms, while by 2012, the figure dropped to fifty-three—a 25 percent reduction (UNITE/HERE 2012). In the meantime, hotels have responded to the recession and an even more competitive market by offering more amenities and services, and pushing for higher customer service standards, in short, offering more with fewer workers.

These changes, which began driving the hotel industry forward in more competitive markets throughout the 1980s, have become standards across the industry. The increased focus on customer service places more responsibilities on the frontline worker, making it more difficult to accomplish everything in a shift during busy periods. This means that housekeepers face a bind in that they have to maintain the high standards and accomplish their assignments, but still do it within their prescribed shifts, because overtime is not available.

Hours and Scheduling

Flexible and lean scheduling has become the norm across the hotel industry. Hotels in San Diego, like in any other major tourist and convention destination, can have wide fluctuations in staffing needs. The challenge this poses to hotel management is straightforward but nonetheless vexing: how can a hotel maintain the right level of staff to meet times of peak demand when there is full occupancy and/or convention and meeting guests one week, but not have idle workers and the same high labor costs when the hotel is relatively empty? Every firm must balance labor supply with demand, but with the hospitality industry, market conditions can vary very quickly and without a strong level of predictability.

Responding to the staffing challenge, the hotel industry increasingly relies on flexible and lean staffing practices. This means staffing the hotel with as few frontline employees as possible during slack periods and boosting staff during busy periods. The reliance on convention center visitors or holiday travel further reinforces this dynamic. During large conventions, or multiple small ones, hotels can become incredibly busy, followed by periods of little activity. Holidays or major sporting events have a similar effect on staffing demands. As a result, management needs to keep a small core of regular, full-time employees on, and either bring them in for mandatory overtime during busy periods, or keep a large pool of part-time and "on-call" staff who may only see twenty hours a week normally, but go up to thirty to forty hours as needed during busy periods. This flexible staffing arrangement allows the company to keep labor costs as closely aligned to demand as possible, but it places the burden of flexibility on staff. Part-time and on-call staff members are faced with the never-ending prospect of being called into work or having too few hours to make ends meet, while full-time core employees are faced with full-time plus overtime hours when demand shoots up. Neither option is preferable to employees. Staff members who work on the part-time end complain about never being able to plan weeks, family meals, trips to see family, even shopping or laundry in some cases. Employees working full time sometimes complain that overtime may be too much work per week, but they see little ability to turn down the extra hours because the pay is better for overtime, and with such low wages, the staff often relish the additional bonus that overtime brings. This type of scheduling, however, does push some of the lowest-paid workers—in housekeeping and front of house or food and beverage service—up to forty- or fifty- and in some cases sixty-hour work weeks. In short, to meet the needs of the hotel industry and visitor demand, the lowest paid workers in the industry have to accommodate to the often highly irregular work schedules that the hospitality industry is driven by.

Wages

Wages in the hospitality industry have largely been stagnant or declined between 1979 and 1995; only recently has there been an upward turn in the median wage since 2000 (Bernhardt, Dresser, and Hatton 2003). In the San Diego hospitality industry, which includes hotels and other lodging firms and their attendant food service businesses, wages reflect the national trends of relative stagnation, with the median annual income of $24,000 per year (ACS 2013). Furthermore, the majority of positions pay less than a self-sufficiency wage for the city of San Diego. With 83 percent of the industry employment below a self-sufficiency wage, the hospitality industry has one of the lowest rates of economically self-supporting jobs. Among the largest industries in San Diego, it has the lowest median wage rate (CPI 2006). Table 9 lists the largest occupations in the industry, their median hourly wage, and the difference from the self-sufficiency wage for San Diego.

TABLE 9. Occupations, Industry Employment, and Wages in the Hospitality Industry

Occupation	Portion of Industry Employment	Median Hourly Wage	Difference from Self-Sufficiency Wage
Maids and housekeeping cleaners	30%	10.17	–3.75
Hotel, motel, and resort desk clerks	13%	11.75	–2.17
Waiters and waitresses	10%	11.46	–2.46
Maintenance and repair workers, general	5%	17.16	3.24
Cooks, restaurant	4%	11.46	–2.46
Dining room and cafeteria attendants and bartender helpers	4%	8.93	–4.99
Food servers, non-restaurant	3%	10.36	–3.56
Bartenders	3%	9.21	–4.71
Dishwashers	3%	9.14	–4.78
Lodging managers	2%	24.28	10.36
Laundry and dry-cleaning workers	2%	10.31	–3.61
Baggage porters and bellhops	2%	9.52	–4.4
Bookkeeping, accounting, and auditing clerks	2%	19.14	5.22
First-line supervisors/managers of food preparation and serving workers	2%	13.87	–0.05
Sales representatives, services, all other	1%	27.11	13.19
First-line sup/mgrs of office and administrative support workers	1%	24.96	11.04
Food preparation and serving workers, including fast food	1%	9.25	–4.67
Security guards	1%	11.72	–2.2
Hosts and hostesses, restaurant, lounge, and coffee shop	1%	9.02	–4.9
Amusement and recreation attendants	1%	9.13	–4.79
Food preparation workers	1%	9.69	–4.23
Concierges	1%	13.85	–0.07
Cashiers	1%	9.81	–4.11

SOURCE: Staffing patterns from the BLS, Cal EDD LMID for San Diego hospitality industry, 2013.

Career Ladders

Career ladders are critical for workers in lower-wage, entry-level positions to move up within a business and earn more, gain more experience, and further their careers. Unfortunately, career ladders in the hospitality industry are very limited. Like much of the service sector, though the firms may have many jobs, the majority tend to be entry level, pay low wages, and offer few avenues for upward mobility.

Hotel operations are typically segmented into three different departments: guest services at the front of house, housekeeping, and, if available, food and beverage service. Class A hotels, or those typically three or four star or higher, have food and beverage services available at restaurants, bars, or other facilities within the hotel. Career ladders within these departments vary slightly, but even if some areas have far greater occupational mobility than others, these opportunities are further limited by the fact that people rarely move across departments. Hotel housekeepers, for instance, rarely move into food service and vice versa. Front desk clerks have few options other than moving into management or administrative positions, but these often require more specialized skills (such as accounting), and therefore on-the-job experience may be inadequate.

Generally, within hotels, there is little movement across these career ladders, and therefore the departmental career ladders become more important for each worker in each department. Based on interviews with hotel human resource managers at larger hotels (those with more than seventy-five employees, approximately 25 percent of the hotels in the downtown core, but with the majority of employment in the hotel industry downtown), the career ladders within different segments of large hotels are all very flat. That is to say, at the most there are three or four jobs hierarchically within each department within which to move up or down. Table 10 displays the typical career ladders in front-of-house guest services, within kitchen departments, housekeeping, and maintenance. Excluded here are management positions, which include accounting/bookkeeping, sales, and other positions, because those positions vary greatly from hotel to hotel in terms of career ladders, they require college degrees and experience, and they are generally not the types of entry-level positions where someone begins a career. In fact, the two largest hotels where I interviewed human resource managers had just appointed supervisors and general managers who were recruited from outside of the area, one through a nationwide search, and the other recruited internally from within the company. In other words, these are not positions usually filled by local residents looking for an entry-level job.

As Table 10 shows, there are severe limits to the career ladders of each department. Front of house/guest services can include valet parking and bellhop staff, but in order to move into a supervisory or management position, a degree is required. Human resource managers report that valet parking staff and bellhop staff/porters are generally split between Latinos who are working full time and spend several years or more in the position, and students and others who typically work part time and fill in during busy periods. As a result, workers in the front of house who are not in front-desk or concierge positions are either spending several years or more in the position with limited upward mobility, or are doing the job part time to work through college or earn extra money (often in addition to other part-time jobs), and the latter often then leave the occupation once they finish their degree or get a better job. In short, there is little evidence that these entry-level positions lead to bigger careers in the firm.

Within food service (waiters and waitresses, hosts), there are few occupations higher up other than the direct dining room/catering manager. This means that like the entry-level positions at the front of the house, serving staff positions do not always lead to a direct or clear career ladder. For those in the kitchen there are longer career ladders, but these require a lot of on-the-job training and experience, and from the sous chef level up (see Table 10), formal training is generally required. Even if someone does start out as a dishwasher or even prep cook, the road up within the kitchen is limited. Even more challenging is the fact that a movement from dishwasher to prep cook brings only about a 25-cent wage increase (from $9.07 to $9.32/hr.), sous chefs or similarly experienced line cooks may earn $12.00 to 13.00 an hour, but it is not until one reaches a head chef position in the kitchen that self-sufficiency wages are found (more than $23.00/hr.). Maintenance workers face a similar problem, where typically there are either janitors or supervisors in managerial positions. Those with some skills, such as general carpentry, plumbing, or electrical skills (fixing smoke alarms, etc.) may earn more and are in a higher position than simple janitors, but in the end, there

TABLE 10. Departmental Career Ladders in Full-Service Hotels

Department	Front of House	Kitchen	Maintenance	Housekeeping
Higher wage and responsibility	Guest services manager	Head cook/Chef	Head of maintenance	Housekeeping manager
	Supervisor	Sous chef	Maintenance worker	Supervisor/ Asst manager
Lower wage and less responsibility	Front desk clerk/Concierge	Prep cook	Janitor	Housekeeper
	Bellhop staff/ Parking staff	Dishwasher		

SOURCE: Author survey of human resource managers in the hotel industry.

are only a couple of levels of upward mobility within the maintenance department.

Housekeeping is by far the largest occupation in the industry, with nearly a third of the workforce working as housekeepers. There are also very few options for upward mobility as a housekeeper. The only steps up from a position as a housekeeper are to a supervisor or managerial position. While these may reflect slightly better pay, there is typically only one such position per hotel at either level, and as many housekeepers have described, these positions rarely, if ever, open up. In other words, housekeeping positions provide almost no avenues for upward mobility within the department. The broader point here is that career ladders that don't have many rungs, and for which the top rungs are largely out of reach because they are filled through external recruitment or have skills and education requirements that are very difficult to attain, mean that the ladders are not really ladders, but instead step stools. Taking Table 10 as an example, there are only two steps up from the entry-level position, and front-of-house operations, where there are more possible upper-level positions, only have four steps. With lots of workers vying for positions on the lower rungs as well as for movement vertically, the likelihood that someone moves up in the industry within their own department or area of expertise is very limited.

The other issue that a close look at career ladders in the industry raises is that of polarization within the jobs. In hotel work, there is a clear skills chasm between entry-level positions and managerial ones. Entry-level positions in housekeeping and janitorial work do not require any special-ized education or training. Moving up into management or even some administrative roles, however, requires not just a high-school equivalency but some college training or even a degree. All managerial positions require some college-level education, plus several years' experience in a supervisory capacity in the industry. Overall, 78 percent of industry employment requires on-the-job training or a high school equivalency, the remaining positions, mostly in management, require some college coursework or a degree or higher, but there are very few stepping stones in between in terms of mid career stepping stones.

We can illustrate this with a career ladder through front-of-house ser-vices. Starting out as a porter or bellhop requires no experience. This is an entry-level position. Moving up to a front desk position usually requires significant experience (several years on average), and often these posi-tions are staffed with employees who have some college experience or even degrees. Approximately half of the front desk clerks I interviewed in San Diego hotels had a college degree. Moving from an entry-level position to a front desk position, therefore, generally entails some col-lege study. And for any managerial position, college degrees are gener-ally required; in some instances staff have advanced degrees in business administration or accounting. The point here is that there are no real intermediary steps between someone in an entry-level position with no high school degree and a position that requires a college degree or at least some college. In the case of housekeeping positions, this is less of a problem, but the career ladder is highly compressed. Housekeepers can move up to supervisory and managerial positions within that depart-ment without a college degree, but there are usually only a few such positions in a large, full-service hotel. In some hotels there is only one managerial position and one supervisory position, meaning that there are very limited chances that someone can move up to the top of this department, even with a lot of experience.

This pattern of career ladder polarization varies depending on the size and type of hotel, but overall there are clear trends. In Table 11, the por-tion of jobs by education and training level are broken down according to the size of the hotel. Staffing levels vary greatly, from more than three hundred employees at the full-service resort hotel, to only fifteen employ-ees at the small hotel. Human resource managers also have large degrees

TABLE 11. Minimum Training/Education Requirements for All Positions among Different Types of Hotels

Educational Attainment	Full-Service Resort Hotel	Medium-Sized Hotel	Small Hotel	Weighted Average
Advanced degree	3%	1%	0%	1%
College degree	11%	25%	4%	13%
Some college	0%	5%	0%	0%
High school equivalency + on-the-job training	10%	4%	10%	9%
High school equivalency	33%	35%	6%	55%
Less than high school	43%	30%	80%	12%

SOURCE: Author interviews with human resource managers of local hotels.

of variation when estimating what the portion of jobs is at different education and skill levels. In the small hotel, anyone working in housekeeping, approximately 80 percent of the staff, was not required to have any high school equivalency.

The overall pattern appears to be one where most of the positions require only a high school equivalency or less, plus some on-the-job training. At the higher end of the skills and education level is a clustering of jobs, primarily in management, that demand some amount of college-level training or degree. Thus, there are not many jobs that have intermediate steps: one either remains in a less-skilled position or moves into management-level work through obtaining a college degree. As many hotel housekeepers describe, there is not much of an incentive to try to get ahead when there is nowhere to go in the industry, at least not without a college-level education. To their credit, Unite/HERE, the union representing most hotel workers in the United States, has programs that encourage greater education and training, including English-language courses, and collaborates with other organizations to improve the quality of jobs and career ladders; however, these laudable programs are few and far between. Also, the union density among hotels is so low that taking a "high road" approach to improving job quality remains very difficult. In San Diego the urban core has a high concentration of hotels, but less than 20 percent are unionized.

This polarization of jobs within the industry, particularly along the lines of career ladders, appears to be long standing, but getting worse. I spoke to a thirty-seven-year veteran of the industry who recalled that in the 1970s there were more positions within the full-service hotels in particular, there were more departments and career ladders, and few managers had college degrees. This has shifted, he describes, because more and more people are college educated today, and cost cutting, increased employee productivity, and subcontracting have removed many of the jobs from the hotel that would otherwise have provided employment and more rungs on the career ladder. For instance, he cites fewer kitchen staff because food is often preprepared and packaged, hotel check-in is now available at an automated service station in the lobby, and the linen services are subcontracted out, so far less laundry is done on site. While quantitative historical data like this to verify the shift toward a more polarized workforce in hotels is difficult to find, this manager's statements are echoed by other long-term employees in the industry.

Race, Gender, and Opportunity

It is impossible to speak about occupational mobility within the hotel industry without giving attention to the changing racial dynamics of employment. African Americans were once the largest minority group working in back-of-house operations, particularly housekeeping, but over the past couple of decades Latino, Asian, and even East European immigrant workers have supplanted them within the hotel industry (Bates 1999; Waldinger 1996). This is clearly the case in San Diego as, according to managers and my own survey, housekeeping, maintenance, and lower-level occupations within the kitchen are almost exclusively Latino. This finding is striking given that the highest concentration of unemployed African Americans (and to some extent Asians) is in the neighborhoods surrounding the revitalized urban core in central San Diego. The predominance of Latino workers in these lowest-paid positions, and the dearth of African Americans, is in part due to the far greater supply of Latinos in the lower-wage labor market, and to their higher rates of labor force participation. These two factors, however, have to be seen in relation to other variables like the preferences of human resource managers and the presence of hiring networks.

Latino hiring networks in many of these low-wage occupations serve to recruit "prescreened labor" from within Latino social networks, but also serve to exclude African Americans at the same time. This is somewhat of a shift and requires further historical contextualization. The growth of Latino workers in the hospitality industry and decline of African American workers reflects several historical trends. The first is the growth of Latinos within the service sector. As many white and African American workers left low-wage, entry-level positions in parts of the service sector, these jobs were filled by Latinos. Much of the economic research on this effect looks primarily at the increasing supply of immigrant Latinos as having a detrimental effect on native-born workers, and in the case of lower-wage jobs this may be particularly acute for inner-city African Americans who are competing for jobs. Increasing labor supply thus reduces wages and decreases the likelihood that African Americans will be hired for positions they once worked in far greater numbers (Borjas 1994, 1995). The argument that this competition results in the displacement of some workers and lower wages for others is based on the assumption that native-born minorities who possess few job skills are most adversely affected because they are all directly in competition for the same positions, that is, that they are substitutable (Abowd and Freeman 1991; Borjas, Freeman, and Katz 1992).

There are drawbacks to this approach, however. First, these studies usually examine the national economy as a whole because urban and regional labor markets have porous borders. Workers and firms can move through these borders in pursuit of less job competition in the case of workers, or lower wage demands in the case of firms. Firms may hire based on very local or specific hiring networks or systems embedded within local and regional social relations. Additionally, there is the alternative interpretation by studies that show the inflow of low-skilled minority workers is sometimes absorbed by the receiving labor market without displacing workers and without undercutting wages (e.g., Card 2001, 2005; Friedberg and Hunt 1995). This line of inquiry usually considers urban or regional labor markets in greater depth. This approach demonstrates that the impact of in-migrating workers depends on the context of the receiving labor market. For example, if intergenerational educational advancement leads to a labor market losing low-skilled labor at a faster pace than it is losing low-skilled jobs, most newly arriving low-skilled workers may be filling what would otherwise be a labor short-age. Thus, ethnic secession in low-skilled jobs may be occurring, but not because a new source of cheap labor is taking jobs away from previ-ously established workers. The inflow of new labor may also increase local demand for goods and services, which can lead to more employ-ment and production.

My own approach draws on more qualitative data at the firm level and matches worker experiences with human resource manager statements about hiring in the hospitality industry. Housekeeping is also almost exclusively female. Of the dozen hotel workers I interviewed, represent-ing five different hotels in the downtown area, none of them stated that men work in housekeeping. In contrast, kitchen jobs are almost exclu-sively male, while serving jobs vary. These gendered divisions of labor within the industry limit the occupational mobility of workers along lines of race and gender. Women of color, primarily Latinas, are typically working in housekeeping jobs for which there are few avenues upward. Latino men are working in the kitchen or front of house. The share of African Americans has dropped dramatically in the industry, and part of the Latinoization in San Diego hotels appears to be the presence of hiring networks and the preference for Latinos by hiring managers.

Managers cite several reasons for Latinos being predominant in these positions. First, few African Americans apply for the jobs. In recent applicant pools (during the previous years' worth of applications) sev-eral human resource managers stated that the number of African Amer-ican applicants was limited to a few out of hundreds. Additionally, these managers cite the higher rate of turnover among those African Ameri-cans who had been hired in the past. When pressed on this, only two cases were mentioned of African Americans who had positions and then left after a short period of time, but such cases are still recalled when asked to describe potential reasons that African Americans are not in the industry, despite a need for entry-level jobs in the local African American community. Another reason that managers cite for a dearth of African American workers in the hospitality industry is the positive attributes of Latinos, and Asians (primarily Filipinos and Vietnamese). Latinos are viewed as hard working and long-term employees. "They don't complain, they take care of their families, and they work hard," described one man-ager. This is not unique to the hospitality industry but is a characteristic of many lower-wage and service-sector employers in San Diego (Kar-janen 2008). Finally, there is the issue of hiring networks. Because so many Latinos already work in the hospitality industry, they refer other family members, friends, and people they know who are looking for work. Managers look favorably on this network hiring process because it offers them another way to prescreen applicants; someone with a personal reference by an existing employee who is trusted is an advantage to the applicant who has the network of already-hired personnel. All of these factors become self-fulfilling systems of reproducing the growing Latino dominance of the industry and the decline of African Americans.

Low Skilled?

One of the striking findings from interviewing hotel workers and their managers, and spending time going over their daily labor processes, is the gap between the perception of what the work is supposed to entail and what the reality of that work is. I have consistently argued that the language of "low-skilled" versus "high-skilled" is inaccurate. It presumes that "highly skilled" people are those with high rates of education and training and that the "lower skilled" are those with less education and training (Karjanen 2010b). Why someone like me with a PhD is "highly skilled" and someone who is a self-taught welder and metalsmith who produces sculpture and public art as well as welds rebar for concrete construction is not is purely a cultural assertion. These skills are not "high" or "low" but differently valued by society. The same comparison holds true for "lesser-skilled" occupations like hotel housekeepers.

There are two different conceptual issues here. The first is how we analyze skill. Space here does not permit a full elaboration of my criticism, but the central point is that the way that labor economists or the Bureau of Labor Statistics measures the relative skill of an occupation is inaccurate. In short, the skill is measured by proxy, the proxy being years of education, or on-the-job work experience. Yet, it is widely recognized that education in itself is a poor proxy for skills used on the job. More broadly, human resource practices, occupational manuals, and the entire system of job skills organization for hiring and wage-setting purposes has been justifiably critiqued for valuing some skills over others, often with a gendered bias (Steinberg 1990). Why is it, for instance, that running budgets on an Excel spreadsheet (accountants) is seen as demanding more skill than taking care of a room full of four-year-olds (preschool teachers)? The second issue for the hospitality industry—indeed, from my experience most of the positions held by members of the "servant class"—is that the industry itself has very simplistic understandings of what skills are used on the job, and what the job actually entails on a daily basis. To be specific, firms in the service sector fail to grasp the depth and complexity of the work by many if not most of their frontline, customer-interacting employees.

It is well established that labor is far more heterogeneous than previously thought. There are in fact very different kinds of labor enshrined within a singular labor process. The cross-training efforts of newer human resource and managerial practices actually promote this heterogeneity: pushing workers to embody a range of possible occupations within a firm or industry even though they are only classified within a single occupation. Thus, hotel housekeepers can perform their core housekeeping duties, but they also act as front-end staff for guests they encounter, they act as concierges for guests who are too busy to call the front desk, they serve as communicators for hotel guests who are not sure where to call in a large hotel to obtain a specific item, information, or service. All of this varied work allows housekeepers to be "more than just housekeepers" in terms of their labor, and yet at the same time be paid as, characterized by, and located within the business as just "hotel housekeepers."

One type of service that housekeepers perform, for instance, is to represent one of the central human interfaces with customers in relation to the hotel. Hotel managers do not see it this way; they see front-end staff as being the "face" of the hotel, but it is often housekeepers who are interacting with customers more frequently. Guests may request towels, spills cleaned, more soap, and so forth, and during these interactions, housekeepers often display skills that have become trendy in more recent human resource management research like "emotional labor" and soft skills. One housekeeper described to me how she has spent several hours in her career consoling guests who are in town for funerals. In one case she arranged to have the hotel provide flowers for the guests free of charge because she was so emotionally moved by the guests' experience flying to San Diego for the funeral of their son, who had died while serving in the navy. Another housekeeper explained that she has helped disabled guests get additional services that the guests were not aware of at the hotel, and even wheeled one guest in her wheelchair to the elevator because they were running late and at risk of missing their flight; waiting for the porter was taking too long. Housekeepers even work as part-time concierges, answering questions from busy guests rushing down hallways, offering advice about amenities for kids at the hotel, and offering extra information that might be helpful.

All of this customer interaction is in excess of the standard house-keeping duties. Part of the job entails "providing excellent customer service" and "responding to guest needs," but what those needs are, and how the housekeepers respond, is left up to the housekeeper. In the few cases I have mentioned here, however, it is clear that the extent of house-keeper interaction can greatly exceed employer and guest expectations, yet little recognition of this occurs in the day-to-day operations. The skill set that many housekeepers deploy involves effective communication, emotional labor, and a range of what are typically described as "soft skills" by employers.

CONCLUSION

As one of the larger low-wage service industries in the city, the hospital-ity industry also has been touted as good for the economy of the city and region, and for providing employment opportunities in the inner city as part of the urban revitalization of San Diego. In this chapter, however, we see that the quality of jobs and lack of mobility reflect similar find-ings in the research. More specifically, wages and occupational mobility are very limited. Wages for the lowest-paid employees have been flat or declined slightly over the past decade in San Diego within the indus-try. And, despite restructuring, cost cutting, and continued profitabil-ity, the industry continues to push employees to be more flexible and accommodating, yet the experience of working in the industry may not directly translate into the types of employment and human capital devel-opment that can lead to greater economic mobility. Although there is some indication that low-wage service work in areas like hospitality and food service or retail work may vary greatly in quality depending on the firm and management (Bernhardt, Dresser, and Hatton 2003; Warhurst et al. 2012), I do not find this in San Diego. Moreover, there is a clear and potentially growing polarization of employment within the industry, particularly along the lines of career ladders.

Career ladders are generally flat and more akin to career step stools. Without many intermediary positions, employees within the industry face either low-wage and lesser-skilled jobs or moving up into managerial positions that require significant amounts of experience and college study or degrees. This job landscape does not offer many options for entry-level workers. If the hospitality industry is touted, as in the case of San Diego, as a means for entry-level workers to move into and up a career and gain economic stability and mobility, then the evidence weighs against this notion unless job quality and career ladders are significantly improved.

Finally, there is the related issue of the skills and demands that workers in the industry do have and are asked to perform on a day-to-day basis. What emerges from studying the broad range of activities of hotel workers is that the skills set is indeed quite broad and in some cases very extensive, and beyond what the actual job description may be for a particular employee. Yet these skills may be rarely recognized by management because the jobs are understood too narrowly. This is not the case with every manager and hotel, but it appears to be the norm. The positive note here is that there appears to be room for upgrading the jobs within the industry to include more responsibilities and activities, as well as recognition of the work that already goes on. This is less an empirical point to be debated and more of a political observation: work can be valued or devalued socially; women, immigrants, and people of color typically earn less and have devalued labor, and the hospitality industry is no exception. Better organizing of employees and recognition of the work actually performed and the gaps and needs to improve jobs should be an industry-wide effort.

4

Working Retail in
the Inner City

I N T H I S C H A P T E R I turn to the other large segment of low-wage
service-sector employment in the revitalized urban core: retail. I first
look at the general trends in the industry that ultimately have an
influence on employment practices and job quality. In the second section I discuss the promotion of retail in the inner city by developers and
planning bodies, and in the final section I look more closely at job quality, career ladders, and case studies of issues related to working in the
industry. Data in this chapter are drawn from secondary sources: Bureau
of Labor Statistics wage data and other data from the California Labor
Market Information Division of the Economic Development Department. These data are combined with interviews and case studies at retailers in the Centre City area.

TRENDS IN RETAIL

Like the hotel industry, competitive pressures forced changes in the retail industry over the past few decades. Recessions in the 1970s and
1980s put great pressure on retailing and forced growing consolidation
of stores, companies, and branches. Notably, this was also the period
when large discount stores or "category killer" retailers began to expand
nationwide. Combined with the growth in corporate consolidation and
chain mergers, this has led to a two-tiered retail structure based on size.
Retailing remains a small business, with the vast majority of stores having fewer than ten employees, and the larger firms being typically mall
anchor stores, like Macy's and JCPenney, or large discount "category
killer" stores, like Walmart or Home Depot.

The growth of the retail market has reached a saturation point in many areas of the United States, with an oversupply creating many regional and local ghost malls across the country. Market saturation occurs when there are more square feet of retail supply in a market than demand based on the market's retail expenditures. This is the reason for the abandoning of many suburban and rural malls in the United States. In such an environment, margins become smaller and smaller and competition in turn increasingly focuses on cost reduction (Bailey and Bernhardt 1997). These shifts, combined with the development of discount retail, put far greater pressure on firms to reduce costs, primarily in the area of labor. Thus, more contingent work, flexible work arrangements, and stagnant or declining wages have been the trend in the industry. In the case of San Diego, real wages for some of the largest retail-sector jobs (cashiers, stock clerks, and retail sales) all saw declines, some as high as 6 percent. This is despite high job growth and long-term openings in the industry.

RETAIL DEVELOPMENT IN THE INNER CITY

Retail development has been central to San Diego's inner-city revitalization. The original redevelopment project in the Centre City Redevelopment Project Area was the Horton Plaza Retail Center, an award-winning suburban-sized mall, enclosed in a multitier structure across three city blocks. Since that project, thousands of square feet of retail space were built in the area. These include dedicated retail projects, as well as retail as part of mixed-use developments. Typically, for instance, high-rise residential or office space may have ground floor retail as part of the project. By 2010 the retail submarket in the downtown area had reached saturation, with a negative net absorption rate (CB Richard Ellis 2013), yet by 2015, nearly four hundred thousand square feet of retail development was in the planning and development stages (Michell 2015). Why then does retail development continue apace if there appears to be adequate supply already in the redevelopment project area? Regional market demand and the dramatic growth of downtown residents is, of course, a key factor, but the city's role as a planning agency and promoter of certain kinds of development cannot be underestimated.

The reasons for so much retail development in the urban core vary. From a fiscal perspective, the city prefers large retailers because they generate significant net fiscal impacts. The accumulation of property, business licenses, and sale taxes for large retailers averages $48,910 per year (City of San Diego 2013), while smaller stores also generate a net positive benefit, but this varies widely depending on the size, location, and annual sales of the store. For these reasons, planners and officials generally look on retail developments favorably; the fiscalization of land use encourages retail developments, like others that generate positive flows to public funds.

Another reason for the growth in retail is that retail and office space have higher rental rates than residential units, typically. There is an incentive to include in mixed-use projects a retail component for promoting financial feasibility. Such mixed-use projects also make the development more attractive to market. Ultimately, developers need to provide adequate pro-forma statements to get approved, and retail as a component can make a project more attractive in that regard.

A more fundamental reason for such strong retail growth in the redevelopment area is the growing demand associated with new housing units. With nineteen thousand new housing units, local and neighborhood retail growth was necessary to keep up with the growth of residential development. Indeed, mixed-use projects and a range of zoning have been a planning priority in the downtown area in order to promote a balance of development types that allow for the co-location of employers, residences, and commercial projects. The co-locating of these development types promotes greater walkability and is part of a smart-growth planning effort.

Retail development in San Diego's inner city has largely been limited to smaller-footprint businesses, two large stores—grocery and office retail—and anchor stores that operate at the Horton Plaza Mall. With several million square feet of retail developed, and several thousand retail jobs created (6,588 since 1980), retail growth has generated a significant number of jobs in the urban core. These jobs provide thousands of entry-level positions for those without work experience, specialized skills, or educational credentials, and even for those who are challenged by English-language proficiency. The next section looks at working conditions in the industry, including an analysis of job quality, and provides case studies of retail operations among firms in the downtown area.

JOB QUALITY

Research on the retail sector points to well-known concerns regarding job quality: notably low wages, lack of benefits coverage, and challenging working conditions (Bailey and Bernhardt 1997; Carré and Tilly 2009; Carré, Tilly, and Holgate 2010; Doussard 2013; Holzer et al. 2011). Some studies (e.g., Holzer et al. 2011) find that for workers at the lower level of the skills spectrum, retail jobs have actually provided more opportunities to have a "good job." My concern here is to examine the issue of job quality in the retail sector and relate it to the broader system of socioeconomic stratification and the reproduction of such forms of inequality over time, thus paying attention to issues like wage growth and career ladders. Overall, workers in the retail industry tend to be younger, have low wages, and have less access to health coverage or retirement plans than workers in other industries. Additionally, as I detail later, they have less control over scheduling and hours, and they face very limited career ladders and skills acquisition through the workplace.

Demographically, retail employees tend to be younger than workers in other industries, with 28 percent being under twenty-four years of age, compared to 16 percent for all workers (Carré and Tilly 2009). In contrast to the notion that retail workers are primarily high school or college students working in temporary or summer jobs, 39 percent of retail employees are between twenty-five and forty-four, and the vast majority in the industry are older than twenty-five (72 percent) (Carré and Tilly 2009). By some estimates, 38 percent of all retail workers and 28 percent of frontline retail workers (lower paid, typically nonsupervisory workers) received employer-sponsored health insurance as compared to 48 percent of all workers (Caree, Tilly, and Denham 2010). Similarly, only 30 percent of retail workers received employer-sponsored retirement benefits in 2001, compared to 48 percent of all workers (Caree, Tilly, and Denham 2010). In addition to being poorly paid and younger, retail workers typically manage less regular work schedules. Working evenings and weekends is common, like in much of low-wage service work. Additionally, employees typically need to be very flexible in being available for work, almost, as some firms I interviewed describe it, as if on an "on-call" basis. This issue has significant effects for families and workers trying to juggle employment with school or other obligations, which I discuss in more detail later in the chapter.

Wages in the retail industry are among the lowest of any in the country, with average hourly earnings nationally at $16.68, and for production and nonsupervisory employees the mean hourly wage is $14.17. Only about 5 percent of the industry is unionized (BLS Industry and Occupation Wage Data 2013), and this figure has declined slightly over the past few years. Nationally, between 2003 and 2013, real wages across the industry have declined, despite strong growth and profitability over the same period. In San Diego, real wages for the largest occupations in the industry— retail salespersons, stock clerks, cashiers, and laborers—have all declined as well between 2000 and 2013 (author analysis of local retail wages adjusted for inflation). In San Diego's retail industry, wages are slightly less than the national average, despite the much higher cost of living in San Diego overall. Average hourly earnings for the industry are $16.11, with 146,000 people employed in the retail industry (author's calculations based on BLS data, 2013) or about 12 percent of San Diego's labor market.

Average hourly or median earnings for the industry, however, do not reflect large segments of the retail industry. Wages can vary greatly depending on the type of store, location, and staffing patterns. For the vast majority of retail in the downtown area, department stores and small stores with fewer than ten employees dominate. Using staffing patterns from the BLS, combined with surveys of staffing patterns of the dozen firms in this study, the following Tables 12 and 13 provide an estimate of wage distribution and average wage (weighted) at these two types of stores. Both of these types of stores make up an estimated 80 percent of retailers in the revitalized redevelopment project area.

As Table 12 shows, department stores are dominated by retail salespersons, followed by stock clerks and cashiers. Many of these occupations are blended in higher-end stores, while in some stores they are separate. On average, however, the five largest occupations—salespersons, stock clerks, cashiers, and laborers—all account for 82 percent of store employment. These occupations all pay significantly less than a self-sufficiency wage for San Diego on average, with cashiers having the lowest pay rate of the large occupations at $9.81, or nearly five dollars less than a self-sufficiency wage. Self-sufficiency wages only show up in a handful of occupations: supervisors, managers, bookkeepers, pharmacists, and customer service representatives. These occupations combined make up less than 10 percent of department store employment. Overall, these

TABLE 12. Occupational Staffing Patterns, Wages, and Difference from Self-Sufficiency Wage in Department Stores, San Diego

Occupation	Portion of Employment	Median Hourly Wage	Difference from Self-Sufficiency Wage
Retail Salespersons	36%	10.77	−3.98
Stock Clerks and Order Fillers	26%	11.14	−3.61
Cashiers	14%	9.81	−4.94
Laborers and Freight, Stock, and Material Movers, Hand	6%	12.08	−2.67
Supervisors of Retail Sales Workers	3%	19.35	4.6
Customer Service Representatives	2%	17.44	2.69
Security Guards	2%	11.72	−3.03
Sales and Related Workers, All Other	1%	11.98	−2.77
Janitors and Cleaners, Except Maids and Housekeeping Cleaners	1%	11.5	−3.25
Shipping, Receiving, and Traffic Clerks	1%	14.43	−0.32
Combined Food Preparation and Serving Workers, Including Fast Food	1%	9.25	−5.5
Merchandise Displayers and Window Trimmers	1%	16.42	1.67
Pharmacists	1%	66.6	51.85
Hairdressers, Hairstylists, and Cosmetologists	1%	11.27	−3.48
Photographic Process Workers and Processing Machine Operators	1%	13.82	−0.93
Sales Managers	1%	51.21	36.46
Bookkeeping, Accounting, and Auditing Clerks	1%	19.14	4.39
Office Clerks, General	1%	14.17	−0.58
Average Wage (weighted)		12.43	−2.32

SOURCE: BLS Wage and Staffing Patterns for San Diego, California Employment Development Department Labor Market Information Division.

types of stores do not provide an average wage that meets self-sufficiency levels in San Diego.

Small retailers have far fewer employees on average, and have lower wage rates. With an average wage of $10.41, small stores do not provide a mean self-sufficiency wage either. Again, the largest portion of employment, cashiers and stock clerks (57 percent of total jobs), pay well below a self-sufficiency wage. Table 13 shows the staffing patterns for smaller stores.

Hours and Scheduling

The retail industry is widely viewed as having some of the highest concentrations of part-time and contingent work. Indeed, retail employment has a far higher portion of part-time employees in the industry relative to other industries: 28 percent of retail workers are part time, and 41 percent of all frontline jobs within retail are part time; other industries average just 19 percent (Carré and Tilly 2008, 2). These figures are more or less reflected by retailers in San Diego. This higher rate of part-time work is complicated by hour and wage pressures that are a function of cost pressures within the industry.

Hour and wage pressures cut across the industry. Of the dozen stores I examined, from large national chains to small family-owned stores, ten

TABLE 13. Occupational Staffing Patterns, Wages, and Difference from Self-Sufficiency Wage in Small Retailers, San Diego

Occupation	Portion of Employment	Median Hourly Wage	Difference from Self-Sufficiency Wage
Cashiers	37%	$9.81	$–4.94
Stock Clerks and Order Fillers	20%	$11.14	$–3.61
First-Line Supervisors/Managers of Retail Sales Workers	9%	$19.35	$4.60
Laborers and Freight, Stock, and Material Movers, Hand	8%	$12.08	$–2.67
Customer Service Representatives	6%	$17.44	$2.69
Counter Attendants, Cafeteria, Food Concession, and Coffee Shop	4%	$9.55	$–5.20
Janitors and Cleaners, Except Maids and Housekeeping Cleaners	2%	$11.50	$–3.25
Combined Food Preparation and Serving Workers, Including Fast Food	2%	$9.25	$–5.50
Average Wage (weighted)		$10.41	–$4.34

SOURCE: Data drawn from author's retail survey 2005–11, wages are from BLS 2013, local area occupational profiles for San Diego, MSA.

out of twelve tied employee hours in part to sales. Some firms have very clear and calculable formulae, others less so, but it is clear that keeping the variable costs of labor as low as possible is paramount to management. The only two exceptions to this trend are small stores that are in part family run (so employees perform some of the work as part of a social obligation), or simply kept payroll steady regardless of sales fluctuations. Most retail managers, however, do not have such luxuries.

The tendency in tying scheduled payroll hours to sales appears more prevalent in larger, corporate-owned stores, but smaller regional or local retail chains also have the same balancing act to maintain. The pressure for store managers is to maintain levels of customer service, store upkeep, and daily operations, while at the same time keeping payroll costs down. With payroll costs the largest variable cost in the firm, and margins in most sectors of retail very tight, there is constant pressure from corporate and regional offices on store managers to hold the line on costs, thereby ensuring profitability. This conflict engenders all sorts of problems for store operations. For the manager, there is a need to maintain adequate staffing, because staffing in part helps generate sales, but sales are needed to allow staffing. A manager at an electronics store described the problem: "It is a catch-22. If I don't have the numbers [sales] then we run short to put in hours at the end of the week. If I don't have people in the store then we can't drive sales. Electronics is something where customers usually need someone to work with them, even it is finding the right cable or something." This dilemma reverberates throughout the retail employees. Front-end workers like cashiers or salespersons may not get all the hours they plan on in a week. If there is a shortage, this can force employees into challenges of their own. So many hourly workers in retail who are independent live within very tight budget constraints, so cutbacks in hours can be significant. I knew a single mother who worked in retail downtown, and her fluctuating hours ("between twenty-eight and thirty-five, with always the promise of forty") convinced her to get another part-time job. This made her more inflexible in her availability.

This raises another issue with staffing: the human resources cost of lean staffing. Retailing has become as flexible in staffing as possible in relation to consumer demand. At the holidays, overtime and overload staffing is the norm; all twenty checkout lanes are likely to be open. On a rainy Tuesday in early February, however, there may only be a handful of cashiers in a store that can normally accommodate twenty or more. This flexible staffing has allowed stores to try and keep labor costs as tight to sales as possible, but it also means that the flexible staffing system places demands on management and employees to be flexible and in some cases be "on call" to come in as needed. This "on-demand" staffing I found at two stores where it had become a de facto store policy (not official) that employees would be asked to be available, if necessary, to fill in during any given month outside of their regularly scheduled hours. This was welcomed openly by some, those employees who were looking to work every extra hour they could, but disdained by others.

An additional problem of lean staffing is that there is not enough excess labor for contingencies. If someone calls in sick or has a car accident on the way to work, and they are the only person scheduled in an operationally critical area, then the store has to scramble to get the position covered. In a six-person department store downtown, a cashier called in sick, and the beer-and-wine sales manager was unable to get to work on time. It was a delivery day, and a semitruck full of merchandise would have to be unloaded at the back of the store and stocked in the shelves and on the floor. The manager had to take over one of the positions at the front of the store and fill in for beverage sales at the back. Fortunately it was early in the morning and did not get too busy, but as the manager explained, this is a substantive change in staffing and operations from years ago.

> Back in the day, we'd have more staff. You'd always have a couple of people in a department. Usually a supervisor, and a helper, sales associate, someone, but today there's usually just one guy. So if Pedro [in beer and wine sales] is out sick, we don't have anyone to cover that department, and that can be a huge loss. Someone comes in here looking for an order they placed . . . we don't know where it is, sometimes he's [Pedro] left a cryptic note on a sheet of paper on the side of some cases of wine or something, but if it is a special order or a wedding or something, we can really be screwed . . . stores don't run themselves.

While lean staffing is the norm now across the industry, this does not mean that the levels of customer service or demands of the staff have been reduced. Since the 1980s, excellent customer service has been central to competitive strategy within the retail sector. Corporate stores typically have rigorous and standardized policies about store appearance and customer interaction, and a broad set of guidelines on customer service. What this means for front-end employees—cashiers, salespersons, and others who interact directly with customers—is that the demands have increased, while at the same time hours in some cases have been reduced. A five-year veteran of a home and garden store described how for her there was never enough time to keep up with the duties of her department. She handled glassware and cutlery. "I have myself and occasionally some help from one of the other sales associates, but it just isn't possible sometimes." As she explained, there are real contradictions with trying to meet the demands of the position in a strictly set amount of time: "I'm gonna get yelled at if the department looks like shit. But I'm gonna get yelled at if I stay later and put in more time to fix it, and I can't punch out and then just do it on my own time because that's against the law and I'll get yelled at for that too." This is further problematized when the store is busy and customers are requiring her assistance:

> On a really busy day it can be impossible, just impossible . . . because you are never getting to get done the stuff you need to get done, you are just helping customers. And some customers need a lot of help. And that's what part of the job is, we are supposed to steward the customer through their "shopping experience" until they are at the register and ready to check out. The other day I was so busy with people I left the place a wreck, but today hopefully it will be slower and I can get my department organized again.

In some cases, employees face great pressure from never being able to complete the work they are supposed to in the allotted hours they have during the week. These types of pressures are what led Walmart managers to lock stores and keep employees working off the clock after hours, and eventually led to several successful lawsuits against the company for unpaid overtime, including a large multimillion-dollar class-action lawsuit. While none of the employees or managers I interviewed in San Diego described this situation, the common response from management appears to be not working people off the clock for unpaid overtime, but increasing the speed of the labor process. This sped-up labor work rate is often done to catch up on work that has not been completed under normal operating conditions. When this effort happens, managers may pull a number of employees and urge them to "work together" quickly to get things done, sometimes incentivizing them with food and beverages, or being able to leave a shift early, but mostly this is interwoven within the normal operations of the store.

For instance, during a busy week when a regional manager was due to visit a retail store in the Gaslamp quarter of San Diego, the store manager asked staff to work quickly and put in an extra effort to clean up the store, straighten merchandise, and prepare for "inspection" by the regional manager. This type of rushed work was evident at all of the retailers I interviewed. In other cases, shipping and receiving clerks and stock clerks explained how unusual and unannounced shipments of goods required extra effort to complete during a shift, otherwise merchandise that had to be put out in time for specific seasonal sales would not make it to the sales floor, displays would not be set up in time for advertised sales, and the overall operations of the store in relation to broader company promotions and events would collapse. In a few instances, employees reported cutting their lunches short or working through breaks simply to get the work done during their allotted shift so that they would not have to face the pressure at the end of the shift to complete the work, or the stress from management for not having completed the work.

These cases illustrate several issues related to job quality in the retail sector. First, there is the issue of hours and scheduling. With competition placing downward pressure on wages, scheduling flexibility is borne by hourly workers and managers to negotiate and manage the contradiction between needing adequate labor in the stores, while keeping labor costs as low as possible. Beyond the daily store operations, however, the pressures for things like flexible scheduling also affect retail workers' lives outside of work.

Flexible scheduling requires that retail workers are available, as one manager describes it, as "on-call" employees. Workers need to provide a just-in-time labor supply in emergencies, with staff shortages, or in periods of high store customer volume. There are no data to compare across industries in relation to this "on-demand" staffing condition, but it is clear that retail is one of a handful of industries where this is a growing human resource practice. In cases of police, fire, or medical occupations, personnel are on call, but those are for public health and safety reasons. People in maintenance and repair occupations—such as airline mechanics, plumbers, and elevator mechanics—may also be called in for emergencies, but again, the reasons are generally pressing public safety or welfare concerns: airline passenger safety, elevator safety, or a break in the water, plumbing, or heating infrastructure. Those occupations are generally well paid, while retail workers face a level of on-demand shift work without the benefit of good pay, nor to meet any serious public safety or health need. They are "on-demand" labor to meet consumer demands and firm staffing needs.

Parents are particularly pressured to manage an on-call employment relationship. A single mother working in retail downtown described how her inability to fill in for overtime or on short notice appeared to make the management want to force her out of the store by cutting back her hours gradually until she went from thirty-five or forty hours per week down to twenty-five. In defiance, she kept her job and took on another part-time job, and then was let go, forcing her to then scramble for a new job because she had gained health insurance coverage with her first retail job, and her employer-provided coverage also covered her five-year-old son. Students also complained of being called to work on short notice, making it difficult to juggle college courses and related academic work with piecing together twenty hours a week of steady employment.

Deskilling and Self-Training in the Retail Sector

Another critical issue related to job quality in the retail sector is the change in who invests in human capital within the workplace. In general, retailers make very limited investments in employee training, with employers providing only 3.7 hours of formal training compared to an average of 10.7 hours of training across all other industries (Carré, Tilly, and Holgate 2010, 3). In some specialty stores—such as specialty shoe stores, watch shops, or jewelers—retail sales staff may have had company training in products, customer service, and other aspects of working in the store. In the case of shoe stores, or shoe sales departments within higher-end department stores, staff may have two or more weeks of company training on shoe fit, orthotics, sizing kids shoes, shoe materials, shoe care, and so forth. In jewelry stores, sales staff may have certifications either as certified jewelers or as gemologists. Specialty and department stores have historically invested in the training and development of employees. With the development of discount retail and "big box" department stores, however, that tradition shifted dramatically.

This shift from investing in training sales staff to not investing in them is reflected in the different retail models that discount retail and specialty or high-end department store retailers represent. Walmart, Target, Kmart, and other discount retailers are based on a warehousing model. The cost savings and competitive advantage these firms have are a function of massive economies of scale, hugely efficient logistics, global supply chain operations, and keeping labor costs as low as possible. None of these companies, for instance, has a dedicated shoe salesperson in the shoe department, nor is there any training in fitting shoes or anything shoe related. Similarly, the function of jewelry or watch salespeople is essentially, as one employee pointed out, "to open the case, ring the item up, and lock the case." The model of discount retail is not to have the employee add any value to the sales process, but rather to serve simply to shelve, stock, or lock up the product, and if needed, to ring the item up at a cash register. In this model, there is no incentive for the company to invest in the training and development of the retail salesperson, because selling, customer assistance, and so forth are not central to the retail model. If the employee does indeed have some skills or expertise that aid the firm in selling merchandise, than that is a boon for the store, but it is not something that is invested in typically.

Even in the case of electronics retailers, employees at two of which I interviewed, training of staff is very limited. These firms rely on a large pool of relatively young, typically male, tech-savvy employees who are capable of providing customer assistance with purchasing complex computer, audio, or video equipment. Again, in the case of the two firms interviewed in downtown San Diego, no training programs were in place for the electronics/computer sales staff. At one store, the lead salesperson in computers had an IT degree, had built his own computer, and was more knowledgeable about the products than the store manager—a typical arrangement of technical product knowledge from what I understand in electronics retailing today.

The central point here is that with the exception of specialty stores or higher-end department stores, the retail industry offers very little in the way of training or development of job-specific skills, or investment in human capital broadly. This is, in many ways, a historical process of deskilling: specialty retailing does require some level of expertise and skill, but greater competition and the shift toward a discount retail model means that the skills are eroded in favor of lower labor costs and warehouse-store pricing. For workers without a lot of educational credentials or specialized skills, the retail sector, particularly with the shift toward warehouse-style discount stores, provides increasingly limited opportunities to learn valuable job skills or knowledge, or attain human capital that would lead an employee to be able to advance into a position higher up a career ladder. The frustration this causes is evident in an African American man I interviewed who just started working at an electronics retailer after being incarcerated for a brief time. "They don't teach you anything here. There is no training, no skill set you get; you are just on your own." He had hoped to learn more about electronics and computers as a means of gaining some knowledge and sales experience, but they kept him largely stocking shelves, and with little indication that he would ever have a chance to gain anything from the position other than a paycheck, he left after a year and looked for a better job.

Another issue related to skills in the retail sector is the invisibility of a wide range of efforts that employees make as investments in their own position-specific human capital. Rather than the firm investing in you, the employee, employees are now investing in the firm by training themselves. Several employees in downtown retailers I spoke with gave examples of this process.

In the case of a home goods retailer that also sold food and alcohol, the employees in more specialized departments all engaged in their own on-the-job self-education. Pedro, the employee who oversaw the beverage department, got the job after an employee left, creating a vacancy. He made the case to the manager that he was already familiar with the department and its stock, and he would be able to use some of his growing knowledge of wine to be the ideal candidate to take the position. He got the job, which did not entail more pay, but it did allow him more autonomy and a more specialized focus within the store. He saw the new position as a promotion because he now had a more clearly defined set of responsibilities and had more responsibility and autonomy in his job. To ensure that he was the "go-to" person in the beverage department, he studied beer and wine through books and magazines. Similarly, coffee sales staff invested their own time to improve their knowledge of the store product. In another store, employees took on developing their own expertise in various areas of product knowledge at a cooking supply store. This entailed not just learning how to use various tools and machines by spending time studying the manuals and trying out the equipment, but personal time reading up on the products, going over different uses and trends in the product lines, and coming up with new ways to pitch and display the products. When asked about the training program or assistance in learning these things, employees invariably said they were hired as cashiers or "sales associates" and had to self-train while on the job.

Career Ladders

Like the hotel industry, career ladders are limited in retail. Strong evidence for this is the very high turnover rate among employees: ranging between 60 and 80 percent. Bigger stores typically have more opportunities for advancement by virtue of their larger and more complex structure. Large department stores, for instance, have the most occupations and the greatest degree of hierarchy. In theory, workers in larger stores should have more opportunities to move up into a career ladder than in smaller ones. Clearly, a small corner store with only three employees—one manager and two cashiers, for instance—does not have a lot of room for advancement. As shown in Table 14, the typical career ladder for entry-level retail sales or cashier positions is greatest in large department stores, the flattest in small retailers, and in-between for the discount retailers. Like the hospitality industry, having only a few rungs upon which to build a career, particularly if there are very few positions at the top of the ladder, makes it unlikely that many workers will be able to have much occupational mobility in the industry.

Discount retailers may vary in their own staffing patterns, but overall, there is a similar dearth of midlevel positions. Though stores like Walmart and Target have executive vice presidents who started out as cashiers or sales associates, these are a very small fraction of the total entry-level career trajectories. The vast majority of positions in discount retail are entry level, with few levels of upward mobility attainable simply

TABLE 14. Comparison of Career Ladders for Entry-Level Sales/Cashier Positions in Different Retail Stores

Large Department Store	Small Retailer	Discount Retailer
Store Manager	Store Manager	Store Manager
Sales Manager/ Department Manager	Cashier/Salesperson/ Stockperson	Assistant Manager
Shipping/Receiving Manager		Shipping Manager
Supervisor		Salesperson/Stock Clerk
Sales Associate		Cashier
Customer Service Representative		
Shipping/Receiving Clerk		
Cashier/ Stock Clerk		

SOURCE: Author interviews with human resource or store managers among retailers in San Diego.

through hard work and on-the-job experience. Many advanced positions outside of sales (such as in accounting) or in management require college coursework or a degree at minimum. Entry-level workers would need to possess these credentials or obtain them while working in order to progress into those types of positions. In sum, the relatively flat career ladders in the industry are an impediment for people moving from entry-level positions to the types of occupations or careers that have greater benefits, economic opportunity, and self-sufficiency wages. We see similar polarization of career ladders in the retail sector as we do in the hospitality industry. Intermediate rungs of occupational mobility within industries or firms that have a mixture of education and experience levels are sorely lacking.

The Career Ladder Roller Coaster

I met Rick outside a large office supply store. He was on a cigarette break. We wound up chatting about surfing, and after he stated, "I'm so sick of retail," we discussed his employment history and labor market decision-making over time. His story is very common among front-end retail workers who are in their mid- to late twenties, even thirties. He began working in retail in high school, and moved around to a couple of other jobs in landscaping and housepainting after he finished his high school degree. His ambition was to get a "trade job" but that never seemed to work out. Painting houses did not seem to be steady enough work or with much career movement, so he went back to working in retail. More than a decade later, he has worked in five different stores, all in entry-level positions: stock clerk, cashier, and shipping clerk. I think of his experience, and that of many others with similar employment histories, as a career ladder roller coaster: people move up, slide down, try to find a better ladder in another store, and move up, then slide down or more often than not get stuck.

For Rick, his challenge is being stuck. He kept switching to jobs in different stores after a couple of years because with already many years of employment, a good track record, and work in jobs outside of retail he wanted to move into a more supervisory and managerial position. In at least three cases he was told that this was possible, even without any college coursework or degree. The supervisory or managerial positions never came to fruition, however. Recruitment of outside personnel, transfers of mangers from other areas to fill vacancies, and a lack of an internal training and career advancement program led to him moving on to other retailers. He has largely moved horizontally for a decade try-ing to find a way up, only to end up switching to a new firm and starting at the bottom again in terms of seniority and experience in the business. He considered taking college courses in business administration to make himself more qualified, but the time commitment and cost has kept him from enrolling. The other factor is that he is unsure if the investment will pay off because he does not have clear signals from retail firms about what managerial qualifications are, in part because he has been told that experience and promoting from within are key; yet he has been unable to gain any promotions, and there are a lot of front-end retail workers vying for a handful of jobs. As he approaches his late twenties, he laments being "stuck" on a never-ending up and down and horizontal career track that has never been able to provide nearly the wages or benefits that would lead to him becoming more economically stable, or allow him to move up in a career.

I returned to the store Rick worked at on my most recent trip to San Diego and asked the manager when he was scheduled in to work next, only to hear that he had moved on, once again. His case illustrates pre-cisely the challenges of moving forward in an industry where there are very flat career ladders and limited internal mobility systems to foster upward progress. This is not always the case; there are some firms that have better job quality than others within the retail sector.

COMPARING FIRMS: DIFFERENCES IN JOB QUALITY

Costco has developed a reputation for paying high wages and promoting from within the company—that is, there is a culture surrounding mobility and an internal labor market wherein workers are incentivized to move up within the firm. This is often contrasted with Walmart, which has far lower pay and relatively fewer career ladders. These differences stem in part from business models and approaches to human resource management. Research on job quality variation does indicate that some firms are better than others. Specifically, Carré, Tilly, and Holgate (2010) find that when looking at consumer electronics or food retailers, two models—service driven and product driven—can equate to better job quality. They conclude, however, that with both industries facing ever-present cost pressures and losses of market share, the likelihood that these strategies will be sustainable is questionable.

Having worked in the industry and based on interviews with management and frontline workers, however, I view the push toward customer service and increased product quality as part of the overall pressures facing the industry. In the case of discount retail, one manager elaborated that the pressures for floor workers—sales associates, stock clerks, and cashiers—are far beyond a standard eight-hour shift. Their business model emphasizes "outstanding customer service," which entails greeting any and every customer within fifteen feet and asking them if they need any assistance, while keeping departments stocked, clean, and in a constant state of flux with new merchandising and marketing materials. He put it simply:

> The reason why Walmart got hit with the overtime lawsuits [when workers were found to have been forced to work off the clock in violation of U.S. labor law] is because the pressures are basically all coming down to the store. Central [corporate management] wants you to stock, clean, and have immaculate and wonderful servicing of customers in a 100,000 sq. foot store with 15 departments, but with only a handful of employees because that's all the payroll hours you can have. It is impossible. You either have

people work off the clock, or you have stuff that doesn't get done. But if you have stuff that doesn't get done or a bad review from a secret shopper or a regional manager dropping in unannounced, then you can lose your job. Basically the business model is do everything with almost nothing or you are fired.

Employees in a range of retail firms echo these sentiments, suggesting that the pressures for high-quality service and product delivery may or may not result in higher job quality, but in fact may be becoming more and more part of the highly competitive retail market. One case in point is an electronics and office supply retailer that offered home computer installation informally for customers. In violation of company policy, the manager allowed tech-savvy college students to take purchased computers to people's homes or offices and install them, connect A/V equipment, configure Internet connections, and then return to the store, all as hourly employees, but without any further pay, compensation for driving personal vehicles, or other remuneration. The manager of this store defended the activity because they have to compete with other stores that offer such services (such as Best Buy/Geek Squad home installation). The pressure to provide a high level of customer service may be laudable from a consumer's standpoint, but the employees do not see their own job quality improve. Indeed, in this case, while the store was utilizing the high skills and willingness and flexibility of the employees, this did not lead to higher pay or benefits. Thus, there is evidence that higher skills will be used to remain competitive, but these skills and their deployment to improve customer service will not improve wages.

CONCLUSION

The cases presented here in the retail sector confirm issues about job quality raised by the aforementioned studies and are well documented over time. Much of the research on job quality and the retail sector focuses on how to take "high-road" versus "low-road" strategies, and a good deal of research has shown what the factors are that contribute to "good" jobs in the industry versus less desirable ones. The concern I have with this approach is that it suggests efforts to improve the jobs, when in most cases even the better-quality jobs in the sector may be insufficient for economic self-sufficiency. Second, there is limited analysis of the possibility of growing polarization and inequality within the industry itself. Are women and people of color congregating more in the "bad jobs" within the sector? Like the hospitality industry, the polarization of career ladders and segmentation of departments makes mobility in the industry difficult, and with the preponderance of women and ethnic minorities in some front-end retail operations, this raises the questions of equity across race and gender as well.

Even in the more labor-intensive and human capital intensive retail operations, such as in computer sales, where retail salespersons need a good amount of technical knowledge to work effectively, it is difficult to qualify jobs in the retail sector for nonmanagerial personnel as good employment. Nonsupervisory and even some supervisory positions in the industry simply do not pay enough or provide the types of career ladders and potential mobility to allow entry-level workers to move beyond being working and poor. Without a dramatic increase in wage-floor legislation that would boost pay, as well as greater worker organization and participation through efforts like unionization, it is difficult to foresee any substantive improvement in the vast majority of retail jobs. With the seemingly strong and potentially growing polarization of retail positions, this means that one of the largest areas of job growth in the economy is poised to provide a lot of entry level, low-wage, servant class–type employment, but with very few avenues for upward mobility.

5

Working on, off, and around the Books

HOTELS AND RETAIL ESTABLISHMENTS are two of the largest low-wage service employers in the inner city, but this only accounts for one part of the broad spectrum of low-wage employment. Another area of employment for inner-city residents is informal or "off-the-books" employment. Traditionally, this type of "street hustling" or, in the emergent informal immigrant economy, day labor or other forms of employment have been viewed as on the peripheries of urban economic activity. I include an analysis of informal work here alongside other forms of low-wage labor precisely because when looked at analytically, this type of wage labor is not marginal, but is in fact integral to the economy of the urban poor and working poor. Indeed, a strikingly large portion of urban residents participate in the urban informal economy, as do businesses, and indeed, the lines between "formal" and "informal" economic activity are so blurred that understanding how closely interconnected these different types of employment are provides a clearer and more accurate picture of the inner-city economy.

Studies of urban poverty, the working poor, and inequality typically have viewed informal employment as marginal to the workings of the urban economy, or the last resort of the most economically desperate. In contrast, when looking at low-income working-poor inner-city communities, informal work has changed, and it is part and parcel of the broader changes in structures of opportunity and the growth of the servant class. This is particularly true in the heavily immigrant populated communities in central San Diego. In this chapter I look at how the informal economy is closely tied to growing urban inequalities and the reproduction of the servant class.

Informal work in U.S. cities has been studied from a variety of perspectives. Much of the research on informal work among the urban poor is ethnographic, detailing how integral and complex, informal work is to poor communities (Duneier 2000). The most relevant work in relation to the San Diego case is the analysis of service work in U.S. cities by Saskia Sassen (1991), who argued that the informal economy was expanding in urban areas because of forces related to the broader economic and specifically industrial transformation going on in U.S. cities, using New York City as her exemplary case study. She argues that several factors are encouraging the informalization of urban economies: expanding high-income populations increase the demand for highly customized goods and services; expanding low-income populations increase demand for low-cost services and products; small firms need to produce customized services and goods in small, limited runs, which requires flexible workforces and/or subcontractors; with relatively low capital costs for entry, many firms operate at small profit margins in a very competitive market where flexible, highly exploitable labor is necessary; and finally, these conditions all encourage noncompliance with regulations regarding wages and working conditions, further inducing informalization in a broad range of economic activities (Sassen 1991, 87). This framework provides a vital intervention in the debate regarding informalization because it suggests that such changes within urban economies regarding informal work are a function, in part, of the industrial restructuring and attendant class structure of the past thirty years within urban economies. My analysis supports Sassen's findings but includes linkages to the labor market and looks at a context where many of the conditions of urban informality such as are seen in New York or Detroit are different, and suggests that the connections between the informal economy of San Diego are less driven by high-wage earners' demand for certain goods or services, and more by economic inequality and responses to dysfunction in the formal economy by the urban poor.

While retail and hotel jobs are quintessentially low-wage service occupations, and these both represent the largest job growth in San Diego's downtown, the growing servant class occupations include work "off the books," that is to say, in the informal economy. Informal work represents a growing and very large portion of inner-city employment where the services provided are not just to visitors and well-to-do residents in the downtown luxury condos, but for other middle- and lower-income households as well.

In this chapter I turn to an examination of the informal economy: where cash and other payments support an integral set of individual entrepreneurs, businesses, and other economic practices among poorer urban communities. The material in this chapter shows that rather than back-alley car repair, street vending, and the penny capitalism that typified urban ghettos during much of the twentieth century and is still present in many parts of urban America, informalization in the present postindustrial metropolis is now embedded within the very working of the "formal economy," generating wages, providing goods and services across both formal and informal divides. Thus, informal work serves multiple, often vital roles in lower-income communities. Informal work, however, is not necessarily an avenue for economic opportunity and mobility, but instead is in part a product of the changing class structure of urban economies. In short, the informal economy fosters the reproduction of economic divisions within the new inner city—it provides lower-income consumers services and goods that are more costly in the formal economy, it provides some income for different segments of the urban economy, and it allows middle- and upper-class consumers access to deregulated and lower-cost labor.

The best way to introduce this complex topic is by way of an ethnographic example. Jimmy, a thirty-four-year-old construction worker, describes one of the salient issues of informal work in the construction industry, subcontracting. We met after his shift as a drywaller, working on a new office building in northern San Diego. He described the issue as follows:

> You know how Ponzi schemes work, Madoff and everyone; it's a giant pyramid. At the top is the con man, and buddies, taking all the cash, then they pay everyone else piecemeal until the whole thing collapses. It's the same in a lot of construction, only with workers. You know, you have the main contractor, maybe a general con. [contractor] and they sub the work out, then the sub [contractor] subs the work out, then the sub subs, and down and down you go until you got guys who are working on a big project,

but nobody knows if they are getting paid right, if they are legal, where they came from, qualified, whatever, and that's a giant pyramid, because everyone just skims their piece off from the ones below them, and those at the top skim off the most of all. Some guys take too much, or they gyp the guy they owe, and so on, and pretty soon, down the chain, nobody at the bottom gets paid [for] what they did.

What Jimmy is describing is a complex set of relationships between what are often considered formal—or state-regulated—economic activities, and informal, or nonstate regulated ones. His account also illustrates how both types of activity can coexist, albeit with potential problems—such as the nonpayment of wages. In this chapter I look at how the urban poor rely on and take advantage of work in the informal economy. Specifically, I look at who does this type of work, what type of work is done, why they do the work, and what these practices tell us about the broader shifting structures of opportunity and inequality in urban economies.

DEFINING INFORMAL WORK AND INFORMALIZATION

By "informal" work I refer to remunerated work that is outside of state regulation for taxation, labor law, zoning, or other purposes, but is legal in all other respects. Thus, this analysis does not include illicit economic activity related to the sale of banned goods and services such as drugs and prostitution. Although there are instances where work may fall into "gray" areas of questionable legality or state oversight, the data in this study are all categorized as either informal or formal. This definition, however, does not mean that there are necessarily two distinct and separate spheres of formal and informal employment.

As Jimmy's account shows, it is vital to examine the relationship between purportedly formal versus informal work. In this case, a developer pays a contractor to do work, formally, with clear accounting procedures and transparency and contracts, but the contractor may subcontract the work further, using only cash-in-hand workers at some point. Indeed, informal employment is not always a separate realm of marginalized work (Guha-Khasnobis, Kanbur, and Ostrom 2006; Hart 1973; Pardo 1996; Williams, Round, and Rodgers 2007, 2009), but in fact involves a good deal of entrepreneurial activity among a range of social classes and is often central to the functioning of the "formal" economy. It is more productive, therefore, to conceive of such employment and the production or movement of goods in terms of a continuum of work with varying degrees of formality and informality (Guha-Khasnobis, Kanbur, and Ostrom 2006; Marcelli, Williams, and Joassart 2010).

THE SCOPE AND SIGNIFICANCE OF INFORMAL WORK

How significant is informal work? Comparatively, in Los Angeles it is estimated that informal-sector workers fill roughly 15 percent of jobs in Los Angeles County and 16 percent of all jobs in Los Angeles City. Using the same methodology, I estimate the informal employment in San Diego County at around 12 percent (Karjanen 2010a). As another proxy, census data show that approximately 6 percent of residents in the inner-city study area report being self-employed, but that is not an accurate reflection of informal work. The figure for informal work may be higher or lower, depending on a variety of factors, most notably, how people define self-employment in the census versus what work is actually going on. In central San Diego, the estimate based on survey data in this study is 17 percent. This includes approximately 8 percent who are working entirely on an informal basis as sole proprietorships. Thus, one in six residents who are working is working informally in some capacity in the inner city, 8 percent rely on informal work entirely, in addition to other sources of income outside of formal labor force participation (such as public assistance), while 9 percent combine formal and informal work in some way.

These findings are not entirely novel. Nationally, figures have estimated informal work or income over the past two decades at between 8 and 12 percent in the United States, depending on the measurement and data used (compare Feige 1990). As a historical phenomenon, inner cities have always had significant informal sectors, but it is difficult to assess this over time due to a lack of data. In two waves of surveys, the change in informal work is roughly 1 percent (in 2003 informal work was estimated at 16 percent, and in 2010 17 percent). Why so many people would work informally in the inner city is subject to a good deal of debate across a range of fields, and it is necessary to examine these theories in order to distinguish how my own findings on informal work differ.

Studies of informal work in urban communities in the United States have varied from more quantitative sociological accounts (Marcelli, Williams, and Joassart 2010) to more in-depth ethnographies of street hustling and ethnic entrepreneurship. There are also studies of day labor, particularly in immigrant-dense communities in the Northeast, Chicago, and Southern California, as well as other research on the ways that immigrants work within ethnic enclaves both formally and informally (Dohan 2003; Valdez 2010; Valenzuela 2001, 2003). This research shows that informal work is closely connected to wider economic transactions, and there is a great need to move beyond the view of inner-city urban informal work as marginal and a result of economic desperation.

How does someone wind up working in the informal economy? Why work informally or illicitly when the San Diego region has seen tremendous job growth, particularly in the nearby downtown redevelopment areas? What impact does working "off the books" have on one's economic opportunities—is it a unique form of opportunism, dead-end, or just part of the spectrum of income-earning activities that residents depend on?

CHARACTERISTICS OF THE URBAN INFORMAL ECONOMY: WHO DOES THE WORK AND WHY?

To better understand why and how people work off the books, Table 15 shows the employment statuses of those reporting informal work of some kind. Although the majority of those working informally are unemployed, a large portion are working full time as well. Also, more than two-thirds of those working informally are men. This is not necessarily the case in other settings, where women are sometimes more likely to work in the informal economy, particularly in developing countries. The differences in gender reflect local and regional economic conditions. In the case of inner-city San Diego, a lot of men have been displaced by the construction-sector slow down, many are recent immigrants, and some are facing a lot of barriers to formal-sector employment. This is also a relatively young set of communities, with a lot of young families, and women tend to be more involved with child care, reducing the likelihood of working either formally or informally (although some actually work informally in child care).

What are the reasons people wind up working informally? Taking the sample data, Table 15 shows the results of logistic regression for informal work (as the dichotomous outcome variable) and predictor variables of demographics and employment status, as well as industry and occupation. Very little research exists on the predictors of informal employment; in large part this is likely because there are no formal data sets available containing informal works as a variable.

Clearly, the relationship between informal work and unemployment is complex. The fact that the majority of those working informally are unemployed suggests that there is strong support for the marginalization thesis: that informal work is done by those who are desperate economically. This is further supported by the fact that the duration of being unemployed is a strong predictor of participation in the informal economy. Also, being a multiple-job holder is a strong predictor. This suggests that people are engaged in informal work in part because they are using the income as a supplement to another job. The data also show evidence for a heterogeneous labor market theory of informal employment; that is, informal work is adopted by a range of different employment statuses, not just the unemployed. People working full or part time with formal-sector jobs also may have informal employment. There are also those residents of central San Diego who are retired but still work informally in some capacity.

TABLE 15. Factors Predicting Participation in Informal Work (logit model)

Variable	B	SE	Exp(B)
Age	0.098	.524	1.02
Race	0.491	.662	0.920
Gender	−0.201	.332	0.105
Employed	−.06	.099	0.062
Temp work	0.238	.441	1.066
Duration unemployed	1.24	.561	1.272
Industry	0.625	.086	0.218
Occupation	.331	.367	0.115
Marital status	.644	.025	0.845
Multiple job holder	1.33	.369	0.115
Children	−0.669	.482	0.211

SOURCE: Central San Diego Survey 2002–10.

As Table 15 shows, race does not serve as a strong predictor of informal work. The issue of how race/ethnicity and informal work are related merits further discussion. While Latinos tend to be overrepresented in informal employment in San Diego, race does not appear to be a strong predictor of informal work. This can be explained by the fact that informal work appears to be evenly distributed across racial demographics. And, secondly, if the sample were much larger, we might be able to detect a greater significance of race. More importantly, however, is that when looking at race independently, it is generally a good predictor of the *type* of informal work being done.

Latinos are predominantly working in construction, landscaping, and housekeeping and childcare jobs, while the smaller portion of African Americans and whites are generally working in car and home repair. There are few Asian residents with demonstrated informal work, but they are in small businesses: tailoring/sewing, auto repair, and restaurants. Perhaps not surprising, there is a clear differential distribution of different types of informal work across racial/ethnic lines. What is significant here is that it demonstrates even further labor market segmentation by racial/ethnic lines even within the informal economy. This provides greater support for the idea of immigrant ethnic enclave economies and labor market segmentation more broadly.

In sum, there are two leading predictors for informal work: either resorting to the informal economy after long-term unemployment (support for the marginalization thesis) or seeking supplemental income alongside other jobs (support for the heterogeneous theory). In either case, both pathways into informal work suggest that these are strategies to shore up income given the marginal location of individuals in relation to the formal economy. If age, race, or gender were strong predictors, then we might assume that this is a phenomenon concentrated in a particular ethnic group or other category, but there is little evidence this is the case. On the contrary, informal work shows up across a broad spectrum of social and economic characteristics.

Looking more closely at the experience of informal work among both employed and unemployed workers, the relationship between employment status and informal work is clearer. Specifically, for employed workers, informality is supplementary, but for unemployed workers, particularly those in long-term unemployment, they face too many barriers to returning to formal employment. This presents a different set of results than the typical perception that informal work is the refuge of the most economically marginalized. In contrast, as the aforementioned research shows, informal work is increasingly integrated into the broader formal economy, and often the boundaries between the two spheres are inescapably blurred. In the next section I compare people who are employed and work informally to supplement their income, and those who are unemployed and who work entirely in the informal sector. There are, of course, people who cross both divides: intermittent job loss or gain, or the movement of someone from full time to part time or underemployment through temp work may mean that people are engaged in a range of income-generating activities.

EMPLOYED WORKERS: ON-THE-SIDE WORK

For people who are already employed, informal work is almost always supplemental to their formal-sector employment, or in some cases it may be as much as their formal-sector employment. This reflects a range of employment situations across the community. For those who have low-paying and irregular work, informal work can be just as important as formal-sector work. For those who have more regular, better-paying jobs, informal-sector work may be far less vital, but nevertheless provides some important returns, otherwise people would not engage in it.

Auto repair is another area where we see full-time employees engaged in informal-sector work. The communities in central San Diego have a large number of auto repair shops. These businesses range from national chains like Midas to small family-owned firms. Some have been in the area for decades, and a few are more recent. Virtually every make and model and every possible car repair need is available in the area—from tires to bodywork to complete engine or transmission overhauls. Despite the plethora of auto repair businesses, however, there is a booming informal economy in fixing cars. From back alleyways to garages, and despite city ordinances prohibiting such work, informal car repairs continue to operate in a range of settings. This is in part due to the economics of auto repair in low-income communities: people may be surrounded by car repair shops, but this does not mean they can afford to have their vehicles fixed there. Instead, residents rely on both formal and informal means to get their vehicles maintained.

This informal auto work is done by everyone from do-it-yourself mechanics, to formally trained ASE-certified auto mechanics who moonlight or work for friends and family, to shops that sometimes stay open after hours for "off-the-books" work by friends, family, and colleagues. If the automobile is what drives much of the U.S. economy, it also drives much of the informal economy as well. The entire range of labor practices and economic transactions is seen in the informal auto repair business.

The Nguyen family is an excellent example of informal work across kinship and household lines. Arriving from Southeast Asia twenty-five years ago, this family developed a well-respected auto repair business that serves customers from all across San Diego County. The business is largely family run, with several of the mechanics being related either by birth or marriage. Two of the young mechanics, Vincent and Jean, work on cars for the family shop from 7 a.m. to 3 p.m., but after 3 p.m. often work on their own side projects for friends or for customers who want something done that the shop normally does not do, like customization or chopping down a frame to low-ride it. Lowrider modifications are sometimes illegal in the state of California, and the shop does not permit the work to be done during regular hours. After hours, however, the two brothers provide a one-stop-shop for many in the Latino community looking to get their car or truck converted to a lowrider. The brothers also provide more standard auto repairs, but prefer to do this type of higher-paying work on the side; they see it as more challenging, and it earns far more than simply doing an oil change or checking a dead battery. The owner of the shop, their uncle, allows this after-hours work because he sees it as a potential way to bring in new customers for more regular work. He is also trying to encourage his sons to start businesses of their own, and he sees this as a way of encouraging their own entrepreneurial development.

I met Rahoul because he nearly sprayed bright orange paint on my rental car. He was on the sidewalk cleaning out his airbrush and compressor when I encouraged him to move his cleaning further down the sidewalk so he would not inadvertently spray any cars with his paint. As he explained, he was in a rush to get to work and he needed to clean his equipment, drop it off in a garage he rents, and get to his regular job. He works at a graphics design firm by day, and nights and weekends he does what he calls "commercial artwork." He airbrushes, paints, and touches up cars, houses, boats, motorcycles, signs, and anything else that people want covered, all as a side project to earn extra money. This work naturally grew out of his background as a graffiti artist, and when he got a "real job and grew up," he kept his interest in airbrush and spray-paint work. As a "side gig," as he describes it, he estimates that he earns an extra couple hundred dollars a month. This, combined with his regular job, allows him to earn a decent salary, but since he does not have a college degree yet and he is in an entry-level position at the graphic design firm, his efforts do not mean that combining both jobs allows him to save much. As he puts it, he "gets through month to month."

As we see from these cases, people working to supplement their income do so for a variety of reasons, and to different extents. Rahoul is earning money specifically to save and pay bills. Vincent and Jean have made part of their daily jobs at the auto shop a side project doing custom work. This earns them a significant income for what they see as easy work that they can use their family business to complete on their own time. These cases, however, are not simply means for earning some extra income. These informal income-earning practices are in part a response to economic restructuring (Rahoul's long-term underemployment), and an effort to gain some level of income mobility when their formal-sector employment does not offer many avenues to do so. For people without any income in the formal economy, however, the role and extent of informal work is different.

UNEMPLOYED WORKERS: MAKING ENDS MEET

For workers who are unemployed and working informally, this typically represents the last resort for many in terms of income generation. The type of work that unemployed people find informally ranged dramatically. A divorced mother of two who lost her job in 2009 and ran through her unemployment benefits eventually went to work in her sister's business, cleaning houses for cash. An unemployed construction worker who gave up looking for work eventually started working as an informal subcontractor or doing odd jobs such as home repair projects.

Pathways to informal work via long-term unemployment usually depend on a number of cofactors. First, industry shifts occur, often causing long-term unemployment. The collapse of the housing market, for instance, dislocated thousands of construction workers in San Diego County, many of whom either moved to different labor markets, or remained with long-term unemployment. Second, some long-term unemployed have moved into informal work due to injury or disability; this typically occurs when someone has been injured in a position where their injury prevents them from working in that occupation. As a result, they are unemployed for a long time in search of a new occupation, and many may not find work despite extensive searching. In these cases, retraining and shifting jobs may result in unusually long terms of unemployment, necessitating informal work as a source of income. Third, someone having difficulty finding work in the formal economy may instead have the opportunity to work informally through networks of friends or family. In such cases, the informal work may become more attractive than formal-sector employment. Finally, there is the issue of immigration status. Less-documented workers (Karjanen 2010b) have higher rates of working informally then those with full documentation. Day laborers are just one example of immigration status contributing to informal employment. Finally, there are usually barriers to formal labor force participation that keep the attraction of informal work relatively high. Although I discuss these barriers to labor force participation more in depth in other chapters, the barriers for formal-sector employment that encourage informal-sector work need to be better understood.

These barriers are raised according to how people see their opportunities in the formal labor market; that is, they are the reasons people cite for not being able to find a job worth applying for. These barriers to formal-sector labor market attachment are varied and differ across gender lines. Table 16 shows the different barriers for men and women who have been unsuccessful for various reasons at obtaining formal-sector work. For both men and women the vast majority face barriers based on either skills deficits or a lack of positions available that they deem worth applying for. For men, skills and a lack of decent jobs are nearly half of the perceived barriers to employment (45 percent). Family conflicts and a limited hiring network are also significant, and all of these exceed the importance of lack of transportation or work experience. In short, for men, the issues preventing them from applying for formal-sector jobs are a lack of openings, followed by skills gaps for jobs they would be interested in applying for, followed by a lack of personal connections to get a job.

For women, family conflicts are the primary reason for not applying for work, followed by a perception of a lack of job opportunities, and then a perceived lack of the appropriate skills for formal labor force participation. Family conflicts include issues like child care, eldercare, or caring for a disabled person, and this in part explains the higher rate of family obligations that deter labor force participation among women. Closely behind family conflicts are the same problems facing men: a perceived lack of skills and a perceived lack of jobs worth applying for. Both men's and women's concern with a perceived lack of jobs goes beyond simply reservation wages, the lowest rate of pay they would be willing to accept to take a specific job. Rather, as discussed previously, labor force participation decisions are a complex interaction between changing economic circumstances and decision-making processes. These barriers also differ across racial lines. African Americans are more likely to report perceived or real job discrimination and a limited hiring network as barriers, while Latinos report specialized skills, language, or documentation as the most significant barrier.

If someone is chronically unemployed, then informal work has attractions beyond simply being able to avoid the problems associated with formal-sector work. First, work is done almost always on a "cash-in-hand" basis, meaning that money is obtainable quickly and without needing to cash a check. Second, working informally allows someone to use the

TABLE 16. Barriers to Formal Sector Employment in Central San Diego among Those Working 100% Informally (percentages)

Barrier	Men	Women
Skills	21	19
Transportation	8	14
Limited work experience	8	12
Ex-offender	2	1
Family conflict	11	23
Limited hiring network	14	5
Discrimination	4	0
Labor market (no jobs)	24	21
Other	8	5

SOURCE: Central San Diego Survey 2002–10.

skills available to them. For lesser-skilled workers this is particularly important in the new service economy. If someone is lacking any specific job skills, then there is always the option of deploying pure labor power—as a housecleaner, landscaper, and so forth—to generate extra income. Third, residents of central San Diego have better access to income-generating opportunities within the local community rather than seeking wage labor in the formal sector in part because they know exactly what the in-demand goods and services are and can offer them at low prices; unlike formal businesses that need to pay overhead, taxes, and so forth, cash-in-hand proprietors can simply charge cash in hand.

Discouraged workers, those who have largely given up on the formal labor market, also participate in informal work. Here we see one of the clearer connections between the labor market dynamics at work as the inner city shifted dramatically toward low-wage service work. This surfeit of low-wage jobs encouraged many people, men in particular, out of the local labor market. Numerous times men working in the informal economy cited the lack of "real" employment opportunities in the formal labor market—"real" meaning a job that paid above a poverty-level wage and had a benefits package.

TOTALLY OFF THE BOOKS: INFORMAL ENTERPRISES

Why do people who work entirely off the books remain in the informal economy beyond simply the barriers to formal-sector participation? For some, a very small percentage, cash-in-hand work may be their main source of income, or it serves as a major source of income in combination with some form of public assistance. Primarily, however, those working entirely informally are somewhat stranded between either fully participating in the formal sector or making a decent living in the informal sector. For those people who are dependent on informal work, the role of informalization varies based on different individual circumstances. The pathways to informal-sector dependence are as varied as there are different people with different labor market experiences.

Karl worked for years in various jobs—construction, warehousing, truck driving, printing, and at temp agencies doing a wide range of manual labor and manufacturing work. He spent several years battling drugs, and a short term in prison left him relatively bankrupt and without any real job contacts when he got out. After several months of bouncing between a couple different jobs, he started doing repair work on the homes of family and friends. He was good with his hands and very mechanically inclined. First it was a garage door opener. Then he painted the garage for a couple hundred dollars and fixed some of the window trim. This turned into a job for the neighbor who saw Karl working on the garage. Since then, he says, he has been doing odd home repair jobs for five years.

Karl's business has gone through some boom and bust cycles, but even through the most recent economic crisis, he still manages to find jobs. If he gets into real trouble financially, he resorts to a temp agency or working with a friend, or he puts bills off until he can get paid. What is notable about Karl's business is that it is entirely informal. He technically operates as an unlicensed contractor doing home repairs. He does not do wiring or plumbing, but he does "everything else," as he puts it. This off-the-books enterprise is just one of many, particularly in construction and landscaping, that operates entirely in the informal economy. Like operators of other small sole proprietorships, he works largely through word of mouth. He doesn't print business cards or drop flyers to prevent a paper trail, and he always gets paid in cash. Additionally, his work is always without permitting or inspection. Even though he avoids plumbing and wiring, he does a good amount of structural work at times on homes, which requires an inspection by the city of San Diego, but he never has the customer get a permit because he is unlicensed. He backs his work up by telling customers that if they have any doubts, they can get a home inspector to look at the work for a fee, or have a builder come in and bid on the job for free, and if either note any problems with the work, Karl will fix it for free. Fortunately, Karl rarely has jobs that are so complex and require a lot of serious renovation that he runs into concerns about the quality of his work. Most of it is painting, minor repairs, replacing things like locks, doorknobs, doors, windows, screens, broken shingles, and so forth. They are small-time repairs, but they would cost significantly more if the customer hired a licensed contractor.

He sees his work in part as a business, but also as a morally upright social service; he provides things that people simply can't afford and would otherwise do without, neglecting their home or apartment. For example, an elderly couple who have lived in central San Diego for decades and were retired, on fixed incomes, needed their front door and a window fixed. They had two estimates for the work, one at $650 and another at nearly $800. Either option was too costly, so they were going to put the work off but worried that this made their home less secure. They heard about Karl's work through a friend and hired him to do the job for $250. As he explained:

> Old people often get taken. People have no morals. You hear of elderly folks getting ripped off all the time. They didn't need a whole new door or window, they needed their door adjusted, the frame screwed in better, and a new deadbolt, and their casement window in the bathroom needed a new handle and to be tightened. . . . I did the job for a reasonable price and still made good money." He adds, "And I got the best advertisement in the world, a happy customer."

His work for older residents he speaks of in prideful terms, referring to it as his "Robin Hood" gig. With the growing number of older retired residents and aging homes, he is often called in to fix jobs that were not completed by someone who began gouging the owners. He comes in to "save the day," as he puts it, by finishing the job properly and without overcharging someone using a ripped-up floor or open window as leverage to extort further payments. He sees this type of illegal activity as exploitive and extortionist, and he wishes he didn't have those types of jobs, but on the positive side he earns a living from them.

He also has some regular customers, primarily two landlords of apartment buildings who hire him to do regular maintenance at their buildings. As he explained, the owners can't afford a regular maintenance contract but don't want to do the work themselves, so if a tenant leaves and has knocked out all the window screens or broken drywall or caused water damage in a bathroom, he gets called in to do the repairs.

Housecleaning is a common type of informal work, primarily done by women. The number of Latina women working as housecleaners in particular appears to be staggering. Cutting the employment data down by occupation and ethnicity, 16.4 percent of Latinas reported working as housecleaners or in some form of janitorial service. In other words, for those working-age lower-income women who reported Latino ethnicity, one in six is working in some form of cleaning service. In fact, no respondents who were women and working in housecleaning services came from non-Latina backgrounds. Some of these women report working for formal-sector firms, but a significant portion also work informally, and many work entirely informally. These jobs are largely structured through social networks and personal connections. According to women working as housecleaners, there appears to be such a strong demand for the service that there are usually plenty of hours of work during the average week. Like many other types of informal work, the barriers to entry are low—all that is needed is reliable transportation and cleaning supplies. Some women have even customized their cleaning to suit individual customer's needs, such as using hypoallergenic and green cleaning products.

As Mary Romero has found (1993), the domination of housekeeping jobs by Latino and other ethnic minorities reflects the supply of large numbers of workers in immigrant-dense cities where they are willing to work informally for low wages and no benefits. Amanda, a single Mexican immigrant who has worked as a housekeeper for several years, describes how she and many of her friends and neighbors (also all Latinas) have plenty of work in predominantly white, but also wealthier Latino, households. Their primary workplaces are in the more affluent areas of San Diego, providing services that are primarily cleaning related, but often expand to include opening gates to let landscapers in and locking up homes, picking up mail, and in one case, removing food from the freezer to place in the refrigerator to defrost. In describing what she and many of her coworkers do, even though they all work independently, she illustrates that even people working entirely in the informal sector are integrated into the system of class stratification in the city. We see the same effects of work among those who work informally as subcontractors to formal-sector firms.

Subcontracting

Subcontracting occurs when a formal business hires someone to do work for cash under the table. This is particularly pronounced in construction and landscaping wherein firms do not face much state scrutiny in employment practices and much of the work is done by immigrants, who form the bulk of the informal economy and who rely on social networks as hiring channels. During a series of interviews in an earlier study (Karjanen 2010b) with day laborers in San Diego, I met Edwardo, who owns a small renovation company, doing drywall, trim, painting, and other work. His main labor source were family members, including extended family that had moved recently from Mexico, and friends and workers who have experience with doing the work or are easily trained. As he explained, the work is generally not too difficult; washing and sanding down stucco can be taught in fifteen minutes, and what he needs are hard workers. As a small firm, however, his business fluctuates. He cannot afford to keep a regular payroll beyond himself and two other employees. When he needs more workers, he goes to his phone and rolls through a list of people he regularly hires. Some of them are usually free, he says, but some are not, having found work on other jobs.

Because he operates on a shoestring budget and often does not get paid until after a job is done, he maintains his small crew as flexibly as possible. He also cannot afford to have them on a regular payroll, paying benefits and taxes. This type of cost would make him unable to get jobs, because he says he is already bidding for work at the very bottom of the market. As a result, his is a formal-sector firm that depends on a flexible supply of informal-sector workers. Without the supply of flexible, cash-in-hand workers, he is adamant that his business would close. If he shut down, as he put it, a dozen people who rely on him for work would have to look elsewhere. His family would also suffer, as would his grandmother in Mexico, to whom he sends money regularly. People working for Edwardo appear to understand this and have resigned themselves to their location in the segmented urban labor market, hoping that an opportunity will eventually come along that they can take advantage of so they can move into a better job.

Jesús, one of Edwardo's regular employees, explained how he understands the nature of the business, but earning twelve dollars an hour with Edwardo on an irregular basis then picking up other jobs as he can is preferable to washing dishes for ten dollars an hour, losing the taxes and taking home less, and working a lot more. In addition, he prefers working in construction to working in restaurants. His last regular job, in the kitchen of a busy downtown restaurant, often saw him working past the 1 a.m. time when he was supposed to finish his shift. This meant he didn't see his girlfriend much, nor did he really see any future in working in a restaurant kitchen. Similarly, José, a friend of Jesús who is distantly related to Edwardo and works part time for Edwardo's renovation business, prefers the irregularity but higher wages of construction to the regularity of low wages in fast food, kitchen, or janitorial positions. None of the food service jobs provided benefits, he explained, and there was no chance for moving up in any career. He is still young, and as he is at least learning in construction, despite the irregular hours and pay, he feels he has more opportunity. Both of these young men described aspirations of owning their own businesses someday, but for now, they were biding their time, trying to save and keep afloat financially.

The landscaping industry also has a high degree of informal work embedded within it, but one distinct advantage is that there are more regular hours due to the nature of the work. Unlike construction, which generally runs on a job-by-job basis, small landscaping firms may have regular service contracts at homes, apartment buildings, or businesses. Several workers in the survey reported working for the same firm, and they describe a similar subcontracting arrangement where they are paid cash but are never "on the books" as regular employees.

Landscaping is a particularly prominent informal sector for several reasons. First, there are limited barriers to entry. All one needs is a truck, some tools, and a mower. The skill set is limited for the most-basic jobs—mowing, weeding, raking, edging, and the like—which typically do not require any formal training. Additionally, state oversight of this type of business is harder than others. There is no place of business like a storefront or factory, so it can be impossible to identify if someone is even running a landscaping operation. Additionally, if someone does actually ask for a business license or other identification, the worker can always say that they are doing it for a friend without any compensation. In other words, the risks are limited and the rewards are potentially very positive in terms of income.

Arrangements that encourage subcontracting tend to be more complex, multijob types of work—such as in construction or landscaping. In these cases, a project can be broken down into smaller subcontractable projects, unlike child care or car washing, for instance, where it is usually just one person doing the entire job.

JOB QUALITY IN INFORMAL WORK

In chapter 3, I discussed job quality in terms of a number of indicators, including wages, benefits, underemployment, and wage growth. Assessing informal work with the same indicators is impossible due to insufficient data. We can, however, look at some of the key indicators of job quality. First and foremost is wages, and this is critical to understanding how informal work relates to the broader processes of class stratification within urban economies. Table 17 shows the average wage by people working informally in different occupations and the self-sufficiency wage for those occupations. It also shows the market-rate wage for the same occupation in San Diego (using 2010 wage data).

Wage data provide some striking insights into the relationship between formal- and informal-sector work and relative job quality. First, wages between the two sectors are typically relatively close for three occupations: housecleaning, child care, and landscaping. Landscaping workers only suffer a pay deficit of thirty-four cents on average per hour, and housecleaners and child care providers actually have a slight pay bonus from informal work: four and twenty-eight cents, respectively. Of course, the informal-sector employment does not include benefits, unemployment insurance, disability, social security, or other advantages of formal-sector work. What is even more striking is that the lower-skill dense occupations, like landscaping, child care, and housecleaning, have the smallest pay penalty for informal workers. Higher-skill occupations like

TABLE 17. Difference in Average Wage in Informal Work, Formal Market Wage, and Self-Sufficiency Wages for Central San Diego

Job	Average Wage	Mean Market Wage	Difference Market– Informal Mean Wage	One Adult ($13.92)	One Adult and One Infant ($24.08)	Two Adults (9.46)	Two Adults One Infant ($13.94)
Landscaping	13.45	13.79	−.34	−0.47	−10.63	3.99	0.49
Home repair	16	27.38 (carpenters)	−11.38	2.08	−8.08	6.54	−2.06
Construction	15	20.24	−5.24	1.08	−9.08	5.54	−1.06
Car repair	18	20.99	−2.99	4.08	−6.08	8.54	−4.06
Housecleaning	10.25	10.29	.04	−3.67	−13.83	.79	−3.69
Child care	12.25	11.97	.28	−1.67	−11.83	2.79	1.69
Transportation	8.5	12.80 (taxi drivers)	−4.3	−5.42	−15.58	−0.96	5.44

SOURCE: California Employment Development Department LMID wage data, and author interview data.

car repair and home repair (here compared with carpenter salaries) have the largest pay penalties. Skilled carpenters earn far more in the formal sector, whereas auto mechanics and construction laborers have a relatively smaller, but nonetheless significant, pay bonus.

The wage data also illustrate potentially important gendered dimensions of informal work. Two of the female-dominated occupations, child care and housekeeping, have the closest wages across formal/informal sectors. This, in part, may explain both the attractiveness of informal work, as well as the lower rates of labor force participation on the part of women. To illustrate this point, take the case of Theresa, the mother of a one-year-old; she takes two other children during the day to provide child care services to friends and family. This allows her to earn money while saving the cost of having to put her own child in child care, and she builds important social ties across friend and kin lines. She also does not have access to a car during the day, so being able to work from home by taking in a couple kids each week avoids the issue of commuting. Other aspects of job quality in informal work are challenging to assess, but do provide greater insight into both the pros and cons of working informally.

Working hours is one of the areas where people working informally report mixed results. While there is a good deal of flexibility in working informally, this varies depending on what specific job someone is performing. Those working as sole proprietors can largely set their own hours, except for certain occupations such as child care, where the client's schedule is usually the priority. Benefits, of course, are not available through informal work. This is one of the central drawbacks, along with potential occupational mobility, career training, and other benefits of being in a formal-sector firm; I discuss these in more detail in the conclusion of this chapter.

Underemployment is a different issue, related to the role and purpose the informal work serves for people. For those who are working a regular job in the formal economy, informal work may be a supplement to their income, therefore they do not mind working for a few hours or working in a position that may underutilize their skills. For those who are fully dependent on informal work as their main source of income, underemployment is often a challenge they aim to overcome. For instance, Johnny, the "hustler" discussed earlier, has a high school degree and nearly completed a certificate in building construction technology, with an aim at working in the construction field, but his military service and health issues had put him onto a different career track in the informal economy. He is working fewer hours some weeks than he would like, and he certainly is not using all of the skills and qualifications that he has, so his underemployment is evident, but he still maintains that he is happy with his work. For those working in large informal occupations like landscaping or construction, either entirely informally or as a subcontractor of a formal firm, again the issue of underemployment varies greatly depending on the individual situation.

A final problem related to informal-sector job quality is the issue of being segregated from formal labor force participation. The isolation of informal work from the formal sector has numerous drawbacks. This occurs in two dimensions. First, there is the relative isolation from social networks and important hiring networks within firms, particularly big firms. For instance, a worker at a large corporation who develops friends and a social network has far greater access to internal and potentially external hiring possibilities that could foster upward mobility than someone who works on their own for cash in hand within the community. Many businesses like to use existing employees, for example, as part of a recruiting network—it provides a prescreening tool to a certain extent— or firms may tend to promote from within their own company. People working largely in the informal sector may be entirely excluded from such preferential hiring segments of the labor market.

This raises a further issue: the longer someone remains out of the formal economy, the harder it is to get a formal-sector job. As one informant put it, "The best way to get a job is to have a job. Everyone wants someone who is already working, with experience, and willing to work for, you know, less, but for more hours." This is a significant problem for people struggling with informal and contingent work: they eventually may lack any credible or verifiable work experience. Mischa, a laid-off construction worker, spent a year working odd jobs and doing temp work before he found a regular job with a small contractor. The contractor went out of business after a few months, and Mischa went back to doing odd jobs for friends and relatives and people he knew who had been asking him to do some work for them. He then got a few jobs with temp agencies, working in warehouses and in construction labor. These lasted a few months more, then he was unemployed again. As he returned to the job market, he realized that he had spent more than two years working off and on trying to stay economically afloat (he had already given up his truck because he could not maintain the payments and traded it in for a cheaper car he could pay cash for). The biggest hurdle he faced now, however, was that he could not get any significant verification of his work over the previous two years. Most of his jobs were informal, some were for temp agencies, but some of his temp employers had gone out of business, like his last contractor. All he had for work references were two temp agencies who could only verify that he had applied, been sent to some employers and did complete some jobs, but the temp agencies have no way of providing any detailed information that would make Mischa a good job candidate—such as being a hard worker, on time, professional, and so forth. As a result, Mischa's informal and temp work has now become somewhat of a handicap in getting a job because it is difficult to verify, and as he explained, "people don't like to see that you have a blank spot for a couple years . . . they wonder what you were up to, like you are trying to hide something, were in prison or on dope or something, even though I was running around working my ass off."

CONCLUSION

Earlier, I discussed how discouraged workers in the inner city may decide to enter informal work as an alternative to formal labor force participation. The cases in this chapter illustrate just some of the complex reasons why this may be the case, and why informal work appears to be expanding in relation to growing urban inequality and an expansion of the urban poor and working poor.

First, in low-income communities, informal work services multiple economic functions that are not provided in the "formal" sector. Informal work provides the opportunity for lower-income consumers to get goods and services that they may not otherwise find in the formal marketplace. Car repair, for instance, can be a lot cheaper if done by a friend or relative, with used parts, than at a garage with new parts. Accounting help or tax preparation, construction, or landscaping are all typically cheaper than in the formal marketplace. The issue of trust and exchange, however, does pose potential challenges.

An additional reason low-income communities may rely on a good deal of informal work is that it may provide an essential form of income generation, either regular or supplementary. This is supported by the two strongest predictor variables for informal work mentioned above: being unemployed for a long time, and having multiple jobs. In short, those who are out of the labor force may be very discouraged and take up informal work, or they rely on informal work to supplement already low or inadequate wages in the formal sector. This is critically important to understanding the transformation of inner-city labor markets. If indeed the growth of the informal economy has occurred, then it can be seen in part as a response to the deregulation of the formal labor market. For instance, without unions, hiring halls, apprentice programs, stable employment, steady wages, steady work, full-time work, perceptions or experiences of hiring discrimination, and a lack of skills for the "good jobs," informal work becomes far more appealing.

Finally, there are the economics of informality in low-income communities. There is clearly a demand for certain goods and services among low-income residents. This is often supplied by other low-income residents. This does not mean, however, that there is adequate market demand to encourage these informal entrepreneurs to go into business. As a resident who does occasional car repairs on the side explained, "There are a lot of people who can afford me, but not as many who can afford MAACO. But I can't compete with MAACO. The market is full of shops out there, and it is cutthroat. Why would I want to jump into that? There isn't enough room for me to open a shop, so I stay on the side." In other words, the formal marketplace is already too competitive to make the risk worthwhile across and outside the community, but there is not adequate income within the community to merit opening a shop there either, and there is also the issue of lots of market competition in central San Diego already. In this light, we can see informal work as partly a function of the inequalities within the urban economy. These are service and good providers who function to serve those who cannot afford "formal-sector" goods and services, while at the same time providing additional income within an already income poor area.

Overall, informal work is a reflection of the marginality of these communities in central San Diego. It is generally assumed that types of informal work, ranging from street hustling and day labor to more hidden, subcontracted work, would not decline as urban revitalization and job creation occur. This has not been the case, however. In fact, there is strong evidence to suggest that informal work has remained steady or expanded in San Diego, despite a radical transformation and redevelopment of the downtown. Why this occurred and continues, I argue, has more to do with the structure of inequality than with poor values or a culture of street hustling.

Informal work in these communities is in part the outer edge of the labor market. It is outside of state oversight, but there is nevertheless a market for informal labor, and it often crosses over and interacts with forms of labor that are within the state's purview. Within this field of work we find discouraged workers, displaced workers, the long-term unemployed, and those who have found a better means to work outside the formal economy. We also see that these workers subsidize the broader system of class relations: providing day care, elder care, maintenance, and other services not only to other poor or working poor neighbors, but also to more affluent households and businesses. As such, informal work is both marginal and integral to the unequal urban economy. It is a means through which socially reproductive functions can flourish outside of the inadequacies of the formal market; this includes both demand for goods and services, as well as the supply of labor.

PART III

Living in the
Servant Class Economy

6

Do-It-Yourself Safety Nets

I N T H E P R E V I O U S S E C T I O N, I looked at how the workplace for two of the largest industries that were promoted as urban revitalization, hospitality and retail, on average are inadequate in terms of job quality. A lack of skills upgrading or experience, stagnant or falling wages, and limited career ladders make these industries less than appealing to many inner-city residents. As some move to the further margins of the economy, working informally to supplement their low wages or to drop out of the labor force entirely, they run into additional problems, like a lack of benefits and labor market attachment, often making it even harder to return to formal employment even if they wanted to.

I also looked at how informal work often ties multiple different domains of the urban economy together. Poor and working poor households both participate in and often depend on informal work. "Formal-sector" firms also employ people informally, as do households with businesses, and then there is the panoply of completely unregulated labor that occurs on a cash-in-hand basis. Much of this income-earning activity is also crucial to people's own self-provisioning given the lack of either market-based or state-provided goods or services. The salient point here is that for the urban poor and working poor the boundaries between formal/ informal and self-provisioning or market-based solutions to important needs are typically blurred. In the absence of adequate or affordable options, people will improvise, draw on social networks, and find ways to self-provide. Much of this innovative, hard-working, and determined self-provisioning I refer to as do-it-yourself (DIY) safety nets, precisely be-cause without any other options, families and individuals will find ways to solve fundamental problems, from income and bill paying to child care. This work is often invisible in scholarship of the urban poor and working poor. We have hundreds of studies of welfare dependency and out-of-wedlock births, but far fewer studies of the herculean challenges that the poor face and the strategies they must develop, though there are some excellent ones that demonstrate the depth and complexity of these challenges (Collins and Mayer 2010; Edin and Kefalas 2007; Marchevsky and Theoharis 2006). My aim in this chapter is to further illuminate the very real efforts and strategies that these disadvantaged communities enact, and to link them back to broader structures of inequality and its reproduction, *despite* people's best efforts.

In order to theoretically frame my understanding of the presence of all sorts of agency and hard work in the face of continued poverty and inequality, I conceptualize the relationship over time as one of *structures of cumulative disadvantage*. This is directly in line with cyclical or cumulative theories of poverty, but updated to locate such systematic inequalities within the context of changing urban labor markets and urban revitalization efforts and changing public policies. The key difference here is that in the communities in San Diego, despite and in many ways because of the urban revitalization that occurred, the problems of inadequate resources that are poverty traps have shifted up the income ladder to encompass the working poor at two or three times the poverty rate. Poverty traps and self-reproducing or reinforcing mechanisms that perpetuate poverty are widely debated, with many policy prescriptions ranging from promoting more types of capital (human, social, infrastructure, etc.) (Sachs 1992), to promoting better youth interventions, primarily through family support and education (Schorr and Schorr 1988), to promoting savings and asset accumulation (Schreiner and Sherraden 2007). There are dozens of approaches, different disciplinary perspectives, and various theories about how to best go about getting families and individuals out of cycles of cumulative disadvantage. Combining all of the studies of poverty and breaking cycles of poverty suggests that those in poverty have massive needs just to reach a level of functionality where we can assume some behaviors, like staying in the labor force and working toward a longer-term career, can occur.

This is especially the case with recent research on low-income families, particularly studies of the effects of welfare reform, showing that the challenges working poor families face are complex, overlapping, and often inadequately addressed by a frayed social safety net. Studies of welfare reform, for instance, find that women being moved off of cash assistance and into the labor market and job programs rarely obtained jobs that meant moving beyond poverty level wages, while at the same time other important considerations that were needed to allow women to enter the workforce, like child care and transportation, are often inadequate (Collins and Mayer 2010; Marchevsky and Theoharis 2006).

In this chapter I look first at the limited access to welfare and low rates of public assistance income in these communities. This demonstrates how limited state supports have become and explains part of the reason for the significant informal economy and how critical social support networks are. In the second part of this chapter I look at how the inadequacies of many critically important socially reproductive institutions, like child care or elder care or medical leave, mean that these families must invest significant resources and experience significant limitations to their economic mobility. Inadequate child care means that women cannot participate in the labor force as often, if at all, reducing the ability of low-income families to gain two incomes.

WHEN THINGS WORK OUT

Marisa has been a navy wife for fifteen years. Her husband, Joe, had just left the navy after several very long deployments to the Persian Gulf, just before the economic recession started to unravel San Diego's economy in 2007. While he was looking to transition into a new job, Marisa lost her job at a real estate company. To make matters even more difficult, they had moved into a new, larger apartment, and the rent had just increased. They were facing a financial crisis and had to downsize rapidly. They experienced the type of quick, downward mobility that many Americans have faced over the past thirty years as middle-class incomes have declined or stagnated, a process that accelerated dramatically with the recession (EPI 2011; Newman 1999). To keep from becoming insolvent and from having to declare bankruptcy, they sold a car to a friend for cash and moved into a smaller apartment; they cut back on cable, Internet, subscriptions, and other expenses, but still had fixed bills like credit cards and Marisa's school loans for her associate's degree. These were manageable expenses, and indeed they were paying off their debt rapidly before the economic crisis, but their budgets were overextended when unemployment hit.

Fortunately, they had a strong kinship network as a safety net. Joe got a job working with his brother-in-law installing car alarms and tinting car windows. This work only lasted a short time, however, as the business had to cut back and lay Joe off. He eventually got a warehouse job, while Marisa took temp agency jobs. Joe then got injured at work and was out for two weeks and then on workers' compensation. To tide them over, they got a loan from his parents, who sold off a timeshare in order to help out; this money also paid off a large amount of Marisa's school loans, making their monthly bills more manageable. Marisa also got help from her mother shopping: they shared a Costco membership, bought in bulk, and occasionally had meals together to save even more money. Marisa also spent some time between temp jobs babysitting for her sister. As Marisa explains, "If it weren't for our families, we'd be living in our car, or in a shelter, or maybe my parent's driveway in a tent, who knows."

By 2011 things for Marisa and Joe had turned around. Marisa was back working full time and considering going to get a BA in business administration with a concentration in finance, looking to improve her options working in real estate finance as a career. Joe heard from a friend in the navy about a position at a manufacturer of marine parts. With a good reference and his background as a naval electronics technician, Joe was able to get the job as a quality control supervisor. Because they were both back at work they needed a second car, and Joe's parents again were able to come through with a loan to allow them to pay cash for their vehicle. This car, a used but warrantied Honda Civic, Marisa now uses to get to work, and she can drive from work to night classes she is taking in preparation for getting her BA degree. Now, with her student loans paid off and a car that she and Joe do not need to make payments on, they are in a far more economically secure position, and have made a successful swing back up to the middle class from their economically dire situation just a couple of years earlier. The key point here is that their rebound and potential upward mobility was a product of diligence, but also the critical intervention of family and resources, notably money. They have gone from literally a week away from filing bankruptcy and not being able to buy food, to planning to become even more economically stable in the forthcoming years and even more comfortably middle class; and much to their relief, with little debt.

I begin this chapter with Marisa and Joe's story because it illustrates how vitally important social support networks can be. Their families allowed Marisa and Joe to stave off bankruptcy and gave them a tremendous boost in potential upward mobility, helping them out with money and even finding work. What of those families or individuals who are lower on the socioeconomic ladder, or who do not have the same type of social support networks? How do the working poor keep from falling further in times of economic crisis? With the elimination of welfare supports, and stagnating or even falling wages for many lower-skilled workers, a new set of economic pressures has unfolded in the past twenty years. Social support networks and other means of making ends meet are not a new phenomenon, but the context today is different from how it was years ago. In this chapter I look at the strategies that the poor and near poor rely on to survive economically while in the second tier of the economy.

In the post–welfare reform era with the stagnation of wages, families and individuals rely on an increasingly complex and overlapping set of resources tied to social networks, friends, families, and public services. This leads to the use of informal services for everything from car repair to transportation, from information such as legal or tax advice to child care. This is not necessarily new; the poor, particularly families, have always relied on social support networks.

THE SHREDDED SAFETY NET

Informal social support networks, or what I call DIY safety nets, are central to understanding the challenges faced by the urban poor. Carol Stack's (1975) *All Our Kin* was one of the first book-length studies of the informal social-support networks of the urban poor. This study debunked the misconception that poor families were unstable and disorganized and instead showed the resiliency of the poor to respond to conditions of deprivation by forming large, stable, lifelong support networks based on friendship and family that were very powerful, highly structured, and surprisingly complex. The economy has changed dramatically since Stack's analysis, but her findings have remained a constant within studies of the urban poor. With the transformation of welfare, the restructuring of the economy, and despite the rapid changes in inner cities, poor urban communities still rely on networks of mutual reciprocity, social support, and community. In the current era, I refer to many aspects of these as DIY safety nets, precisely because the ostensible responsibilities of the state have shifted to individuals, families, churches, communities, and so forth. As such, self-provided emergency safety nets are even more critical with the working poor and near poor caught between often insufficient public services (for instance, the eight-year wait list for Section 8 housing in San Diego) and, for those who are at the higher end of the working poor spectrum (over 200 percent FPL), incomes too high to qualify for public programs.

In central San Diego approximately 9.5 percent of households were receiving public assistance income in 2000 based on the decennial census. This figure includes CalWORKs (California Work Opportunity and Responsibility to Kids) funds that households received, but does not include Supplemental Social Security Income, food stamps, or other funds, such as disability payments or veterans' benefits. This figure is higher than in most parts of San Diego, and higher than the county and state on average, but it must be contextualized with the income and unemployment rates. Unemployment rates are higher than average in central San Diego when compared to the city and county, and overall a higher concentration of people seeking work who are at the margins of the economy. In short, we should expect there to be higher rates of public assistance income, as in any lower-income community. Yet, despite the economic challenges, there is a lower uptake rate than there should be given the economic data; in other words, a lot of people who may qualify for CalWORKs or other forms of assistance do not take advantage of them.

Part of the reason for the lower than expected uptake rates for public assistance is the rate of noncitizens in the inner city, but another significant factor is people's reticence to use public assistance programs. The vast majority of residents in central San Diego view public assistance as a stigma. Nearly 90 percent overall think that people should rely on public assistance as a last resort.

Notably, this is higher in the predominantly Latino areas of zip code 92113, where nine out of ten people feel that public assistance should be a last resort option for low-income people (see Table 18). Overall, use of public assistance through CalWORKs is lower than other sources of

TABLE 18. Public Assistance Usage and Attitudes in Central San Diego

Zip Code	Public Assistance Use	Reliance on Public Assistance as a Last Resort	Other Sources of Income (VA benefits, child support, etc.)
92113	14.80%	90%	15%
92102	10.73%	88%	13%
92101	2.26%	85%	14%
Total (weighted averages)	9.47%	89%	14%

SOURCE: Central San Diego Survey 2002–10; U.S. Decennial Census 2000.

income such as VA benefits and child support, in some cases by a wide margin. This suggests that residents are more willing to use sources other than public assistance to shore up their finances, and then rely on other sources of income like informal work or formal-sector employment to make up the difference.

As Hector, a thirty-year-old concrete-and-masonry worker, pointed out, with his family size (six, including four children), he and his wife, Jessica, actually qualify for a number of public assistance programs, but instead they rely on his income and his wife's part-time income as a cashier. The rest of the time Jessica takes care of their two youngest children, while her mother takes the children on the days Jessica goes to work at a retail store. Hector admits that they have used food stamps, but only sporadically, as necessary. For example, when they found, unexpectedly, that they were having a fourth child, they realized that the family income was not going to cover all of their food needs. Hector justifies his use of food stamps as the right thing to do for the health of his children. "We did not plan on such a large family," Hector explains, "but that's life, you can't feed your kids just milk and rice and beans. If we did not have kids, then we wouldn't need food stamps. We [he and his wife] don't need the stuff, but they [his children] should eat good for their health." Hector's comments bring up an important dimension to the justification of the limited use of public assistance—children. Most families reliant on a program state that they would not use the program if they did not have children, but they will take advantage of the resources because virtually every program requires the presence of children, or someone with a disability, to enroll. As Jessica put it, "Anyone with kids knows how expensive things get. If you don't have family to help out, then there is the county or Y [YWCA] or other groups [civic groups administering federal and state programs]."

Another reason that uptake rates are not as high as they could be is that enrollment is not easy. As she and so many other parents have expressed, the qualifications and processing of applications requires a great deal of time, and possibly money—getting rides, taking the bus, getting child care, photocopying forms, and so forth—that there is not much of an incentive to apply for programs unless someone really feels an urgent need. Even in such cases, however, the needs are often justified on the part of applicants by the presence of children or disabled family members—again, the main requirements for most programs. CalWORKs, for instance, has a long list of eligibility restrictions. In general, these include:

- Reside in California and intend to stay
- Have children or are pregnant and:
  - One or both parents are absent from the home, deceased, or disabled
  - Both parents are in the home, but the principal wage earner is either unemployed or working less than one hundred hours per month at the time they apply for assistance
- Be a United States citizen or a lawful immigrant
- Have a Social Security number or have applied for one
- Have a net monthly income less than the maximum aid payment for family size
- Have less than $2,000 in cash, bank accounts, and other resources ($3,000 if sixty years or older)
- Provide proof of regular school attendance for all school-age children
- Provide proof of immunizations for all children under the age of six
- Cooperate with child support requirements
- Participate in welfare-to-work activities
- Perform thirty-two hours of work-related activities per week for a single-parent household or thirty-five hours per week in a two-parent household

Simply obtaining all of this paperwork can take weeks. Documents required for the intake interview include a range of possible items. Many of these documents are puzzlingly unattainable, according to some residents of central San Diego. How does one provide a "statement of school expenses," for instance? Is that something you provide with receipts or something the school provides with some form? wondered a mother of twins I interviewed as she was preparing to assemble a CalWORKs application. At minimum, applicants must provide any of the following as needed:

Proof of income, such as:

- Pay stubs or other proof of earnings
- Social Security and Veterans benefit award letters
- School grants/loan statements
- Child support papers showing awards by the courts
- Unemployment printouts or stubs
- Disability/workers' compensation award letter or stubs
- Statements of any other income

Cost of living and asset documents, such as:

- Rent and utility bills showing the address and person billed for the rent and/or utilities
- Property tax statements
- Real estate, mortgage, and personal property loan statements
- Cost of medical bills or receipts
- Cost of medical transportation
- Child care receipts
- Proof of court-ordered child support
- Statement of school expenses for household members

Personal property and/or resource documents, such as:

- Vehicle registrations and payment book
- Checking account statements
- Savings account statements or bank records
- Insurance policies
- Property trust deeds
- Mortgage bills

Verification documents, such as:

- Identification for anyone over the age of eighteen who lives in the home
- Social Security cards

- Documentation of naturalized citizenship status/noncitizen status
- Proof you applied for disability benefits or unemployment benefits
- School or training enrollment/attendance documentation
- Registration for work with employment development

Applying for CalWORKs is not easy; in fact, despite some streamlining, obtaining documents and preparing for the intake interview can be very time consuming. Rita, a mother of two children, described her exasperation with the health clinic that had her children's immunization records: they would not release them unless she went to the clinic in person, because they insisted she had to sign for them. When she did get a chance to go to the clinic, the staff produced the wrong records, stating that with all the Spanish last names sometimes the records can get confused. She called for two weeks after the initial trip to make sure that the proper records were being copied and provided for her to pick up. She received a phone call back, asking more follow-up questions to verify her children's identities, then the records were copied and available. A similar problem occurred with her older child's school attendance records. All of these forms must be filled out with intake forms, copied in multiples, and brought to the intake interview. Missing information or documentation, or unclear documents, requires that these be fixed and a return interview scheduled. The forms are available at county DHS offices, or on the Internet; however, most people appear to need to get them from the DHS office, which requires a trip simply to get the paperwork to initiate the process (not surprising given that those qualifying for CalWORKs are often limited in their access to the Internet).

All of this, of course, does not mean that someone will be approved for CalWORKs; it simply means that an application will be taken. Some may be rejected, some may have special circumstances that require further follow up—such as the verification of participation with County Social Services regarding child support—and these additional processes can take up to several weeks. If public assistance is only used as a last resort, emergency stopgap measure during periods of unplanned crisis, then it is not a very responsive one; people usually have to wait weeks to determine if they are approved, and then further time to actually get the benefits processed. As one woman who qualifies for CalWORKs stated: "Why spend months battling an office that doesn't care about you just to get some income support that they make you feel bad to take? I have some dignity."

As Daniel Dohan (2003) has found for residents in low-income immigrant communities, the stigma associated with public assistance and other factors makes such programs the last resort. Rather, use of public assistance is a product of a range of unexpected crises and problems that have built up over time; reliance on social programs becomes the last resort to cover an unplanned emergency or a crisis, and it may be used in conjunction with other income (Dohan 2003). The challenges of using public assistance are simply part of the broader context regarding economic restructuring and the plight of the working poor.

How people have responded to these changes is the focus of this chapter. I describe these methods as do-it-yourself safety nets because they reflect the ways that the working poor and near poor have developed new economic strategies or expanded existing ones to make up for stagnant or lost incomes. As anyone who lives or works in a low-income community will attest, "money comes and money goes, but it does not stay around that long." This chronic economic insecurity presents daunting challenges in the wage of labor market and state welfare restructuring. What then are the DIY safety nets that people have developed or rely on? In the following sections I detail the different mechanisms that have emerged both formally and informally to make up for eroding wages, benefits, and public assistance.

CAREGIVING

One of the benefits of having kinship and other networks is the social and economic support they can convey. These networks also typically make some form of reciprocity obligatory. Aging parents, children, grandchildren, disabled family members, and relatives returning from rehabilitation centers, hospitals, and wars all require some form of assistance, and much of this is done informally among family and other networks. State and federal programs, churches, and social service organizations only provide limited assistance, but for child care, elder care, or care for the sick or disabled, family is the primary locus of support. A third of central San Diego residents report being caregivers to someone during the average week. This caregiving can be stretched across a range of different types of care: for children, the elderly, or a combination of caregiving needs (sometimes family members get sick or injured). A focus on caregiving responsibilities relates to the broader political economy because it is a critical socially reproductive function that has once again been increasingly pushed onto communities, families, and individuals as state programs are cut back, made more difficult to obtain, or are inadequate. The two areas I focus on here specifically are elder care and child care.

Child Care

Child care is one of the biggest hurdles for working families. The cost of even subsidized child care services can be prohibitive for low-income parents. Single parents, in particular, of course, are in a bind because they have only one income, and without someone in the immediate family to care for children they face the quandary of how to obtain care. Access to high-quality child care in low-income communities has been a significant problem for decades, but particularly acute since welfare reform. Working mothers and immigrant mothers are particularly challenged in using formal child care arrangements due to the inadequacy of care. My findings in this regard are similar to Sarah Mahler's (1995, 154) where women would prefer to provide their own care for their own children, but due to overcrowding, cost, and limited availability, even with sliding scale or free care, the costs as well as scheduling, transporting kids, and a lack of trust in formal providers means that informal care is often preferred. This situation forces working poor families into a bind: go to work to keep up with costs but pay the higher price of child care, or attempt to find informal care arrangements. Child care costs can vary widely. Recent reports put California child care costs for full-time care as high as college tuition or more ($5,000–12,000 per year) depending on the type of care (Child Care Aware 2012).

Subsidized Programs

Subsidized programs have expanded, but there are challenges to obtaining access to them, and gaps in the type and quality of care according to parents. In order to get subsidized child care one has to apply to get on the CEL, or the Centralized Eligibility List. Spaces for children at various centers are then provided based on the CEL listing. Families are listed on the CEL based on need, which is a formula taking into account eligibility guidelines, family size, and income. For instance, a one- or two-person family can earn no more than $3,283 per month, while a family of four can earn no more than $3,908 per month (San Diego County CEL 2012). While this income limit covers many poor families, it does not cover the near poor—those earning approximately 200 percent of the federal poverty level. The income cut offs are near eleven dollars an hour for each parent. Lower-income families are given higher priority, so this reduces the likelihood that more moderate and higher-income families that qualify will participate in the program. Moreover, if someone qualifies for subsidized child care, this does not mean that they will get it. The CEL has a wait list that may require someone waiting five to ten months before they can get affordable care.

Nationally, few eligible parents actually take advantage of government-subsidized child care. Parents who are low income and have irregular work schedules are more likely to use informal child care arrangements. For the families in central San Diego, the likelihood of having irregular work hours is high. This is one of the central reasons for choosing informal arrangements over formal ones. Among low-income employed families that did not receive child care help from the government or another organization, only 7 percent reported that they had asked for such help. The others presumably did not feel they needed assistance, did not want assistance from a government program, did not know that assistance might be available, or did not think they would be eligible for assistance. For those with regular full-time jobs, the preference is for formal child care arrangements. This may or may not be the case depending on the number of children in the family. Families with employed mothers are also more likely to use formal child care arrangements; this is especially true if the mother works full time (Zaslow et al. 1998).

Another problem is the irregular working hours of low-income families. Those performing temporary or contingent work are often unsure of their schedules, and it is difficult to book a spot in child care if they do not have any clarity of their shifts. With more than 75 percent of cashiers, food prep workers, nursing aides, orderlies and attendants, retail sales clerks, and wait staff working nonstandard hours, those with the fewest resources are forced to choose between working or child care (Collins and Mayer 2010, 94). In some instances with temp work, people may have a lot of work for a project, but then be out of work for a spell;

what they need is intermittent child care, but this is not always easy to come by because one week there may be a spot for a child, but the following week there may not be. In short, there is a disjuncture between the labor market flexibility encouraged by contemporary labor market and employment policies and the limits on child care flexibility. Caught between the two are low-income working parents.

Celia, a twenty-five-year-old mother of two whose husband works from 8 a.m. to 5 p.m., also works, in her case part time in retail and part time as a temp worker. She often works for inventory control companies in the retail industry. These jobs place workers for a week or a few days in a store to do an inventory audit, and then the job is done; they may not have another job for a week or a month. In the interim, she works part time at a retail store downtown, and her frustration with finding flexible child care is palatable: "Nobody wants to take you just as 'drop in' child care, they want to sign you up a week or year in advance, and there often is competition to find spots." Celia pointed out to me that there were more doggie day care centers in downtown San Diego than licensed child care centers (something I later corroborated).

An additional problem of the low-wage workplace related to child care challenges is the issue of mandatory or coerced overtime. Retail, warehousing, food service, and other low-wage service jobs that require a lot of customer interaction need people to fill in when others are sick, quit, or otherwise cannot make it for a shift. Sometimes people are called in simply because there may be a regional manager visiting a store and the staff is brought in for a few additional hours to make the store presentable. As Celia pointed out, putting in the extra time wasn't required, but it was essentially a given that if you didn't you would be "looked down upon, not working as a team, and therefore when someone needed to be let go, you might be the first one." In other cases, lower-income workers may actually want the extra hours and overtime, particularly if it is paid in time-and-a-half wages. This can be an important source of extra income, especially for those who are underemployed and looking for more hours to work. On the other hand, this causes a child care problem: who takes care of the kids on short notice if a free shift or hours have come up? To address these problems parents often rely on informal child care arrangements with friends or family, but there are challenges with informal care as well.

Informal Child Care

The reasons people provide for relying on informal child care arrangements in this study include flexibility, cost, barriers to formal state subsidies, and the social relations of trust and reciprocity of using kin or friends for child care. In some cases, families have mutually supporting or shifting child care systems. Day shift workers may take care of children in one part of the family or social network, while night shift workers take the kids from another part.

Informal arrangements are more flexible in part because they do not have the same regulatory requirements. A parent can always "drop off" a child with kin or an informal sitting service if they have been called in for work or have to run an important errand, but this is not necessarily the case with formal care centers. As a reflection on this reliance on informal child care arrangements, in central San Diego I identified more than informal child care centers (many simply family members caring for a number of children), while there were only six registered centers. In the revitalized downtown, as my informant Celia noted, there are more dog sitting firms than child care centers.

An additional reason for preferring informal arrangements is the social trust and reciprocity engendered by child care. Although a small percentage (14 percent) of children in the survey relied on grandparents for regular child care, these families used them almost exclusively, and if they did have grandparents to provide child care, then it was more likely that they also participated in other informal care rather than formal care. For these parents, it does not make sense to rely on a costly or formal-sector care provider when there are grandparents, cousins, and perhaps friends or informal providers who can take care of the children. This child care support system has been well documented as a central social support mechanism among the urban poor and near poor (Lamb and Ahnert 2007), but what has potentially shifted is the relative importance of it in the wake of welfare reform and more women entering the labor force.

Relying on this type of care, however, does have its disadvantages. First and foremost, it is not as reliable as formal care centers. This places the labor force attachment of parents at greater risk if care cannot be found or is too irregular. For example, a parent who relies on a grandparent for child care has to leave work if they do not have a backup provider and the grandparent gets sick, has an accident, or is otherwise unable to take care of the child. In some cases this can mean job loss. Ian, a single parent of two children, a welder by training who was working in a machine shop, had steady employment and used his mother as a day care provider. When she became ill and was unable to take care of his two children for a week, he had to shuffle to get the children into a child care center. This required several days off of work to do so, and when he returned to work he was told that his hours were cut back, "because of lack of business," he was told. He had no proof, but he feels it is due to his need to take care of his kids for a week. Two weeks later when his mother was recovered, he kept his kids in the formal day care center, but it was costing him twice as much. He only paid his mother for expenses and a small sum for her "trouble," as he described it. Even with subsidies in the formal provider, he still was paying twice as much as he was with just his mother as a care provider. He felt it was necessary to keep the kids in the child care center to ensure that he would not lose his job or lose more hours. Eventually, he did resume more work hours at the machine shop, but he harbors resentment against the employer for cutting back his hours after a child care problem.

Another problem with informal arrangements is that they can end at any time. Family members move, change jobs, and leave the child care business, and friends may have their own schedules change. This is not to say that formal-sector child care centers do not open and close with changes in funding or demand, but they do so far less frequently. The chronic insecurity of having to arrange child care and seek some level of child care provider stability is a cost in itself; and it can erode the strength of labor force attachment.

For those who are "near poor" and do not qualify for many subsidies, or who do but find it too difficult to get into a nearby center, they face the balancing act of costs of care versus wages. As many economic studies have found (Anderson and Levine 1999; Kimmel 1998), the high cost of child care can be nearly as much as the earned income of the care provider. In many instances, it simply makes more sense for one of the parents to stay home and care for the child rather than paying for the care and spending all their earned income on paying for the care. There are more than a dozen women for whom this is the case in the community survey. One of them, Aliyah, explained that because of her husband's good job as a mechanic for a commercial truck repair business, they did not qualify for child care subsidies. Her income from her work as a restaurant hostess was less per week than the child care costs for their daughter. As a result, Aliyah took care of her daughter full time but would have preferred to work if it was possible. Without family or an affordable provider, however, there were no viable options. Because she withdrew from the labor force for three years, she lost out on what she saw as valuable job experience. In short, a family with young children and one high-income earner and one low-income one is penalized occupationally, because it is not economically viable for both earners to go to work.

Problems with child care result not only in difficulties keeping a regular work schedule, but also performance at work and lost opportunities. A significant percentage of working parents face child care conflicts related to work or schooling or other issues. Based on surveys of parents in central San Diego, these problems range from minor issues, such as being unable to run an errand (35 percent), to missing a day of work (23 percent), to being unable to take a promotion or relocate for a better job (15 percent). The most common problem is the need to change work hours if child care is not available. Nearly half (45 percent) of parents had a problem during the previous year scheduling work hours because of child care problems. These difficulties may reduce the likelihood that an employee is successful at work or can move up a career ladder. Several people, 8 percent, described not being offered or unable to take a promotion because of conflicts with child care.

One woman, Nadia, a cashier at a large retail store, was offered the option to move into an assistant manager position within the company. The promotion would mean that she would earn significantly more, but she would also have to work more hours and much earlier in the day than her current position. This meant that she would have to find child care for additional hours, beyond what her parents and husband could provide. With her new pay increase, her combined income would push her and her husband beyond the income limit for subsidized care, but even if she could get subsidized care, it would mean that the additional income would go almost entirely to paying for the additional child care hours. Several people I spoke to who have informal child care arrangements reaffirm Nadia's experience, but with a sadly ironic twist. They were caregivers themselves for other children, but they had to place their own children into the care of others while they looked after a different family's children.

Elder Care

Elder care is a growing concern in the United States, but especially for low-income families. According to a recent MetLife study, the average cost of assisted living in California was $3,845 per month or $46,140 per year, while care in a skilled nursing facility was $7,470 per month or $90,885 per year (CALA 2012). Publically subsidized programs include HUD-funded affordable senior housing, locally funded senior projects with redevelopment and foundation money, and facilities backed by churches or other organizations. The economic resources available to caregiving families vary widely. Ann Bookman and Delia Kimbrel (2011) point out that upper-middle-class and affluent families usually have adequate funds for elder care, and poor families can often rely on subsidized services, such as home health care. The greatest challenge for families are the working poor and those with moderate incomes, who are too "rich" to qualify for subsidized services but unable to pay for care themselves. This leaves many residents to do their own elder care, while balancing work and their own caregiving for children.

My survey of residents in central San Diego shows that 24 percent report being a caregiver to someone at some point during an average week. The types of care people provide range from shopping to cooking and cleaning, to spending time with elderly parents or grandparents. Some families simply "check in" to make sure people are okay. This rate is lower than the reported 40 percent nationally (Abutaleb 2013) and is in large part due to the large portion of migrant and younger families who live in the area: their parents and grandparents are either in other countries or other states.

The challenges of elder care among low-income working families also produce conflicts between work and family time and caregiving time, but with very different issues and potential problems. This is a growing challenge as an aging inner city demands more and more elder care options, but with limited resources to provide for them. As much of the research shows, caretaking for older generations is largely an individual task, often informally, without market-provided or state-subsidized care, and typically done by older women. Care is primarily provided for by immediate family members, then extended family, with care duties being rotated as necessary to accommodate people's schedules and obligations. Caregivers tend to be female, older, and have lower rates of labor force participation. In my surveys there also was evidence for competing demands: 21 percent reported child care responsibilities, 9 percent indicated that they had quit their jobs, and 20 percent reported other work conflict. Although the majority of informal care is provided by one person, most elders receive help from other caregivers as well. People who provide help offer a range of services to elderly residents, but less than the primary caregiver. This means that a significant portion of residents with elderly people to care for rely on other family, paid help informally, and formal-sector services.

The effects of limited elder care are similar for those with limited child care. Conflicts with elder care can disrupt work, prevent workers from taking other opportunities, and become a challenge in itself for working families who do not have the time or means to care for an aging family member. In central San Diego elder care results in people having to change work hours (18 percent), miss shifts (12 percent), arrive late for or leave early from work (22 percent), or miss running important errands (35 percent). As Table 19 indicates, these issues can range from affecting employment (and hence earnings as well, and potentially promotions) to getting more job training or attending school.

For families caught in the middle of multiple caregiving obligations, this makes both the costs high and the strategies to deal with caregiving very time consuming. This is to say nothing of the emotional and physical toll that caring for young children and elderly adults can take on families trying to care for three generations. Strategies for DIY caregiving safety nets are limited by all of these factors; time, money, and the capacity to arrange them are very real costs for low-income families.

TABLE 19. Costs of Elder Care Responsibilities

Changed Work Hours	Unable to work a shift	Missed Days of Work	Arrived Late for or Left Early from Work	Unable to Take Promotion or Relocation	Unable to Go to School or Training	Unable to Run Important Errands
18%	12%	11%	22%	15%	3%	35%

SOURCE: Central San Diego Survey 2002–10.

COMBINING STRATEGIES

It is abundantly clear that people do not rely on any single strategy to serve as a DIY safety net when they are in a period of economic insecurity or crisis. They typically combine multiple strategies, and these often become mutually dependent. Thus, the range of resources and strategies people use to shore up their economic position in times of need or urgency are varied and complex. Like any challenge, people often combine strategies when addressing financial crises or simply falling short in paying for expenses. Kin, friends, shuffling debt, working out payment plans, taking on odd jobs, and a host of other tactics allow people to stay afloat, but it does not ensure much in the way of financial stability. In fact, just the opposite is true; having to constantly micromanage finances across various different resources requires a lot of effort, creates a lot of complexity, and prevents any steady accumulation of savings. To see why this happens we can turn to the case of the López family.

The Lópezes have two daughters, and the parents both work. Miguel and Laura are in construction and housecleaning, respectively. When the construction industry employment collapsed during the housing crisis, Miguel could not find work, and Laura's hours were cut back. She found work with friends and former coworkers, and Miguel did odd jobs for a while, but they fell behind in their bills. To keep their car payments going they borrowed a couple months of payments from relatives. When their car needed a costly repair, Miguel's father loaned them his car for a while until they could save up the money. They sold some household goods, particularly jewelry and electronics, and relied on their one credit card for a couple weeks in order to save for the necessary car repairs. When they finally got their car fixed, they had to pay the credit card, which they had used for a lot of basic expenses, including their daughter's back-to-school clothes and materials. They hoped that by the time the car could be fixed and the credit card was due, one of them would have found more work. This did not happen, unfortunately, so they then had to start paying the credit card down in installments—effectively, a very high-interest loan. They also fell behind on their utility bills. To prevent losing service, they set up a payment plan with San Diego Gas and Electric. They also borrowed some money from Miguel's father. When Miguel finally did get a regular job, several months after being laid off, the Lópezes faced the complex task of paying down the credit card, getting caught up with their utility bills, paying back family members, continuing to pay for the car and rent, and trying to get back on track financially. Throughout the process, it was impossible for the Lopezes to save, and they had already worn out much of the goodwill and social support of family members.

DUCT TAPE DOESN'T FIX EVERYTHING

Dominica and her husband, Jason, have lived in San Diego most of their lives, having moved from El Centro years ago. Jason worked in construction until 2009 and when I met him in 2010, had been unemployed for more than a year. They have survived on Dominica's income as a nursing assistant but are falling behind in bills, having already sold their older, used Toyota truck and cut back on everything but critical expenses: food, clothing, housing, utilities. They have a five-year-old daughter and fortunately a very supportive network of family across San Diego County. There are limits to what families can do, however. With two aging parents and busy siblings with their own families and economic challenges, I asked Dominica about their fallback safety net if they run out of options to pay bills and their family can no longer help out (already they have borrowed five hundred dollars from Dominica's parents, and Jason's father purchased some of his tools to provide some cash as well). They have not exhausted their options, such as selling more personal belongings, or putting off bills, but Dominica's $29,000 salary does not go far enough for them to stay financially secure. Already they have gone through what little savings they had, along with their daughter's nascent college fund ($850), and Jason has been looking for work, even odd jobs like lawn mowing, but they admitted they were very worried about the future. Dominica described their situation as we talked in their living room.

DAVID: What happens if your husband can't find a job?
DOMINICA: We have family and friends, but you know duct tape only goes so far . . .
DAVID: Duct tape?
DOMINICA: Duct tape. It can fix a lot of things when nothing else will, but it doesn't fix everything.

DAVID: So if your family can't fix it . . . then what?

DOMINICA: Pray to the Lord.

JASON: [Overhearing and shouting from the kitchen] Amen!

DAVID: Amen.

DOMINICA: Amen.

My emphasis here is that these practices are a product of people being unable to afford many of the licit services and goods available, and also in the absence of any state support. Inevitably, the costs of DIY health care or plumbing do rise, sometimes catastrophically—injuries or pneumonia that go untreated get worse and require hospitalization—causing an even greater financial crisis. Improper home or car repairs done by a friend or family member may fail, causing even more damage and higher costs in the long run. Again, the issue of struggle against both structural inequities as well as being at great risk for substantive harm and financial crisis is an ever-present force in people's lives. A broader but critical point I make here is that when faced with fewer resources, due to low income, low social support, or the erosion of state benefits, people must engage in riskier and riskier behavior, precisely the opposite of what families and individuals living at the economic margin of viability can afford to do. There are also costs and casualties of being reliant on others that do not show up in data sets or surveys. These costs can be far more personal and costly, and result in long-term consequences.

SLEEPING WITH THE ENEMY:
NOT ALL SAFETY NETS ARE SAFE

I met Claudia as she was taking her son to school. He had just started fourth grade, but her car was being fixed and they were late for the bus, so she was walking him to school. For Claudia, her situation began deteriorating with car trouble. Two years earlier her son's father, Gordon, was stopped for a traffic ticket and found to be driving without a license and uninsured, and when authorities discovered that he was undocumented, he was deported to Mexico. He had been in sporadic contact with Claudia but unable to return to the United States, and Claudia eventually lost all contact with him. Two years after she last spoke to her son's father, she had moved on and moved in with a new boyfriend. He turned out to have an alcohol problem and would occasionally become abusive. He did have a good job, however, and kept her car repaired, paid rent, and generally was a "good provider." Without family nearby (her family is in the Inland Empire and Mexicali, Mexico), she decided to take up an offer with friends and move in temporarily to get away from her abusive boyfriend. This, unfortunately, was two years after she had first moved in with her abusive boyfriend, with physical and emotional abuse as a cost.

Claudia's situation is unfortunately far too common. It reflects the deepest gendering of poverty: a situation in which a lack of economic opportunities in the labor market, a lack of resources, a lack of family supports, and limited safety nets encourage or coerce women into maintaining ties with a man who may provide some economic stability, and for whom there is hope he may be a sound father figure or partner, but at a high price, and with the risk of being exposed to violence or worse. She eventually saw her relationship as one where she was prostituting herself to an abusive boyfriend in exchange for some economic stability and what she hoped would eventually be some better opportunities for her son. Free rent, car repairs, and household expenses, as well as gifts, were positives in her and her son's lives, but they did not compensate for the costs. When Claudia began to fear for her safety she finally left.

The cost of staying with her boyfriend for two years was high. She was left emotionally and physically scarred, and she often had irregular work schedules because she did not dare leave her son alone with him. She was constantly taking time off from her retail job to take care of her son or drive him to a babysitter. Ultimately, Claudia moved to El Centro to stay with her family, in part out of concern for her own safety. Her story highlights how in the absence of nearby socially supportive safety nets, and without other resources to draw on (she earned too much for public assistance but had difficulty balancing work and parenting on such a low income), people may be encouraged to rely on others who are not the most helpful in the end. Claudia in part took advantage of an economically supportive boyfriend, but one who extracted a high personal toll and eventually forced her to leave San Diego altogether.

I hesitate to argue that Claudia's reticence to leave her boyfriend was a "strategy" or some form of self-help safety net, but the more time I spent with a social worker who counsels battered women in San Diego, the more it became clear that relationships are often held together despite severe consequences, simply for economic reasons and holding out the hope that things may "turn around." The difference in the case of interpersonal violence is that this is not a strategy typically maintained by women, but rather, one perpetuated by men; one that in turn may continue to perpetuate cycles of violence, poverty, and economic insecurity among targeted women. Indeed, battered women, abused children, and economic dependency are all too common, and have been exacerbated by the processes of welfare reform (Brandwein 1999). As numerous studies of post–welfare reform have demonstrated (Brandwein 1999; Tolman and Rosen 2001), abuse toward women, in a range of forms—sexual, emotional, and physical—causes women to maintain their own economic and social marginalization from both their own families and even public assistance, sometimes isolating them and in turn fostering even greater dependency on the abusive partner or husband.

I end with Claudia's story to illustrate that while DIY safety nets may be useful, vital in fact for many facing economic crisis, not every safety net is safe; not every social network or relationship is healthy. For Claudia and many other women, the price of reduced social safety nets and a lack of a strong personal social network or kinship network can be dependency on too few people, and in her case unfortunately, this became a very violent and ultimately damaging relationship.

CONCLUSION

The DIY safety nets discussed here are likely not striking to most Americans. The critical point here is not simply that these are critical resources that can mean the difference between becoming completely financially ruined or surviving a crisis and moving back to the middle class, as we saw with Marissa and Joe at the beginning of this chapter. Rather, the presence of such widespread DIY safety nets further illustrates the differential costs that lower-income families and individuals must take on; these are costs that in many ways are not new, but have shifted or increased as public programs have been cut, modified, or eliminated altogether.

Moreover, the shift in burdens for critical socially reproductive functions such as caregiving, or basic needs such as housing, further illustrates the massive and often dysfunctional separation of the market-driven and neoliberal approach to policy reform over the past two decades, and the everyday realities for low-income people. Welfare reform was designed with a vision of work and workers that put aside historical understandings of a need for socially supportive resources to foster work and family balance. In contrast, welfare reform imagined a labor market wherein workers were "free" to pursue their best interest and "was on his or her own in doing so" (Collins and Mayer 2010, 9). As Collins and Mayer put it, this specific ideology imagined people "unencumbered by family responsibilities or disabilities" (9). This terribly skewed vision has fostered the further entrenchment of a series of barriers for low-income people to attempt to overcome.

Again, we see here that the development and reliance on DIY safety nets is not a product of randomness, but a specific response to economic and social policies undertaken over decades that have reshaped the inner city in San Diego. The erosion of good jobs and the publicly driven expansion of low-wage jobs, combined with financial services deregulation that enabled fringe banking growth, all contributed to the shifting of critical economic and socially reproductive functions from states and employers to lower-income communities.

These are not just issues for those in poverty, however, but for the working poor more broadly. Furthermore, these challenges are rarely ever occurring at different times for families or individuals, but instead often occur simultaneously, and over long periods of time. These types of challenges and the inability to overcome them contribute to further cumulative disadvantage. Marshaling resources for these efforts, particularly caregiving, requires giving up something else. These opportunity costs may be steep: a raise, a promotion, a better apartment, better health, saving for education or a down payment on a car. These challenges further contribute to the overall structural barriers to economic security and mobility that have been laid out in the labor market and in the workplace.

Asset Poverty and the
High Cost of Fringe Banking

T HERE IS A GREAT IRONY about San Diego's urban revitalization. Despite a plethora of large banking establishments in the downtown area and a good concentration of retail banks, poorer adjacent neighborhoods in central San Diego have a dearth of retail banking. Financial services are available, but they are what are sometimes called "fringe banking." These businesses typically have higher costs than conventional retail banks, but are often the only means that the urban poor and working poor can access financial services. If there are serious opportunity costs or direct cost borne by low-income households for not having adequate socially supportive services or income, as discussed in chapter 6, here we add to the structures of cumulative disadvantage. Since obtaining critically important assets like transportation or accumulating assets for savings and investment for things like education and training are critical for the urban poor, then having a well-functioning financial services system to aid in this is crucial. Unfortunately, this is not the case.

A TALE OF TWO HOUSEHOLD BUDGETS

Clarence is a very successful African American man. I met him after a church service just east of downtown San Diego; he no longer lives in the neighborhood, but he still tries to attend Sunday services when he can. He studied accounting, eventually in his midcareer earning an MBA with a focus in accounting, and developed a strong professional track record in the banking industry. By the time he was in his mid-forties he was already an established banking executive managing large corporate financial transactions. In the 1990s, during a recessionary period in

California, he was able to purchase a small apartment building and put enough equity in his home to refinance it and pay it off in only a few years. Today, he earns enough from his rental property and salary and investment income to pay cash for his "not new, but pre-owned and gorgeous" Mercedes Benz, as he described it. By most accounts he is the epitome of African American success, having worked hard and not only moved up into a comfortable middle class, but surpassing that and becoming fairly wealthy by most standards. As a result, his household budget, with a wife and two children, is rarely under stress. He pays nothing for housing, as his home is paid for; he does not make a car payment, because his cars are all paid for in cash. "One of the most powerful forces in the world," he explained to me, "is the power of compound interest. And you want to be paid that interest, not be paying it out." In other words, Clarence can afford to pay cash for what most Americans have to finance. As a result, he uses his income primarily for day-to-day expenses and investing. He hopes to purchase more real estate, he invested in properties outside of California, and he has a large investment portfolio in financial assets, earning him capital gains and dividends every year. In sum, he is a member of the investor class and doing very well. The central points of this chapter are brought to light if we compare Clarence's household budget and economic status with that of Washeed, an African American man, also married with two children, who works as a pest control technician for a nationwide company. He gets health insurance from his employer, and earns $31,000 a year. His wife works as a dietary counselor, earning $22,000 a year. Each month their net pay is about $3,000. Out of this income their expenditures fall into the categories outlined in Table 20.

Estimated annual interest charges are about $300 per year in addition to the costs above. It is clear that the $3,000 each month does not leave much room for splurges or unanticipated expenses given that basic expenditures generally run over $2,900. The economic differences for Clarence and Washeed are far greater than income alone. One can save and accumulate assets, the other has a hard time saving and finds it impossible to invest in any assets. Clarence does not have to borrow to purchase goods or services, while Washeed relies on credit. One family has a great deal of economic security and has more than an adequate cash reserve in the event of an economic crisis; the other family faces

TABLE 20. Sample Monthly Budget for a Household with $53,000/year
Income, Central San Diego

Rent (three bedroom apt)	$1,250
Car payments (two cars)	$275
Credit card payments	$100
Furniture financing	$99
College savings	$50
Food/household supplies/laundry	$600
Phones	$150
Utilities/cable/Internet	$175
Car insurance	$45
Gas (automobile)	$160
Total	$2,904

SOURCE: Author interview.

chronic economic insecurity, with only college savings (limited to several hundred dollars a year) as an emergency fund.

Washeed, like many in central San Diego, is on the economic margins, where credit costs more, where consumer goods and penalties can cost more, and where policies and economic practices structured throughout the economy accumulate into a significant economic disadvantage. This is not a new phenomenon, as numerous studies have shown the costs of being poor are greater than those of being affluent. These costs show up in differential access to affordable consumer goods, housing, transportation, and so forth. That the poor have less-favorable financing terms and experience more fraud in consumer transactions still rings true with more recent research (Barnes 2005). These costs rise significantly when looking at the lost assets that could be accumulated with better access to banking and credit systems.

THE WEALTH GAP: CHALLENGES TO ASSET BUILDING

Living with economic precariousness and lack of economic stability make saving and planning, as well as investing in things like education, far more difficult. As a result, one of the further costs the poor face is greater difficulty in investing in critically important things like housing and education, both of which boost long-term wealth and promote economic mobility. In particular, there are three areas where asset accumulation is challenged among the urban poor: saving, home ownership, and invest-ing in education or human capital. In this section I look at each of these challenges for the poor and working poor in central San Diego, and end with a discussion of how difficulties with asset accumulation present a further barrier for economic mobility.

The issue of asset accumulation shows great promise for improving the economic mobility of lower-income and poor households (Schreiner and Sherraden 2007). Assets can convey a range of social and economic benefits, from providing a means to save for financial emergencies, to leveraging big purchases such as cars and property. These benefits are also social and psychological, as most working poor in central San Diego express a strong desire to have an economic cushion—savings or some form of fungible assets that can absorb the unplanned economic crises that beset them. This is particularly vital given the increased risk that the working poor are exposed to. In order to accumulate assets, however, households need three things: enough income beyond expenses to store the assets, a mechanism of storage (savings, pension plan, etc.), and the ability to defer short-term consumption for longer-term savings.

The potential benefits of asset accumulation are significant. Assets can have a range of economic benefits, especially in the longer term with intangible ones like home ownership. First, assets can increase income, primarily through interest and dividend payments, as well as capital gains when investments are sold. Second, assets can decrease costs by reduc-ing the need to pay for certain goods or services—having a reliable car that is owned outright can be far less expensive than a car being paid for in installments that is less than reliable. Owning a home instead of rent-ing, in the long term, in most circumstances, can yield significant savings as well, as it promotes increased equity and further asset accumulation. Third, accumulating assets can increase income through providing better employment opportunities. This may be the case where spatial barriers due to limited transportation prevent workers from getting a better-paying job, or perhaps just to work more hours (Raphael and Rice 2002), or in other cases it may allow people to move into their own business or invest in a business that they currently run. Using assets to invest in human capital (like education) or specific services (such as convenience stores that offer notary services) can boost income. There is also good evidence that just having assets can improve labor market performance and working hours, ostensibly because people are incentivized to earn more because they can save more (Bynner and Despotidou 2001). Of course, investing assets in these potential future gains requires removing liquid or relatively liquid assets from current holdings. This involves risk: what if the investment does not pay off, or during the period of investing, there is a financial emergency and what little economic cushion the household had is now tied up in either equipment, a vehicle, or education? The problem with asset accumulation, of course, is that the poor tend to be far less likely to attain and keep assets throughout their lives.

With rising debt levels, particularly among lower- and middle-income consumers as a portion of their overall income, the issue of saving and accumulating assets has become even more problematic. More than one in five Americans (22 percent) is asset poor (Bynner and Despotidou 2001). A widely used definition of an asset-poor individual is one who lacks sufficient net worth to subsist at the federal poverty level for three months if her income were cut off (Brooks and Wiedrich 2013). While 22 percent of Americans fit into this category, there is also a serious issue of asset disparities. Roughly one in six Americans owes more than they own: 15.5 percent of Americans have zero or *negative* net worth, and these percentages only get higher among subsets of the population such as women (38 percent are asset poor; 18.8 percent have zero or negative net worth) and minorities (43 percent of blacks, 39 percent of Latinos, and 35 percent of Native Americans are asset poor; and overall, 44 percent of these three groups have zero or negative net worth) (CFED 2008). Furthermore, for every one dollar of net worth held by white households, households headed by minorities have just 13 cents (CFED 2008). This type of disparity in assets and wealth has significant consequences as people move through their lives.

Similarly, households in central San Diego are highly asset poor. When asked how many could come up with a thousand dollars from savings or some other source in an emergency, only 12 percent said they had access to such resources, and half of those respondents said they would have to borrow some of the funds from family, but could get the money. This illustrates how little in assets the working poor have. This is not to say that all the working poor are asset poor and do not save. One couple living in Logan Heights has saved five thousand dollars, part of a college fund and rainy-day fund. But even in this case, the financial buffer is too low given the potential economic crises that can occur in a family of four. Why are households so asset poor? For residents of central San Diego the greatest hurdle in terms of asset accumulation is income. Too many residents live paycheck to paycheck.

For those that do manage to save some, particularly for recent immigrants, they may be supporting families or extended kin in Latin America or elsewhere, which means there is little savings left over for investing in things like savings, education, or a fund for a home purchase. This is why most of the proposals for asset accumulation, like the reasonably successful Individual Development Accounts (Schreiner and Sherraden 2007), do not work well in very poor communities. Even with pretax withdrawals available, or preplanned payroll deduction programs, participation in such savings plans runs up against the chronic economic insecurity that people live with. Very poor residents and those who cannot earn enough to save need liquid assets precisely because they never know when an emergency might occur (again, this is one of the issues with fringe banking; having access to cash instantly versus tying it up in a bank is a cost for those with a chronic inability to plan ahead because one lives on a financial razor's edge). This is in part why proposals relying on behavioral economics to make saving "easier" (Mullainathan and Shafir 2009) still ring hollow. Take someone who earns poverty level wages and usually keeps only twenty to thirty dollars in cash after cashing a paycheck and paying bills. That small amount is the emergency reserve; it may seem like just pocket change, but that is what is on hand in the event of an emergency. A related issue is simply banking system access.

THE UNBANKED

Nearly half (38 percent) of central San Diego households are unbanked (Central San Diego Survey 2002–10). This estimate is higher than the national average (28 percent) (FDIC 2012). Moreover, 55 percent do not have a savings account, nearly double the national average of 29 percent (FDIC 2012). Understanding why people do not save and instead rely on fringe banking is critical for understanding the penalty faced for being low income in the financial services market. If we look at the difference between reliance on fringe banking versus retail banking, the costs versus potential savings ratio is great. Fringe banking costs are very large relative to people's income in central San Diego. Thus, promoting savings and eliminating the reliance on fringe banking represent great opportunities that can be greatly beneficial to low-income families and individuals. Overall, what the high portion of unbanked in central San Diego shows is that just as many low-income households are effectively excluded from mainstream financial services; they are also excluded from society's mechanisms to encourage saving. There is in fact a very real inequality in financial services and supports. Two-thirds of the tax benefits for pensions go to the top 20 percent of American income earners while the bottom 60 percent receives only 12 percent of the tax benefit (FDIC 2012). Most low-income workers do not have jobs with savings plans.

Accumulating savings is also clearly an important step in asset development, and access to regular financial services can be critical in this regard. We know that low-income families are far less likely to hold savings or assets. These families often find it difficult to save and plan financially. Living paycheck to paycheck can make it difficult to plan, or accumulate enough to save. Also, living on the edge of financial viability means that families and individuals are constantly exposed to the risk that a financial emergency will push them over the edge of economic security. There is good evidence that lower-income families and individuals, particularly if incentivized with the right program, can save. Studies of IDA (Individual Development Account) programs, for instance, have proven effective in establishing some level of savings. One drawback, however, is that most of these projects demonstrate success for the near poor, or those at twice the FPL or more. For those who are very poor—at poverty or less—savings is still a massive challenge (Schreiner and Sherraden 2007).

Why do people avoid conventional retail banks, and what are the costs of being unbanked? Table 21 shows the reasons for not using banks in central San Diego. These include a lack of cash assets or income, being unemployed, perceptions that they are not needed, and so forth. The first column (very poor to working poor) refers to residents at or below the poverty line; the second column refers to those up to three times the Federal Poverty Line (the "near poor"). The reasons are varied and complex. Often they overlap. Some people view banks as nothing more than a rip-off: "Charging you fees to hold your money. I can hold my own money for free, thank you very much," as one man described his

TABLE 21. Reasons for Not Using Formal-Sector Retail Banks for Central San Diego Residents, by Percentage of Federal Poverty Level

Reasons for Not Banking	Very Poor–Working Poor (up to 200% FPL)	Near Poor (300% FPL)
Don't have enough money	24%	17%
Unemployed	11%	9%
Don't need one	10%	9%
Inconvenient	10%	9%
Citizenship issues	10%	8%
Fees are too high	5%	7%
Bad credit	4%	8%
Owe the bank money	4%	7%
Don't trust banks	3%	5%
No branches nearby	3%	4%
Other	16%	16%

SOURCE: Central San Diego Survey 2002–10.

attitude toward banks. In some cases there are real policy issues or financial literacy problems that can be addressed; for example, people without proof of residency or documentation of citizenship or work visas may not be able to get a bank account, or they may fear violating the law or being reported to immigration, and so they do not use banks.

Behavioral economists and community advocates have long questioned the seemingly puzzling fact that many urban poor prefer to rely on check cashing and other businesses for obtaining money or cashing paychecks, rather than opening up a bank account, particularly a savings account, to save money and build assets. As we have seen already, the economically poor are not always financially illiterate. While it is true that financial literacy and educational programs can have a positive impact, the reasons for eschewing the banking sector in poor communities are far more complex. Central San Diego is a case in point.

First, there is a dearth of financial institutions. In the downtown core, zip code 92101, home to many commercial banking offices, there are dozens of banks and ATMs. These serve the downtown businesses, consumers, visitors, and residents. Outside of the urban core, however, in 92113 and 92101, there are only a handful of banks—four in total to service a population of a hundred thousand. Nationally, there are typically twenty banks per hundred thousand (Avery et al. 1997). Part of the answer to the question is simply that there are very few banks conveniently located within the community. There are about ten ATMs, some from major banks, many of which are often out of order, and the reality is, as one retail banker suggested, "That's not a community which is going to be profitable, the average deposit account will have eighty dollars in it perhaps, and most of the income will be generated with fees. People don't like the fees and don't seem to trust banks, so opening up a branch there just isn't good business." His assertion reflects community sentiment. People tend to avoid retail banking for a number of reasons beyond simply the lack of them nearby. The major factor from the residents' point of view is that they do not see the benefit of retail banks, at least as they conventionally practice. The concerns are multiple: high fees, inability to see tellers (unless you pay a fee), tellers who may not speak Spanish, fees for minimum balances, fees for transfers, fees for use of an ATM . . . as one man described, "Why would I get an account? I cash a $250 check, they take $15 for an account every month because I don't keep enough in there, they take $40 if you overdraw the account, they take two or three dollars if you don't use their ATM, . . . come on, I'll just keep my cash in my wallet or locked up and pay myself [save the fees]."

Another reason for shunning the banking sector is the need for liquidity. As we saw in chapter 6, lower-income households rely on highly liquid, flexible assets. Bills need to be paid by creatively shifting around money and funds. This cannot be done if a bank is holding the money, does not have a branch or an ATM nearby, and charges fees just to obtain the money. Having cash on hand avoids all these problems.

Another reason for the need for liquidity is that many families are supporting others through remittances. An estimated 25 percent of people earning income in central San Diego wire money abroad. This is often done all in one stop at a check cashing business, or even some corner stores that have both check cashing and wire transfer services available. Thus, many consumers make a trip to the convenience store and check cashing store a payday activity. A recent immigrant from Ecuador stated, "I get paid, then go right to cash the check; some gets sent to family back home, then I get some groceries, and whatever is left goes in my pocket."

As other scholars have found, there is also the issue of trust (Newman and Chen 2007). Many people in low-income communities have a great distrust of banks. People are not only concerned that some of their money may disappear but have experiences losing money in banks. For instance, two families I spoke to about bank accounts declared that they would never use a bank again because they were "crooks." One family lost several hundred dollars in a bank transfer to purchase a car. They were moving funds from one bank to another, and the funds never arrived at the bank that was being used to make the down payment on the car. The receipt for the transfer was lost on the drive to the dealership, and the couple who were going to purchase the car never were able to prove that they transferred the money and lost it. They had to put off purchasing the car. Another family told a similar story of how they would transfer money between accounts from checking to savings at an ATM, but that sometimes it would work, sometimes it didn't, regardless of getting a receipt or not. In one instance, the money was transferred from a savings account to a checking account to pay for the rent that month. The transfer did not go through for some reason and the check bounced, with a $35 returned check fee being charged. Selena, the woman who held the accounts, showed the bank the receipt and the transfer date, and after six months, the bank agreed to refund her returned check fee. "I was so angry," she explained, "that I closed my accounts and I don't deal with banks anymore. They just want to take your money. That's how they make money. Fees and telling you you made a mistake. I didn't have a mistake, I had my receipt; they were trying to cheat me."

Clearly, there can be a great deal of frustration with using a bank. "It's your money; shouldn't you actually be able to get it?" That is the refrain I hear many times talking to people in central San Diego about retail banking. ATMs don't work. ATMs may not be safe and are in low-lit areas, and people do not trust the machines will give them accurate information. Banks that are open strange hours, or are not open when you need them to be open. As Schneider and Tufano (2007) point out, low credit scores, even for someone who has never had any delinquent payments or does not owe any debt—they may just not have a credit record yet—means they can be denied a savings account. In other words, banks are not necessarily working hard to find ways to bring poorer customers into the financial services industry. Indeed, even more barriers are being erected to prevent lower-income people from being bank customers.

Not banking, of course, has costs. The use of street finance, which I refer to as alternative banking and credit services, is widespread in central San Diego. The costs of being outside the mainstream of financial services, as numerous scholars have pointed out (Blank and Barr 2009; Caskey 1994), can be very high.

THE COSTS OF STREET FINANCE

Street finance is the product of two important trends. First, the rise of check cashing outlets, pawnshops, payday lenders, and other fringe banking operations developed in response to the growing inequalities emerging in urban economies. Stagnant and declining wages for lower-skilled workers and lower-income communities while at the same time growing shifts in wealth upward toward the wealthy and investor class saw retail banks take flight from the inner city to the more affluent financial services markets. Additionally, retail banks sought increasing fees from customers beginning in the 1970s, and a consolidation of banks and subsequent branch closings through cost-cutting measures in the 1970s and 1980s resulted in far less access to deposit accounts on the part of the urban poor.

This type of street finance is costly, with the average annual costs of relying on fringe banking outlets being several hundred to more than a thousand dollars a year. In Table 22 the estimates from average annual per capita costs for nonretail banking services by zip codes are listed. As Table 22 indicates, total average costs for fringe banking dependency average $462 per year. This is a significant cost for very poor to near poor households. In general, there is a tremendous penalty simply for being outside of the formal banking system.

Pawnshops, Payday Loans, and Other Forms of Street Finance

It has become popular to decry many economic problems of the urban poor as the result of a lack of financial literacy. The reality, however, is that the poor, working poor included, know a lot about money. They know how much things cost. They know how many hours they have to work to purchase things. They know how much their utility bills are. They know

TABLE 22. Average Costs of Using Street Finance, Central San Diego, by Zip Code

Type of Fee	92102	92101	92113	Total (weighted average)
Car title loans	$175	$0	$300	$290
Check cashing	$112	$12	$310	$265
Refund advance loans	$85	$88	$152	$90
Payday loans	$112	$31	$36	$75
Pawnshop loans	$38	$0	$11	$12
Total average costs				$462

SOURCE: Survey of Central San Diego.

how much car repairs cost. They have a great deal of financial literacy, just not the type that financial planners and advisors to low-income communities teach in financial literacy courses. I call it street finance: simply put, the ways that lower-income people manage money given severe income constraints, often outside of conventional household economics. I distinguish this from fringe banking (Caskey 1994), in that street finance encapsulates an entire range of financial strategies and practices, whereas fringe banking refers to the economic institutions operating in poorer communities that are typically not part of the mainstream banking or financial markets.

The types of street financing vary, but include several businesses that have grown enormously over the past twenty years in poorer urban areas. Pawnshops, check cashing stores, and other businesses offer a variety of products to the under- or unbanked. These include payday loans, car title loans, tax refund loans, and pawnshop loans. These are all means of generating income either on a regular basis or as a last resort before more significant economic hardship occurs. The incidence of this type of income generation is widespread. In central San Diego, pawnshop loans are reportedly used by 18 percent of residents, car title loans by 8 percent, tax refund loans by 26 percent, and payday loans by 21 percent of residents.

Street finance has emerged out of the very real need to manage swings in income; unplanned expenses can be very challenging if you barely have enough at the end of the month to cover the rent. What happens if you are short, get laid off, have an unpaid medical bill due to an accident, or have an unexpected increase in insurance premiums, rent, or utilities? The increasingly common response is to rely on what assets one has and engage the fringe banking industry of check cashing stores, pawnshops, and payday loan operations. As the following conversation with a long-time resident of central San Diego illustrates:

> QUESTION: "Why are there so many pawnshops in poor neighborhoods?"
> ANSWER: "Are you for real? That's our bank. When you need cash, you cash in your stuff."
> QUESTION: "What if you don't have any stuff?"
> ANSWER: "[laughing] Everybody's got stuff... even poor folk got stuff. My buddy works at a pawnshop, he's got a room full of DVD players, and nobody wants them. You get one for sixty bucks now, even less, how much is it really worth? You can barely give them away."

There are very important consequences for remaining chronically in a low-income or economically unstable condition. How people respond to such conditions vary, as do the results. One of the main ways to address income insecurity, particularly during periods of crisis (say an unexpected bill or expense), is to resort to alternative income-generating activities. This can include selling items, borrowing from family or friends, even coworkers, taking out payday loans, working on the side, or even taking in a roommate. All of these practices are typical responses to income insecurity. It is precisely why we see so many pawn and payday loan stores in poorer communities. During the time of this study (between 2000 and 2012) there were zero pawnshops in the wealthy area of La Jolla, while in the study area there were eleven, including the flourishing Monte de Piedad, a Spanish-language chain that not only provides payday loans but wire transfers and a pawnshop. This fringe banking sector did not emerge overnight, but is a result of both historical and market forces.

Abandoned by conventional retail banks, poor communities have often welcomed pawnshops as they provide an immediate injection of cash in emergencies. They are seen as potentially exploitive by many, because they pay so far below the resale value of the items, but they also perform a vital service; they move goods from low-income residents in central San Diego to other consumers, providing low-income residents with an immediate supply of money.

Of course, the reasons people sell to pawnshops varies. Sometimes it is to pay an immediate or overdue bill, sometimes it is to get rid of goods no longer needed, and in some cases it is to raise money via a pawnshop loan until the loan can be repaid. The key element here is velocity. If an individual or a family has exhausted their options and is short the rent, mortgage, or car payment by the end of the month, selling items can immediately cover the cost. For instance, a family of three with two working adults, people I have known for many years, faced a minor economic crisis when Marcus, the husband, lost his job and was falling behind on car payments. The dealer sent a notice that if they did not get a payment by the end of the month, they would repossess the vehicle. Fees and additional costs for getting the car would be too onerous, plus Marcus needed the car to look for work. In order to keep the car he took a variety of items from their apartment, including a bike, a game console, a "bucket" full of games for the game console, and a number of other items. The son was upset about losing the PlayStation, but the parents promised to get another once Marcus got back to work. All total, they earned about $200 for what they pawned, enough to make two $120 car payments and stop the risk of possession. They were still behind, but it gave Marcus, a delivery driver with a class 2 license, two more months to find a job. Fortunately, he did find work and was able to get back on track financially, but the family had to rely on the pawn company and part with a lot of household items, including some family jewelry, to keep the car. In this case, the pawnshop was their last resort, as there was simply no way they could shift money from another expense as they were already behind on some other bills and there were no family or friends they felt comfortable borrowing from, even for thirty dollars.

In some cases, pawning items is a way for low-income or economically displaced residents to raise capital or shift careers. This occurs for a variety of reasons: the small amount of money involved and problems with commercial banks make those less appealing avenues, sometimes someone is switching careers and can sell off no longer needed tools or equipment, or sometimes someone is moving and does not want to have a yard sale. When the construction industry collapsed in the wake of the housing bubble burst, pawnshops in central San Diego were inundated with construction equipment. Many construction jobs, particularly among small firms, demand that workers provide their own tools. When the jobs dried up, particularly for small firms, many of these workers decided to pawn their tools. Circular saws, reciprocating saws, sanders, nail guns, even air compressors were being brought to pawnshops. The supply overwhelmed demand and some people were getting turned away with tools no matter how low they were willing to sell them.

Aaron, a twenty-four-year-old Latino who has lived in central San Diego for his whole life, worked his way into construction with his father, first as a laborer, then as a carpenter. He was fortunate to learn on the job with family and then later had enough of his own tools and the skills to work in the industry, partly "freelance," as he calls it. He worked primarily for small companies or for friends and family, and he moved from job to job largely through personal referrals. He describes the boom years of 2000–2007 as "the best work in my life; there were too many offers, I had to turn jobs down." Then in 2009 he was unable to get enough work to pay bills. By 2010 he was broke and out of work, and he gave up looking for construction jobs and moved with his girlfriend to Los Angeles. Before moving he took all his tools that he couldn't sell to a pawnshop and got what he describes as "pennies on the dollar, but I had to get rid of them and move on." All told, what he got for his tools did cover his one-way U-Haul rental to Los Angeles. For Aaron, his reliance on the pawn industry was a product of economic collapse in his field and his need to simply offload tools and move to another city. It was both a matter of convenience and a means to raise some money to help with the move given that he did not have any unemployment compensation—as a sole proprietor, he did not always work "on the books," and he did not work long enough with those firms that did hire him as a subcontractor to qualify for unemployment. Even when he did, the contractor did not pay properly, but paid him just cash, making it impossible to qualify for unemployment insurance.

When I asked about taking legal action or reporting the employer he said it wasn't possible. "Take on a contractor? Spend four, five, six thousand dollars on a lawyer and ultimately get nothing or very little, just unemployment benefits? Not worth it, man. Plus, once I did that I'd never get work, blackballed, nobody would hire me." The critical point here is that many of those who work informally, or who aren't paid properly, particularly in industries like construction, do not have the safety net of unemployment or later social security to fall back on. They have been economically marginalized in the formal labor market, and that encourages even more reliance on usurious and predatory lending practices in the fringe banking sector. As Aaron put it bluntly, "A lot of people made a lot of money off me."

Car Title Loans

Another resource the urban poor rely on is car title loans, often called "pink slip" loans. A title loan offers cash from the lender; in return, the borrower signs over the title of a vehicle. Usually, these loans are due in thirty days. The loans do not require a credit check and only limited income verification. This makes the loans very appealing, but the loan has a high cost. Some lenders charge annual rates of as much as 180 percent. While the loan is being paid off, the borrower drives the vehicle, but if there is a default or missed payment, the vehicle can be repossessed. In California, title lenders operate in a largely unregulated environment that places no cap on interest rates for any loan over $2,500. As a result, few title lenders offer loans for less than that amount, making these very large and potentially very costly loans to pay back.

Reliance on a car title loan is often a result of someone being asset poor: the only real asset a person can draw on for external finance is their car. With low home-ownership rates in central San Diego, this is an especially challenging issue. Unlike many parts of the United States where people had housing they are able to draw on for home equity lines of credit, few working poor in central San Diego have been able to do this. Vehicles, however, are almost always the largest asset the working poor have. It is critical for getting to work, but it is also something that can always be sold or drawn upon with a car title loan. The challenge with these so-called pink slip loans is that they can, like other forms of fringe or street finance, become very expensive and over the long term, cost far more than just interest charges.

Natalie, a secretary at an insurance agency, took out a car title loan as an emergency after her husband abandoned her and her six-year-old son and left her with $3,000 in back bills and credit card debt that she had been unaware of. Desperate and without many family members she could turn to, she took out a car title loan for $2,500 to cover expenses until she could find a way to move to a cheaper apartment or in with a friend. After she moved to a cheaper apartment, sold some of her furniture, and negotiated with the credit card company for a repayment plan (while she researched legal options against her ex-husband), she began making the payments on the loan. One month she was told that she had missed a payment and was charged a late fee and penalties. She claimed she made the payment, but the loan company said they never received it. She then made a double payment, but the company only credited her for one. She had to then go in person with the canceled check to prove that she made a double payment. The loan company then agreed to credit her but charged her a fee for having to make the credit. When expenses became too difficult to manage and she was late with an additional payment, the loan company doubled her interest rate and charged her an additional fee as a late charge, moving her new interest rate to 125 percent APR. At the rate she was going, she would have to pay nearly $6,000 for an original loan of $2,500, and on a car that was only worth about $10,000. She eventually decided to cut her losses and sold her car, paid off the loan, and purchased an older, less-reliable vehicle in cash. In the end, she had to sell her original car, and she lost nearly a thousand dollars in interest and fees.

Refund Advance Loans (RALs or Tax Refund Loans)

Refund advance loans or RALs are a growing business in poor communities, for those receiving an Earned Income Tax Credit (EITC) in particular. These loans are essentially drawn against the future amount of a tax return. National research has shown that the average $200 preparation fee paid by low-income tax filers only enables claimants to receive their tax refunds about one to two weeks earlier than if they did not use the service, and tax preparers and lenders take more than $1.5 billion in fees annually from earned income tax credits loans (Theodos 2010).

Every winter and into the spring, ads blanket local television and newsprint for people who need cash fast with offers for an "instant" cash tax refund. The idea sounds simple and is very hard to resist. If you are short of money and expect a refund from the IRS after you file your taxes, then why not pay someone a small fee to handle the filing and give you the refund up front so you do not have to wait for the check from the IRS? This is particularly alluring for those lower-income households that do not have bank accounts, and so would have to wait even longer for an IRS tax refund instead of getting it done via direct deposit; who need the money sooner to insert into the ever-shifting budget of fluid cash flows; who are willing to part with a small fee to have the convenience of having the taxes taken care of and your refund provided up front; and lastly, for those qualifying for the EITC, which is a significant portion of the urban poor, the instant tax refund is often seen as an ideal instant injection of needed funds.

As David Shipler points out, tax time for poor communities is not April, but January, when people receive their W-2s and can run out to tax preparers: "With cunning creativity, the preparers have devised schemes to separate low-wage workers from as much of their refunds . . . as feasible. The marvel of electronic filing, the speedy direct deposit into a bank account, the high-interest loan masquerading as a 'rapid refund' all promise a sudden flush of dollars to cash-starved families. The trouble is, getting money costs money" (2008, 15). This is certainly the case in central San Diego. Every spring tax refund businesses, ranging from large corporations like Jackson-Hewitt to smaller mom-and-pop shops, some catering specifically to recent immigrant and Latino residents, operate tax refund loan businesses. The fees charged in central San Diego range from $100 to $300, depending on location. In central San Diego 26 percent of residents take advantage of RALs. In some cases, such as in zip code 92101, the rate of EITC recipients using RALs is 45 percent. As Table 23 shows, there are also high costs to getting the RAL loan, ranging from as much as $221 on average in 92113 to $85.

Why would people pay such high fees to secure an early refund? There are several reasons, often interrelated, and part of the complex annual budgeting of low-income households. First, there is the need for cash in a lump sum to pay off debts. Some families rely on their spring RAL

TABLE 23. Earned Income Tax Credit Use and Return Authorization Loan Use, Central San Diego, by Zip Code

	92113	92102	92101
Low-income returns that receive EITC	48.4%	39.8%	18.5%
Average amount received from EITC	$2,017	$1,876	$929
Average fee paid for RAL loan	$221	$170	$85
EITC recipients using RAL loans	26%	31%	35%

SOURCE: Central San Diego Survey 2002–10.

to pay off debts accumulated over the year. Getting that lump sum payment up front is "like Christmas in March," as one resident describes it. He uses his EITC to pay off bills that are past due, to pay for Christmas presents that were put on credit back in December, and to cover expenses that emerged over the previous year, especially unanticipated ones.

The reasons people are willing to pay such high fees to get RALs vary and are typically far more complex than simply the desire to get money quickly. As the case of Andre and Marta illustrates, quick cash infusions to household budgets are far more significant than just a means to pay bills. Andre has two children and his wife, Marta, is on disability. She was injured in a car accident and is working on getting back to a job. In the interim, he also needed a brake job on their car, something he hadn't planned on, and one of his sons had an unexpected dental problem that had to be resolved. He paid for the brake job on credit, set up a payment plan with the dental office, and paid cash for a lot of other expenses between the end of the year and the RAL, which was due to arrive in February. When the RAL was processed, this allowed Andre and Marta to pay off the car repairs, the dental bills, the Christmas presents, an overdue utility and cable bill, and a personal loan to Andre's brother, and it provided enough money for a gift for Marta and Andre's godchild, who was born a year earlier. This RAL cost them around 10 percent of their refund, but it also allowed them to clear all their debt in one moment. It also left them with a bit of money to put in the bank and to splurge on pizza delivery for two nights and rent movies. "That was our living large," Andre explained.

Andre and Marta's use of their RAL indicates how broad the impact of the RAL is. They are willing to pay the upfront fee because the RAL eliminates accumulated debt, and with that erasure, a lot of stress. Chronic indebtedness carries untold burdens through stress and anguish as it stretches family budgets and makes living on the economic knife edge far more precarious. One bad stroke of luck, and debts may not be payable—pushing what most working poor dread: complete economic collapse and bankruptcy. Unlike many studies of bankruptcy that suggest that the poor are eager to run up bills and then leave them—used as justification for bankruptcy law reforms—the exact opposite is the case. Most poor fear bankruptcy and work very hard to avoid falling into it. This is why there are so many high-cost street financing mechanisms available: money is made staving off economic crises among the urban poor. Thus, for Andre and Marta, their RAL was expensive, but what it bought was more time, more economic freedom, less worry, and a sense that they were staying afloat, even if they knew deep down that their long-term economic health was not so good.

The other important function of the RAL for Andre and Marta, as for so many others, is that it allows them to fulfill and maintain important social obligations and social support networks. Andre had borrowed thirty-five dollars for gas and milk one day from his brother. His brother knew that Andre and Marta were tight for money so he did not bother them for the thirty-five dollars, but Andre realizes how important it is to pay people back; he himself has loaned money to friends or family and never seen it paid back and that has soured his relations with those people, some of them close relatives. So when Andre was short at the gas station while he and his brother were driving back to town one day, he borrowed the money from his brother and promised to pay it back. The RAL allowed him to keep his promise and maintain that relationship and social support network. Andre and Marta were also able to get a nice gift for their godchild. Again, they were short of money when she was born, but with the RAL they could not only demonstrate their good standing as godparents, but also their generosity within the family network. This expense is not just part of a family obligation but an investment. By showing they are diligent and generous, Andre and Marta are also demonstrating that they are worth helping if they ever have an urgent need. This raises a broader point discussed later—that social support and kinship networks have to be maintained, and this takes resources. When they are not maintained, those networks can erode and with that erosion so goes financial and other help that may be vital in times of need.

Payday Loans

Payday loans are another emergency stopgap measure. The growth of the payday loan business is a testament to the growing reliance of millions of people who cannot stretch their income until their next pay period. They are not living paycheck to paycheck: they are falling short; they cannot make it until their next paycheck. If there are no other sources of income, or an unexpected bill is due, then the payday loan can be a last resort. There are also short-term and installment loans in the high-risk credit market. Even during the recession, these financial institutions grew in central San Diego. Generally, low-wage workers who rely on check cashers end up spending 2 to 3 percent of their income just to get their pay. If low-income workers cannot repay payday loans on time, they may pay interest calculated at annual percentage rates as high as 470 percent.

Payday loans are a growing mechanism to keep an individual or family from falling off an economic cliff. Typically people who use this mechanism rely on a two- to three-hundred-dollar loan until their next pay period. This covers bills and living expenses until payday. It is widely popular among the very poor, those who are at the greatest financial risk; the problems with payday loans are now notorious and have spawned legislation in a number of states. The basic loan process involves a lender providing a short-term unsecured loan to be repaid at the borrower's next payday. Typically, some verification of employment or income is involved, though some firms now don't require even employment verification.

Much of the research on payday loans shows that once people realize there are such high interest rates and that the long-term costs are exorbitant, then they apply for them less often. Fortunately, in central San Diego the survey data show that only 6 percent of people are using payday loans. Even so, that translates into hundreds of thousands of customers just from within the communities in the inner city.

Why do people turn to payday loans then? As much of the scholarship has described, the full costs of the loans are usually not understood by the consumer (McCoy 2005). Additionally, people feel that this type of loan is a "one-time" situation that they will not have to resort to in the future. Another important factor is that some people do not have any other options; without friends or family or a standard commercial bank to fall back on, where else can someone legally get urgently needed money? This demand is what drives payday lending. What it tells us more broadly is that there is a large segment of the urban poor who are financially in very risky circumstances and have few safety nets other than what is typically seen as usurious lending. This is a two-sided issue: on the positive, some people have described to me how such loans helped them stave off being kicked out of an apartment for back rent due, or avoid having the power cut off, or to eat when funds were too tight, but the down side is that beyond the fees and interest being extremely high, the risk is that the borrower will fall into a deeper cycle of debt.

This "debt trap," as it is often described (Center for Responsible Lending 2009), is when someone who cannot pay for food or bills takes out a payday loan. When they get their paycheck, they pay the loan, plus a fee; if they cannot, they can roll the loan over, but with more fees and possibly even higher interest. Now that the consumer is short of money, they have to take out another payday loan to keep up with the first. This vicious cycle can be very costly. For example, if you borrow $500 and repay it in four monthly installments using a payday loan (with a $17.50 per $100 finance fee for a fifteen-day loan with seven "rollovers"), you would end up paying $700 in financing fees (an ARP of 426 percent) for a total of $1,200. What can be done if someone falls into this type of debt trap? One solution is to continue to move funds or debts around from other areas of the individual or family budget.

THE COST OF CREDIT

When funds coming into a family budget cannot cover current spending, in the absence of government transfers the only way to make ends meet is through private borrowing, and in recent years Americans have accumulated unprecedented levels of debt, most commonly by running up balances on credit cards in a desperate effort to make it from one month to the next. Contrary to popular belief, most families become mired in consumer debt not because of frivolous shopping sprees, but in response to economic shocks lying beyond their control—family emergencies that force them into a downward spiral of debt and borrowing (Sullivan 2008; Warren and Tyagiy 2003). Credit, of course, costs more if one is a higher risk borrower, and by definition, those with lower incomes have higher risk. This makes credit far more expensive for lower-income households.

Getting a credit card or a loan for any reason can be a blessing or a curse. If it is the first step to developing a credit history and using that good credit to leverage a bigger and important purchase, such as a car or home, then it means a person is on the road to asset building and potentially greater economic security. On the other hand, if the credit card or loan cannot be repaid adequately, debt accumulates, and eventually a crisis ensues, then that poor credit history can create problems for lower-income consumers in a host of areas. I have already highlighted the issues with credit and employment screening, but poor credit can also affect loan rates, credit card rates, the ability to rent an apartment, even getting utilities or a cellular phone service.

Customers with San Diego Gas and Electric, for instance, who have poor credit must pay a two-month deposit before power can be turned on at their residence, typically around $150. People with little or poor credit can only get auto loans at the 14–18 percent interest rate in some cases. Many central San Diegans with poor credit report visiting car dealers with ads stating $99 down and a verifiable job means being preapproved. For those with good credit, the rates can be as low as 3–5 percent, but up to 18.25 with poor credit. Sandra, a customer service representative for a hospital, did not maintain her Toyota Corolla well, and it was damaged and in need of a new clutch, brakes, and windshield. It was not worth putting the money into a car, but she was still working through paying off a credit card she had fallen behind on when she had some unanticipated expenses—some of which were to help out her sister who was just out of jail and needed help getting a place to stay and pay for the first month's rent. Sandra went to a car dealer advertising what she describes as a "teaser" rate of $99 down and $99 per month. "But that was only if you had perfect credit," she stated. "And if you had any little thing on your report, there goes the $99 down $99 a month deal. Now they got you in, they know you need a car, and they know you don't have great credit, so they make it sound like you are getting a good deal anyway, like they are doing you a favor. The salesman says to me that his boss won't like it, but he will push to approve me for a loan for seven years at 15 percent. That's almost what my credit card is! You know, they are always trying to get you some way or another. They pushed it on me like only $189 a month is a great deal . . . kept saying that 'you can afford that right, a car for just $189,' but I'm not stupid, I know that I'll be paying zillions in interest at that rate." Sandra's frustration borders on anger; she feels like she has been playing by the rules, working hard, and still if there are some incidents that occur out of her control, she pays the price, and it is more than what is fair. Unfortunately, this is such a common perception among the working poor—that financial services in particular but any business that sees you in a vulnerable position takes advantage of you.

THE COSTS OF TRYING TO BUILD CREDIT

Enrique is the type of Latino immigrant who reflects the American ideal of immigrant entrepreneurship: the notion that anyone can "pull themselves up by their bootstraps" and be successful if they work hard enough. He arrived from El Salvador after fleeing the Salvadoran civil war in 1981. He has struggled to get his own business going, however, and his efforts were set back when someone stole his identity and damaged his credit. He spent several months just trying to determine what his options were and researching the problem, and after two years of having credit problems due to the identity theft, he had finally begun to address the problem through a whole range of legal filings. Eventually he did get his credit restored, but in the interim he had to spend money on getting a slew of less-than-ideal loans to get his business (hauling and recycling with his truck) off the ground. He estimates that he spent three years and three thousand dollars trying to get his credit restored, money he could scarcely part with.

As Enrique's story demonstrates, the poor or those with no credit also face far higher costs simply to establish a credit rating. Despite this being a critical step to accumulating any asset, such as financing two critical life purchases—cars and homes—the poor face challenges here as well. Thus, they are limited in their ability to leverage their income to make these larger purchases. The prime example of a barrier to building credit is the steep cost of securing credit with a prepaid, unsecured credit card. These typically have higher rates and fees than any standard credit card. In Table 24 I compare two different credit offers in 2013, based on credit history and score. They show a stark difference on a number of costs and fees. The unsecured card is essentially a very high-cost, high-interest revolving credit card with a steep set of fees. Compared to the good credit offer (zero interest for a year and a half), the differences in securing credit are obviously very real. Overall, the cost for simply getting an unsecured card, for the first year, is at minimum more than $353.

With the extremely high cost of unsecured cards, who actually would use these types of financial products? Very few informants expressed an interest in or use of these types of cards. Of the few people who have used unsecured cards, they did so to build credit only for a brief amount of time so that they could then start saving money as part of a broader financial plan. These people were all middle-income residents, earning

TABLE 24. Unsecured versus Standard Credit Cards

Interest Rate and Fees	Unsecured	Standard (with Good Credit)
APR	29.99%	0% for first 15 months, then 10.99–20.99%
APR for cash advances	29.99%	23.99%
Set-up fee	$75	$0
Annual fee	$75	$0
Monthly maintenance fee	$12 (billed annually at $144)	$0
Cash advance fee	Either $5 or 5%	5%
Foreign transaction fee	3% of each transaction	$0
Late payment fee	Up to $35	Up to $35
Returned payment fee	$35	$35
Credit limit increase fee	$30 for each $100	$0
Additional card fee	$30	$0
Paper statement fee	$4.95	$0
Minimum total fees first year with paper statements	$353.40	$0

SOURCE: http://www.bankrate.com, July 2013 credit offers.

over forty thousand dollars per year, and some had just gotten a job allowing them to really take advantage of their new earning power.

Notably, no Latinos in central San Diego reported an interest or use of prepaid or unsecured credit cards. There were several reasons for this. First, the cards, as discussed previously, are extremely expensive. For low-income consumers, this is a very costly entry point to start a credit line. Additionally, most residents preferred to build their own credit through purchases they already had to finance, typically at high rates, such as for cars. One Latino couple, Selma and Christopher, have two cars: one is a Honda Civic, and the other is a near-new Toyota pickup truck that Christopher drives. He works in landscaping, has his own business, in part off the books, but partly through registered work as a subcontractor. Selma is an office worker at a large nonprofit organization serving Latinos. The Honda was the first car, purchased when Christopher was working in the restaurant business. Their previous car, bought used, broke down and was not worth fixing, but with their jobs they were able to finance the Honda, albeit at a high rate because they did not have any credit. After four years they paid off the Honda, and they had established a reasonably good credit rating, despite some occasional setbacks. Then Christopher worked his way into landscaping and eventually decided to save up money and start his own business, using in part the good credit standing from paying off their first car to finance their second one. They built credit through their already must-have purchase of automobiles and saw no need to get an unsecured card. They also do not use credit cards; they have one, but it is only an emergency source of funds that they rarely rely on. As such, Selma and Christopher are still struggling to make it into the middle class, but they have done so without having to rely on unsecured credit to make borrowing cheaper.

Who does pay for costly credit then? People who have had economic crises, fallen behind in payments or declared bankruptcy, and need to repair or rebuild their credit are the most likely users of unsecured credit cards. Like many of the fringe banking products that lower-income residents must rely on, unsecured cards that allow someone to rebuild their credit rating are often evidence of a vicious cycle of problems; the card is seen as potentially one way to break the cycle. The problems begin with something that causes people to fall behind in payments they already owe, either car loans, medical bills, unsecured debt like a credit card, or even a personal loan from a bank. The duration might be short, just a couple months of falling behind, but that may be enough to damage even a good credit rating for a significant period of time. In this case, unsecured cards are seen as a possible way to hasten the way back to credit worthiness.

MOVING THE DEBT AROUND

Another strategy used by the working poor and near poor is to constantly rotate payments. One woman described this practice as a form of financial Russian roulette. The hope is that by simply deferring payments to bills, only paying off the ones that are so far past due that there are imminent repercussions (losing phone service, eviction, etc.), people hope to buy enough time until things improve economically. In short, people keep shifting payments until something comes along, a job, a check, a loan, a car sale, and so forth. This last gasp effort can keep a family or individual afloat financially without resorting to bankruptcy or falling into collections with any single bill collector. In this way, people try to buy time until they can get back on their feet financially. This entails making the minimum payment required with a business and pushing it back as long as possible. Some companies are amenable to rescheduling bills and can set up payment plans. The risk here is that once you have pushed all the debt holders as far as possible, slipping up in payments means that they may push your account into collections, cancel service, send an eviction notice, and so forth.

A number of families and individuals who participated in this study described "musical chairs" with credit card debt. They had done well during the 1990s to build up good credit, and some now had several credit cards, but during the recession these had turned to emergency lines of credit rather than just standard revolving consumer credit. Rotating debt means getting a new credit card or using an existing credit card to shift existing credit card debt to. The new debt, often with a low or 0 percent annual percentage rate but with a service fee, is rolled onto a new credit card. Essentially, this is a 0 percent, fixed-term loan with a fee. The credit card companies are buying the debt service off one another, and the consumer is trying to keep the interest low by paying an annual fee. People rotating this type of debt from credit card to credit card can keep their 0 percent interest rate but do pay a fee, sometimes as high as 5 percent of the balance, with no maximum.

In extreme cases, people use cash advances on a credit card to pay an immediate bill, then pay back the cash advance by the due date on the card. This only works if the person does not have a credit card balance, as the cash advance, with a much higher APR and a very high fee to begin with, is paid *last* by the credit card company if the person is paying in installments. Thus, if someone has a balance they are paying off each month, then they take a cash advance, they will have to pay off the balance first, and then the cash advance at the end. Over time, the interest payments can become exorbitant, higher than payday loans. This is a strategy only available to those with adequate credit, typically those who are more likely than not to be earning more than twice the poverty level.

The use of credit often becomes integrated into other strategies. For instance, rotating bills around, that is, putting off one bill until it is about to go to collections and paying it, then saving up to pay the next bill as it approaches collections might be combined with using a credit card to pay for living expenses. That strategy then allows thirty days to pay the credit card bill. For instance, for someone being paid every other week, they may run short of cash for food and gas for the car in the second week, so they use the credit card to pay for those items and any other vital expenses, and use what money they have on hand to pay for the critical bills that are due or past due. The hope here is that their income will increase or expenses will drop the next week and they can catch back up by paying their regular expenses, plus the credit card. This type of emergency budgeting, however, only works in the short term. In the long term, if someone has to rely on credit cards for regular living expenses and then can't pay the bills down, they wind up with a large amount of expensive debt to pay off. In such cases, if they have good credit, they may be able to get a lower interest rate card and transfer the balance, but if not, then they have effectively taken out a high interest loan just to live. This, unfortunately, appears to be too common.

These strategies are aimed at shoring up income, providing emergency cash when necessary, and stabilizing family incomes as a personal, last resort safety net. They are standard practices for growing ranks of not just those in poverty, but the near poor, those who earn up to twice the poverty level. Given the high cost of living in San Diego, other areas of personal and family expenses are often put under pressure. These areas are where income is not just needed, but also goods and services, notably child care, elder care, and housing.

CONCLUSION

People resort to fringe banking for a variety of reasons; the most widely stated reason is the immediate need for short-term cash. Being on the financial fringes, however, comes with significant costs. Relying on very expensive short-term credit erodes wages and can lead to damaging cycles of debt (in the case of payday lending). The widespread result of low-income communities and the working poor relying on these forms of fringe banking and street finance is that financial instability in terms of financial services and high borrowing costs becomes the norm, further eroding low-income household financial resources. Strategies like expensive short-term borrowing and reliance on kinship networks or using credit, for those with access to it, are stopgap measures; they are emergency financial management. This is a financial services system with very little benefit to the consumer except as an emergency stopgap to prevent eviction, the loss of utilities, or vehicle repossession. These types of financial services are predatory in the sense that though they may be used for convenience (such as in check cashing), they are also widely used as very expensive emergency measures.

This chapter illustrates the huge gaps in financial services in the inner city. These gaps have a clear and direct bearing on other areas of those who are poor or working poor. An inability to accumulate assets, higher costs of credit and financial services, and predatory practices by street finance that can quickly escalate into damaging debt cycles all contribute to a type of chronic low-level equilibrium trap (Nelson 1956) wherein it is very difficult for the poor to accumulate any income for investment, and therefore the poor are constantly facing limited options for paying for critical needs such as transportation or education.

8

The Low-Income Trap
Barriers to Economic Mobility

I DISCUSSED BARRIERS TO ECONOMIC MOBILITY in terms of career ladders in chapter 2, and I covered barriers to small business formation despite the great entrepreneurial efforts of many in the informal economy in chapter 5. In this chapter I turn to barriers to economic mobility from an entirely different perspective. Here I look at how being low-income can in and of itself be a barrier to greater economic mobility. This is in many ways what the cyclical approach to poverty, with the attendant ideas of poverty traps, suggests: without adequate resources, people will, on average, intergenerationally, have a hard time getting ahead economically.

Taken more broadly, as we piece together the lives and challenges of the poor and working poor in San Diego, it becomes clear that there are structural problems all across the local economy. We saw in the first section how economic development and urban planning failed to address the real needs of the poor and working poor, following essentially a supply-side, pro-business, "give business whatever it wants, build stuff, and hope it all works out for everyone," approach. In fact, the local labor market became clogged with low-wage, dead-end jobs, industries and workplaces did not have the types of employment that people need in some of the largest local industries, and in the local community all sorts of issues from a lack of fair financial services to inadequate social services meant that the depth and number of barriers to getting ahead begin to look quite extensive. In this chapter I shift to a different set of hurdles, ones that are in place when those seeking greater economic mobility try to obtain it. Overall, we can argue that the servant class economy is one where not only are the structures of opportunity limited, but also the barriers to movement are increasingly severe, making the relative probability of escaping the bottom of the urban-class strata far less likely. To use a gravity metaphor: there are far more things keeping people sucked down than there are avenues for them to struggle up. As inequality in the United States and our cities continues to grow and become more and more persistent over time, we need greater insight into these gravitational forces that are pulling our systems of socioeconomic stratification even further apart.

THINKING ABOUT ECONOMIC OPPORTUNITY AND MOBILITY

In this chapter I flip labor economics regarding economic mobility on its head by showing how, through a variety of often interacting forces, simply starting out in a position of low income is in itself, either directly or in some instance indirectly, a barrier to economic mobility. I define economic mobility as attaining greater income and benefits through wage labor, and I assume that gaining greater work experience, skills, or education are critical to improving one's ability to earn a wage over time. Conventional approaches in economics assume that being poor is not a barrier to mobility; on the contrary, these approaches propose that people should seek to work harder if they are poor and those that do not simply do not deserve economic mobility (they have the wrong mentality, there is a culture of poverty, etc.). The problem here is both theoretical and empirical.

The blind spot of the rational actor approach in labor economics is an inability to recognize that job seeking and overall economic mobility is highly resource-dependent. Getting a job, keeping a job, and finding a better job, either through advancement in a career ladder or through obtaining more education or training, all require resources. I refer to these resources as "mobility enabling" because without them one's chances of moving up within a career ladder or finding a better job are diminished. Mobility enabling resources are things like adequate transportation, adequate freedom from personal or familial obligations, adequate education and training, or adequate motivation and perseverance. Social support, social capital, a social network, even a typed résumé and clean khakis can all be considered vital resources; a lack of them can be a real stumbling block. Take the example of a young woman, Keisha, recently returning from prison and drug rehabilitation. She did not have any family to draw on. She did not have any significant job references for the past few years. A job counselor at a local social service and advocacy organization that runs a program for reintegrating ex-offenders described the woman's résumé: handwritten on pink-ruled notebook paper, with a phone number and two employers, four years earlier and a year apart. Her skills listed were "good listener" and "customer friendly." The job counselor asked her to type up her résumé and provided some advice on how to improve it. The woman did not have a typewriter, however, so the job counselor spent an hour working with her in the office to type up a proper résumé. If it were not for the job-counseling program, Keisha may very well have been at a significant disadvantage given her résumé; fortunately, she is getting support in that area and also in terms of job interview skills and how to handle her drug and criminal record with potential employers.

All of these resources and characteristics are the types of requisites that standard labor economics assumes workers have, despite some economists, particularly feminist ones (see Folbre 1994), who have pointed out the flaws of this assumption. Nevertheless, these resources are necessary to enter the labor force and stay in it. Economic mobility within jobs, specifically within a single industry by moving up a career ladder or by moving into a different industry or occupation, also requires these resources, and despite pronounced debates within our culture about some of these challenges (how can a woman go to work and be a mother taking care of kids or breastfeeding at the same time!).

Specifically, all of the requirements of economic mobility require resources to make it happen. Labor force participation and attachment (getting a job and keeping it) and occupational mobility (moving from a less desirable job to a better one) all have associated costs. To put it in economic terms, labor force attachment, retention, and mobility have transaction costs. That is to say, it is a cost necessary for market entry and exchange. In the case of low-wage workers or anyone seeking to enter the labor market and sell their labor (for a wage and benefits, etc.), they must provide up-front costs to do so. Arriving at a job interview, wearing appropriate clothing, having the clothing clean and pressed, arriving on time, having the social and cultural capital to present oneself tactically in an interview (interviewing skills), having the skills and knowledge or credentials for the position being applied for (human capital), being healthy (workers who appear chronically ill, possibly due to lack of health care, may not do as well at a job interview as someone who is radiantly healthy), and so on—these are all investments that the job applicant has to make, and for low-income workers, these transaction costs and human capital and other investments may simply not be possible.

Indeed, research on low-wage workers and labor force attachment, particularly since the welfare reforms of 1996, have found that job retention and training demand a great deal of resources. As Rangarajan points out, "Programs can mitigate the costs of employment by helping clients with some of the additional costs of work, such as child care, transportation and health insurance. Most states offer some version of these support services, but such factors as administrative complexities, lack of knowledge about availability of benefits and reluctance to interact with the welfare system have kept utilization rates low" (2001, 14). She also suggests that upfront expenses be paid for during the early part of a worker's employment period. As workers usually have to absorb many employment beginning costs, but do not get paid typically for at least a couple weeks or longer, it may be critical to keep people on the job by providing financial support during the beginning of employment. In the remainder of this chapter I look at the challenges central San Diegans face in gaining economic mobility because of a lack of adequate resources.

LOW INCOMES, THE DIGITAL DIVIDE, AND EMPLOYMENT SEEKING

A significant challenge facing low-income workers in terms of job seeking is the need to keep up with employers' shift toward web-based hiring. As employers increasingly move toward electronic, primarily web-based, human resources management, this includes not only managing one's personnel records, but also applying for jobs and even applying for promotions. What is particularly a problem for the urban poor is that many of the entry-level positions in the city for lower-skilled workers (retail sales, cashiers, and even restaurant positions) are increasingly with major retail or restaurant chains, and these jobs are shifting toward Internet HR management (even McDonald's has switched a preference to online employment applications). This poses a new challenge for people seeking employment among urban poor and minority communities, and the trend appears likely to grow. An HR manager at a major retailer explained to me that it is an excellent prescreening tool: "If someone can get on a computer, speak English, upload a résumé, has an e-mail address, types in their ID information[,] . . . it saves us a lot of time in the scheduling and interview process. We can eliminate a lot of basic questions right away simply because we know they have navigated our hiring page and submitted an application." Research on this digital divide in job searches shows that there is a clear and growing trend of job search activity among whites, with nearly double the rates of Internet access, job searching, and successful Internet-based job searches (Kuhn and Skuterud 2000). The barriers here for many low-income job seekers are multiple. First, there is a persistent digital divide among poor and minority communities in the United States (Warschauer 2004), with fewer Internet connections at high speed (the speed required to apply for a position generally), and fewer computer literacy skills. This is particularly pronounced in rural areas, but it affects urban communities as well, as local resources, such as public libraries, often are not equipped for Internet demand or for assisting users with computers if they do not already have the skills to use the Internet (Healy 1998). Overall data show that nationwide half of poor households have personal computers and 43 percent have Internet access (USEIA 2011), while in central San Diego communities the figure is slightly higher: 52 percent have computers, and 45 percent have Internet access. One of the drawbacks of these data, however, is that they do not clarify what types of computer and what type of Internet access are available. Many people have only partially working or outdated equipment that will not run the Internet browser required for some websites, and many have low-speed connections, making job applications and searches virtually impossible. Overall, less than half of lower-income residents of central San Diego have these resources, and when broken down across racial lines the figures drop much further for African Americans and Latinos. The consequences of this trend are that many minority communities and the poor in the United States are becoming increasingly isolated not just from information technologies, but older, recent immigrant, and other populations may increasingly be unable to access many formerly non-Internet-based employment resources (Hogler, Henle, and Bemus 1998). Although job placement and career preparation programs and schools do provide readily available access to the Internet and free computer time (at the edge of downtown, San Diego City College's job placement office offers free use and assistance with job searches on a daily basis for anyone attending a class), these are not always accessible to members of low-income communities.

To assess job-seeking methods in central San Diego, Table 25 shows the distribution of job-seeking methods by ethnicity. The responses in this study are similar to national trends across racial and ethnic groups. As the table shows, whites tend to have approximately double the rates of Internet-based job searching as Latinos and African Americans. Asians are close behind, with 22 percent conducting Internet searches for employment. As other research on the digital divide indicates, part of the problem here is that Latinos, particularly nonnative English speakers, may be at a disadvantage in web-based hiring practices as most employers do not have multilingual sites (although the number in Spanish and English appears to be increasing). For African Americans the issue has tended to be access; they have far lower rates of Internet access at home and lower rates of computer usage in general. Accessing Internet-based hiring for African Americans, therefore, may require using a public library or other public service provider who can provide computer access, and that requires time and potentially money for transportation. Again, here the barriers are not simply a matter of access, but the cumulative disadvantage that different minority groups, or anyone who is unable to afford Internet access and a computer, must contend with.

TABLE 25. Job Seeking Methods in Study Area (percentages)

Job Search Method	White	Latino	Asian	African American	Native American	One or more races
In person	12	15	9	5	n/a	17
Newspaper	27	7	22	9	n/a	14
Job posting	10	8	9	14	n/a	5
Career center	12	9	4	12	n/a	12
Word of mouth	10	38	30	41	n/a	22
Internet	27	14	22	10	n/a	20
Other	2	9	4	9	n/a	10

SOURCE: Central San Diego Survey 2002–10.

It is not just private-sector employers that have shifted toward Internet-based hiring. Nonprofit and government entities have also moved in this direction. A case from an applicant to the San Diego Community College District illustrates how the application process requires significant resources. I met Ronaldo by accident in the new Logan Heights library, an architecturally stunning $14 million building providing Internet, computer classrooms, and nearly four thousand square feet of space. Ronaldo was in the midst of several online job applications for various positions. The most frustrating case, he explained, was the Community College District. The district had two jobs that were a good fit for his skills and background. He registered in the human resources system, created and uploaded his files, and created a username and password to manage his job applications. He prepared a scanned copy of his credentials, and went through the lengthy application and online questionnaire. Twice the system froze, and he had to return the next day to attempt to complete his application. After a third day of attempting to submit his application, it went through, and he waited for a reply.

When he didn't get any phone call after two weeks, Ronaldo checked the e-mail account he had used when registering, but he had no message regarding the job (he did have several offers to refinance his house, something he doesn't actually have, and a message about getting rich while working from home). He assumed that he didn't get the position, but wanted to know that his information was in the system properly so that he could at least reapply for a different position in the future and not have to go through every part of the process again. After trying without success to reach the human resources office on the phone, he sent them an e-mail message. A few weeks later he got a reply that they had his information in the system, but that his first application had not been successful, and that he should check his application status from the human resources website, something he wasn't aware of.

All told, his unsuccessful application and follow-up took an estimated fourteen hours. He bemoaned the fact that he couldn't do this from home, but it didn't make sense to purchase a computer and pay for Internet access when it was free at the library. He did, however, have to invest a tremendous amount of time just for a single, unsuccessful job application. The broader problem this points to, however, is that the San Diego Community College District *only accepts applications online*. This limitation effectively screens out a large segment of the inner-city labor force. Staff are available to answer questions about the site, but do not provide any assistance with completing an application. In other words, this type of employment application system already screens out most people who do not have regular and reliable access to a computer and Internet connection.

While only 25 percent of unemployed job seekers regularly report using the Internet for job searches (Hadass 2004), far fewer low-income unemployed appear to use the Internet for job searches. At the same time, many employers are moving entirely to online hiring or prefer online hiring to in-person/paper applications. One of the potential problems with online hiring systems is that the applicant pool can become skewed toward those with greater access to the Internet and greater computer skills (e.g., updated browsers are needed for most websites, and a high-speed connection is essential for most applications). At Starbucks, for instance, relatively real-time openings can be searched by location and applied for fairly easily, but this tends to advantage those who are actively searching online; these job seekers can find out about positions quickly and apply instantly. Those with less frequent access to the Internet are therefore left out of the hiring queue at many entry-level service positions in retail, food service, and even nonprofit and educational institutions.

This is clearly a concern for the urban poor, who have less Internet use, but also for older workers who may not be computer literate. While there is still a great deal of research needed on how the digital divide affects the employment of inner-city workers, the data here suggest that this trend puts many low-wage workers at a significant disadvantage.

INCOME AND THE COMMUTING PROBLEM

For much of my analysis I have argued that the spatial mismatch does not pose a great challenge for inner-city residents to the extent that they have lots of entry-level jobs nearby. This does not mean, however, that there is not a need to commute to work. Like any Sunbelt city, San Diego has a great deal of sprawl and extended industrial parks and other employment-dense lands outside of the urban core. For many residents of central San Diego, attempting to move upward in a career path may entail looking for work farther away from home, raising the issue of commuting costs, adequate transportation, and some level of a spatial mismatch.

As much research shows, for inner-city residents the continued spatial relocation of employment across metropolitan areas (such as to the suburbs or industrial parks) presents particular problems in getting to work (Kasarda 1989), and this is particularly true for low-wage workers (Stoll 1999). Indeed, there is strong evidence that individuals who own cars are more likely to be employed and further, conditionally upon being employed, are actually more likely to earn more than individuals without cars (Holzer 2001; Taylor and Ong 1995). As a result, several researchers and public policy scholars have argued for policies promoting car ownership among lower-income workers, particularly those transitioning from welfare or public assistance programs or prison (Ong and Blumenberg 1998). The conceptual problem with this research is that it presumes a very simplistic model of commuting to work based on often simple understandings of space and cost. Space is measured as distance between residence and job, and cost is assessed, often indirectly by whether or not one has access to a car or takes public transportation. As Raphael and Rice describe, "Reliable private transportation positively affects employment prospects. To start, commute times are lower using private transportation . . . reducing the fixed costs of employment and freeing up time for alternative uses. Lower commute times may result in greater work hours for some workers while affecting the labor force participation of others" (2002, 3). The drawback with the purely econometric approach to this problem is that it does not fully elaborate the complexity of the interaction between time and the cost of not having access to reliable transportation. What is not examined is how these types of transit can produce other costs and potentially long-term expenses indirectly, thus requiring a whole new calculation of commuting costs and methods. For example, taking public transportation can be cheaper than driving a car, particularly if the car is old and in need of regular repairs. However, the cost of public transit is not simply the cost of bus or train fare; it also may produce other costs due to reliability and timing problems. For instance, if a parent takes the bus to and from work, but the return trip during rush hour is too unreliable to make it home in time to ensure walking to the nearby daycare center to pick up children before the center closes, this produces a new set of costs directly related to commuting.

In this specific case, the parent either has to pay an often exorbitant fee associated with being late to pick up the children, or has to hire someone to pick them up (unless of course there is a friend or relative capable of doing this for free). If the bus is late, then the children may also need to be fed via a take-out or delivery meal because the parent may not get home in time to cook. We can add to this the potential cost for women facing a late-night bus ride and a walk home alone that might be unsafe—sometimes, they call a cab. In short, commuting is not a fixed issue but a constantly shifting matrix of calculations based on changing circumstances.

This type of scenario is precisely what occurred to a number of parents I interviewed who did not have reliable or trustworthy friends or relatives who could serve as a backup to take care of young children. In one case, Sally, a mother of two young boys, returned to work two and a half years after her second child was born. She got a job working in a store in Fashion Valley, a large mall complex a few miles away from her apartment. Her husband works for the phone company and often drives a company truck, and she was able to use her car to commute, but the car required significant, costly repairs, so they decided to sell the car and start saving for another one. For several weeks she took a combination of bus and train to work, but the bus schedule was so erratic that she often was late picking up her children from the daycare center. Each time this happened the additional cost consumed nearly all her net earnings for that day. She looked for a provider who would be open later or that was less costly, but they were both beyond walking distance from her apartment, and she did not like the reputation of the facilities. Adjusting hours with her employer was not possible, and with limited credit, and limited savings for a car, even a used one, she and her husband decided that she should look for work closer to home until they could get a new car. After several weeks she did get a position through a friend at a local store. It paid less than what she was earning previously, but she could commute on foot usually, and this meant that she could keep her children in daycare, picking them up on time each day she was at work.

What we see in this case is that the spatial and cost barriers to labor force participation, job attachment, and potential occupational mobility are limited by the complex interaction of commuting costs and other family concerns. In Sally's case, although she did find a job closer to her home as a receptionist, her new employer is also a small, family-owned business. She had to take a slight pay cut, and she knows that she has no real career ladder within the firm; she will not be looking at a promotion or pay increase, or improved benefits over time. Also, she does not gain any new experience working in her position as a receptionist. In contrast, her position in Fashion Valley was with a large national firm, and part of the attraction of that position (in sales) was that there was clearly the possibility of moving up within the organization. In short, the job nearer to home was preferable in terms of commuting costs and other important (and incalculable) risks to her children's well-being, but less preferable in terms of wages and occupational mobility. Her frustration remained palpable as she explained how she felt that she had to compromise between "a good job or being a responsible parent."

How does income figure into the difficulties faced by Sally and her husband? As she explained, if they were earning more (she had to stop working during her pregnancy, and they incurred a lot of expenses with the arrival of a second child), then the car repairs might have been possible, or at least purchasing a new (used) car would have been a realistic option. Unfortunately, for the several weeks they attempted to save up more for a down payment (thereby reducing their monthly payment and their annual percentage rate on a car loan), the problems of combining unreliable public transit commutes with child care proved too costly, and she made the decision to find a job closer to home. This decision, she explained, was also made in relation to the cost of buying a new car. Her husband had had a credit card debt problem in the past, making them less than good borrowers for a car loan—their rates were far higher than the often advertised "no money down, only $99 per month, your job is your good credit!" advertisements in the paper. So taking the job closer to home meant that they could save more for a vehicle and hopefully pay for half of it, and only have to finance the other half. Thus, for the case of Sally and her family, the limited income meant a crucial resource related to commuting directly, and adversely, affected her labor force attachment and her potential occupational mobility in the future. In this case, the inability to afford needed car repairs or replace the automobile has a direct impact on her current and future employment and earnings. Moreover, we see here the interaction among commuting time, vehicle costs, and child care as mutually reinforcing barriers to economic opportunity. Of course, Sally's experience is not unique; other studies have shown the costs associated with commuting for the poor, but my aim here is to illustrate how the costs actually interact within a complex system of decision-making as part of the broader process of facing barriers to economic mobility.

INCOME, CREDIT, AND JOB SCREENING

Over the past fifteen years there has been dramatic growth in companies using credit histories as a pre-employment screening tool. The Society for Human Resource Management has reported that 35 percent of firms use them in the hiring process, almost double the percentage who did so in 1996, with a majority of employers using credit checks at least occasionally (SHRM 2010). A national survey of retail employers found the proportion using credit checks to screen applicants increased from 37 percent in 2001 to 48 percent in 2005 (Nielsen and Kuhn 2009). Employers often rely on credit reports to verify employment history and social security numbers. This does not necessarily mean that employers do not hire people with poor credit—about 80 percent of human resource managers hire applicants with questionable credit—but this leaves 20 percent to be rejected simply due to credit reasons (SHRM 2012).

More recent data shows that nearly half of all employers are now using credit checks. One of the particularly challenging problems for low-wage workers is that many of the industries and occupations that offer entry-level positions have even higher rates of credit check use. Retailing, for instance, has dramatically increased the use of credit checks, and any jobs that require handling money, even entry-level positions such as cashiers, regularly require credit checks. Many government jobs, including TSA screeners and many Homeland Security positions created after 9/11, have credit screening thresholds, and even limits on the amount of uncollateralized debt an applicant can have (for TSA it is five thousand dollars).

Despite the increasing prevalence of credit checks in selection, there is almost no research on their validity or even on how firms use them. The extent of credit screening as a barrier for low-income inner-city residents to get and keep employment is not known. Even though it has been used as a screening tool for fifteen years or more, data on turned-down job applicants are not available, although there are plenty of anecdotal cases that both scholars and the media have pointed to as an unfair hiring result or employer practice.

In San Diego, inner-city residents in this study indicated a small, but nevertheless significant percentage of people had difficulties with credit reports and employment. Table 26 shows the percentage of residents who responded to questions about credit issues and employment. While only 8 percent of respondents said they were denied a position based on a credit report problem, the broader issue of credit reports being a very real or potential barrier for low-income workers is significant. Overall, 18 percent of respondents stated that they have experienced at least one problem with credit reports and employers—nearly one in five low-income residents. Nine percent were asked to reapply when their credit report was better. Additionally, some workers were either denied a promotion (2 percent) or warned that credit problems could hurt their standing at work (5 percent). While being denied a position is a barrier to labor force attachment, these other concerns are directly related to occupational mobility: being passed over for a promotion or potentially losing a job is a serious problem; it puts employment and promotion at risk precisely for those who are in great need of steady income. This problem also exposes to employment problems people who may actually have fine credit but who have been the victim of fraud or simply credit bureau errors. Again, these are challenges that have a great impact in communities that are poor or among ethnic minorities, as fewer of these individuals have access to credit reports or monitoring, which generally require monthly fees, high-speed Internet connections, or computer access (Mossberger, Tolbert, and Stansbury 2003).

In some cases, these problems are compounded, and there are few easy solutions, causing long-term damage to both a person's employment

TABLE 26. Credit Report Problems and Employment, Central San Diego

Type of Problem	Percentage Reporting
Denied a position	8
Denied a promotion	2
Warned about the problem	5
Asked to reapply when credit report was better	9
Other	1

SOURCE: Central San Diego Survey 2002–10.

prospects and economic mobility. One of the more complex but increasingly common cases is Donald. He is twenty-five and recently moved back to San Diego to live with his aging mother after he lost his construction job in Nevada. He spent several months applying for other construction jobs (he has a variety of skills and trained as a carpenter), but with the housing market collapse, finding a job in construction in Southern California in 2010 was impossible, so he applied for a range of jobs, looking for anything that he could commute to without having to spend too much time away from his mother. The position he was most hopeful for was as a maintenance worker for a condominium complex. It paid well and he could use his skills in construction, but the property management company turned down his application for credit problems. The company requires every employee who may have access to buildings, and potentially to residences, to pass a credit check. Having credit problems is deemed to make an employee at greater risk for potentially stealing from residents or the property management company. He understood the reasoning but was not sure why he had a credit problem. After getting a free copy of his credit report he found that there was still a record of a very late payment to a credit card and a continuing small balance that was past due. Although he did not owe very much money, the company still did not want to risk him as an employee. Further complicating things, Don claims that the credit problem is not his fault; when he moved from San Diego to Las Vegas to take a job with a general contractor, one particular credit card did not process his change of address, and his mother in San Diego just kept saving the billing statements in a big folder until he came to visit. He had forgotten that he still had a balance on the card, and by the time he found out that it had not been paid, the initial fifty dollars in items had ballooned with late fees and interest payments to more than three hundred dollars. He fought the credit card company on the charge and eventually came to an agreed payoff amount, but his credit report was severely affected, and efforts to get it changed have not had any results. Adding to the problems, he still had a five-dollar interest fee on the card that he was unaware of after he settled with the credit card company, which was erroneously listed as a "late fee" and showed up as a delinquent account on his credit report (even though he had already settled the account). Don admits that he was at fault for not double-checking on the change of address for one of his credit cards, but he is angry and frustrated with the company and credit reporting agencies for, as he put it, "shutting down" his ability to get a decent job. When I followed up with Don a year later, he had gotten his credit report as "clean as it can be" and had found a job.

Don's case is one of many, and he is on the more fortunate side of this problem. His credit improved and he was able to get a job, but what of those who often rely on credit for emergencies? What happens to someone if they have to resort to using all of their available consumer credit and fall behind on payments? This is obviously a serious problem for low-income Americans, but does this also hinder their occupational mobility? Can using a product supplied by the financial sector in an emergency actually damage one's employment and career chances? As the next case shows, this can and does happen, and the consequences can grow over time, with few straightforward solutions.

One of the more challenging cases about consumer debt and the consequences falls into the category of what Warren and Tyagi (2003) call the "two-income trap," where families have been engaged not in reckless personal spending, but a bidding war for schools and housing that has decimated their ability to save and forced indebtedness, particularly in emergencies. This is precisely the problem with the Callahan family. Tom and his wife, Joan, had moved to San Diego, purchased a home, and had a son. They bought at the near peak of the housing boom, spending almost half of their monthly income on their mortgage. When Tom lost his job in 2009, he worked at a temp agency, and the family had to rely on credit cards to cover an unexpected car repair and dramatic increases in their son's preschool costs. With an associate's degree in business administration and two years of accounting experience, he found plenty of short-term, project-based temp work, but none of them paid nearly what he was earning before he was laid off, and he eventually lost the family's health coverage and COBRA coverage. They signed onto the family health plan with Joan's company, but it was much more expensive. As their income shrunk and their bills increased, they relied more and more on consumer credit, hoping that Tom would get a job soon and they could start paying off the debt they had accumulated. A full-time job with good pay never materialized, however, and by 2011 they were facing either foreclosure or personal bankruptcy, or selling their house at a massive loss and moving to an apartment. Eventually they completed a short sale, got an apartment, and sold off all their furniture and a car, but it took nearly a year to pay off their credit card debt, including late fees. The entire process severely damaged their credit, and Tom has now found that even some temp agencies will not hire him if he would be involved in anything related to accounting or handling cash. He is more than welcome, however, to apply for a position as a warehouse worker, laborer, or landscaper, as one temp agency advised him. Eventually he did get a job as an accounts manager with a nonprofit organization, but he is still earning much less than he did before, and he cannot apply for other positions, he fears, because of his credit record. As he put it, there is a great deal of discrimination against those who have had bad financial histories or luck. He explained that "accountants aren't supposed to have financial problems, we are supposed to be great money managers. . . . Who wants to hire an accountant that basically went bankrupt and couldn't pay his bills?"

A related problem is identity theft or credit card theft and the potential problems this creates for lower-income job seekers. Lower-income communities are particularly hard hit by identity theft because of the range of scams that circulate among those desperate for cash. In some cases, people are offered stimulus funds or tax refunds if they fill out what is purported to be an IRS form with personal information. Additionally, lower-income communities have lower rates of credit bureau report requests to ensure their identity is not being used to open other accounts. The problem becomes even more pronounced because both the opportunity and the demand are present. With low-income communities facing a range of economic difficulties, and the limited security that poorer consumers rely on to safeguard their identity, these are often crimes of opportunity.

A case in point is Tanita, a mother of two children, with an ex-husband paying child support. She relies on a cousin to provide child care during part of the week. This became an opportunity for her cousin to use her and her children's social security numbers to get two credit cards, and as a result Tanita was left with several thousands of dollars of debt, fees, and late payment charges. Tanita's cousin has since left the state, and Tanita has struggled for nearly a year to get the charges eliminated. Her credit score and her children's credit scores are now compromised until they get repaired, which could take years, she is told. She faces potential limits to getting a new car loan, credit cards, or even opening a bank account or getting a promotion at work. Although she works in social services and does not handle cash at her job, she knows that a supervisory position that handles budget and financing information requires clean credit. In another case, a grandfather caring for a granddaughter used her personal information to open a credit line for his small business, planning on repaying the eight-thousand-dollar loan quickly, but he then passed away, leaving a financial disaster that ultimately forced the family to sell off the business and liquidate assets to pay back the loan.

Each of these above cases raises a final issue regarding credit screening and employment. As two dozen of the people surveyed in Table 26 reported (9 percent), they were told to get their credit report fixed or pay down debt, then to reapply for a job. The difficulty, of course, is that paying down debt or fixing errors take time and money, and they are especially difficult when someone is seeking work! As a job counselor I met after a church meeting pointed out, "Here is someone looking for a job, so they can get back on their financial feet and pay down a debt, and here is the business owner saying, 'Hey, get a job and pay down your debt before you get a job!'" In other words, simply being in debt or falling behind on payments can become a significant barrier to employment. This leads to a vicious cycle: the people who most need a job (generally those already having credit problems) are not able to get or keep a job, resulting in more credit problems and with few avenues (other than bankruptcy, which is devastating to credit) to remedy them. Employers often justify these policies in vague terms and do not cite concrete evidence of any connection between bad credit and poor job performance. Because minority populations tend to have poorer credit scores, these credit-check policies have a greater impact on minority job applicants than on nonminority applicants (Nissim 2010). As a range of past financial problems can show up in a credit report—repossessions, collections, charge-offs, or even carrying high credit card balances—the number of potential barriers that can prevent people from being hired or even promoted is high.

INCOME AND SKILLS UPGRADING

For those who already have a job and are seeking to increase their human capital for a promotion or a better job in a different firm, are the resources needed to obtain those skills or training in part too great to allow lower-income workers from obtaining them? The data presented here suggest that the answer in part depends on what types of skills—formal university coursework versus a certificate from a technical college, for instance—and what type of demographics the worker has. The vast majority of participants in this study had an interest in improving their education and skills (75 percent), but only 8 percent actually were actively taking classes or completing training programs to do so. Why is there such a stark difference between wanting to invest in human capital on the part of low-wage workers and the actual ability to do so, and what types of skills or education do workers want to attain?

Table 27 shows the types of skills and credentials workers in this study would like to attain. It is clear that education and skills upgrading is highly valued, two-thirds of those surveyed stated a desire to increase their current education and training. The most sought-after credential is a technical or trade certificate, which includes occupations that require licensure or credentialing in the state of California, such as becoming a certified hairdresser, nail technician (to work in a nail salon), HVAC installer, or welder. The next most sought after credential is a high school degree or equivalency.

With such a high rate of people expressing a desire for greater education and training, and these being critical investments in human capital, why are there such low take-up rates in education and training among those surveyed? The barriers are numerous, from time to motivation to

TABLE 27. Skills and Credentialing Sought by Inner-City Residents to Improve Job and Career Outcomes

Skills Sought	Percentage
High school degree or equivalency	24
Technical or trade certification	33
Associate's degree	13
Bachelor's degree	18
Other training	5
Graduate or professional degree	7
Total	100

SOURCE: Central San Diego Survey 2002–10.

funding, and in this chapter I focus on the interaction of income and time in relation to attaining more skills and training.

Getting a GED (General Educational Development) certificate requires paying a hundred-dollar fee, and taking a practice course may cost an additional seventy-five dollars, although some online test prep courses claim to be free. Study centers are offered at numerous locations in San Diego, but those require time and transportation to attend. A person often takes GED courses two to three times before being able to complete it. Parents, those who are unemployed, and men tend to have high dropout rates and lower completion rates of these types of courses (Tucho 2000). Postsecondary education and training is similarly found to have different success rates depending on demographics and income. Those at risk for not completing any type of postsecondary training are typically older than postsecondary students on average, attend part time rather than full time, work full-time while enrolled, are a single parent, and have dependents other than a spouse (Reder 2007). The case is similar for those seeking technical training and specific trade skills or certifications. When asked about why a GED was so difficult to get, an older Latino man said simply "time, money," and his wife elaborated that "if you have to take time from work to study, then who pays for you to take the class and all the other bills?" Indeed, the very perception that getting a GED will be more costly than simply taking a course and a test is part of the complex decision-making matrix that lower-income workers must navigate: is there time, is there money, who will watch the kids, what if I get called into work late, what if I miss the test day, is there a refund, can I reschedule the test, will it really help me in my job? Should I bother!?!

In part, many people simply described the GED as a problem of motivation, time, or perceived payoff. College classes or programs also pose similar barriers, as much research has shown. As a career counselor describes the situation, "Some people just haven't got the right attitude, but a lot of people may want to take a class, say at San Diego City College, but really can't justify spending the time and money to take a history class or something when they are working or have kids, or are trying to make ends meet." This quote is telling, because it reinforces a critically important concern that low-income workers convey frequently: that some of the credentialing necessary (such as a college degree, even a two-year degree) requires a lot of coursework that may be seen as unnecessary and as a waste of time and money, but nevertheless is necessary for the degree. People in the building trades or low-wage service industries frequently decry that they need the technical training and skills from a certification course, not a "full-blown college degree," but that most of the "good jobs" require a degree. But this is only part of a more complex picture regarding educational and training investments people may or may not make.

The problem is compounded for those with dependents. How does a working parent obtain more skills or training if not provided by an employer? San Diego Community College District for in-state residents is very affordable in terms of tuition; approximately $865 covers the fees per term, assuming a specific number of units. This does not include up to $1,500 in books and supplies as well as transportation and other expenses, however. There may also be other fees, but if we include the costs of attending outside of campus, say child care or lost income from work, then the price grows dramatically.

A case in point is Salvador, who has worked in construction for a decade and wants to shift gears toward working in HVAC as an installer or even inspector. He plans to enroll in the program at San Diego City College for HVACR consultant certification. The HVAC program at the school is called the AIRE (Air Conditioning, Refrigeration, and Energy) Program, and it trains people for a range of career options that include air-conditioning and/or refrigeration contractor, service manager, dispatcher, HVAC or refrigeration service technician, manufacturer service representative, HVACR consultant, and control systems designer/commissioner. The AIRE Program also prepares students to enter into Green careers that include solar energy technician or contractor, solar system design engineer, and HVAC and solar integration specialist, but these require the associate's degree in AIRE, a program that focuses on high-efficiency HVACR, advanced controls, and alternative energy systems. At $46 per unit, this is $2,760 for tuition, plus $3,000 in books and supplies, plus other fees (health service fee, liability insurance fee, and parking permits total $100 more). The cost on average runs around $6,000. This is far more affordable than some college programs, particularly the for-profit ones, which run as high as $40,000, but it still is a significant investment. Salvador has decided he needs to hold off on attending the course indefinitely not only for cost, but because he has two children, and his wife has only just returned to work, but she has unsteady employment at low wages. He qualifies for some grants and financial aid, but the prospect of taking out loans he finds unappealing.

Salvador is considering taking the courses one at a time over a few years, paying as he goes, and attending only at night. At this rate, even though class schedules are flexible, he would have to take the courses at night, and study other nights. At the same time, the program would take three years, not just two. At which point he suggested that nobody will know what the jobs will be like, "maybe it will be another construction boom, or bust." After attending the first class, he wondered whether he was making a mistake or not; all of the other students were much younger. Why would a company hire him if they could hire someone half his age and pay them less? He had heard worrisome stories of friends and relatives who had gotten associate's degrees in different fields only to find that there weren't any jobs, or they weren't actually paying what the recruiters said they would be paying. Thus, they could have saved all the time and money and just stuck to their old job. Eventually Salvador dropped the program, for now, he says . . . but he hopes to return if he feels confident that the investment will pay off.

The point here is that despite tremendous resources for education and seemingly very affordable prices, investing in human capital among the urban poor carries significant risks and unclear rewards. For those struggling to meet monthly bills, and understandably somewhat risk averse, obtaining labor market skills that are potentially but not certainly useful for several thousand dollars may not be the most practical goal. Many jobs that offer higher pay and benefits, particularly those that are salary based rather than hourly, demand at least a two-year college degree, and some a bachelor's degree. The problem again, however, is that there are clear barriers for working adults to obtain these credentials, particularly for parents, and income plays a major role in the decision-making process around skills upgrading.

It is conventional wisdom that the highly competitive global economy demands more skills, and that successful workers who want to see pay and job improvements need to have a college degree. Indeed, the data over the past thirty years in the United States make this point abundantly clear. Yet, talking about the need for investing in human capital formation and actually providing feasible and affordable pathways for working adults to achieve that goal is another matter entirely. Again, the issue here is that extant research typically views costs very narrowly. Things like child care, transportation, and the behavioral economics of deciding risk versus reward in terms of investing in skills and education are not fully appreciated in either their depth or complexity.

CAREER TRAINING AND FOR-PROFIT COLLEGES

One of the notable changes in education and skills upgrading in the past decade has been the expansion of for-profit colleges and universities, as well as specialized schools such as those that provide culinary training. While these may be rewarding and critically important avenues for educational attainment, there is also tremendous risk for those without the resources to afford the tuition and fees. A case in point is Victor, a friend of Salvador.

Victor has always enjoyed cooking. Until his mother's early death from cancer, he cooked many meals with her. His first job was busing tables in a restaurant, and as he graduated from high school, he decided to enter culinary school. He left after the first term, twelve thousand dollars in debt and with no credentials or specialized skills. It was, as he describes it, a decision about "cutting his losses." After studying for a term, he became worried about the amount of debt he was taking on, and the difficulty in finding a job after graduation. Like other students enrolled in culinary programs, the subject of numerous lawsuits now, he felt that he was misled by the enrollment counselors about how much he could earn. "They always said that top chefs can make a hundred thousand dollars . . . and you think well I'm going to be a chef and make a lot of money, it will be worth the effort and the money, but then you hear that you get a job as a prep cook." Indeed, his suspicion appears to be borne out by several pending class-action lawsuits, particularly among California-based culinary schools (Trachta 2010). For now, Victor has started working with his brother as a customer service representative at a mortgage refinancing company and is working to pay back his school loans. He still considers working in the restaurant industry, but only if he sees a viable career trajectory with adequate remuneration; for now he does not. He describes feeling cheated, and now about a third of his yearly income is going to pay back his school loans as quickly as possible.

These types of experiences are well known among those in low-income communities. As Salvador, who dropped out of the HVAC program, described, it was experiences like Victor's that made him pause and rethink his most urgent economic priorities. The same sentiment can be heard across much of central San Diego among those seeking to get more education or skills, questioning whether the benefits would outweigh the costs.

These sensible questions have a very real empirical basis when looking at the potential return on the investment in education in the for-profit and specialized career training schools. Many of these programs charge anywhere from four to nine thousand dollars for a term of study, with overall costs ranging from only a few thousand dollars to seventy or even eighty thousand. This in part explains the recent federal regulations requiring for-profit colleges and universities to disclose program costs, graduate placement rates, and levels of indebtedness by graduates. Victor decided that this type of a program was not worth the risk and that he should simply get a job and work his way through the industry if he really decided that becoming a chef was his career goal. The problem, however, is that there are few options for upward mobility within the restaurant industry without spending years learning from the bottom of the kitchen job ladder up to the top; this work requires long hours, offers relatively low pay, and provides few opportunities even after many years as a line cook or sous chef. Victor has decided not to take this route at present because he needs to earn money. "I would like to consider it, but realistically, I can't afford to; you can't earn enough, not what I need now with saving, helping my family out. It's weird, it's like it would be a luxury to take a low-paying job just so I could get the experience, but it is what it is," he explained.

BANKRUPTCY AND LEGAL PROBLEMS

The poor, as Sandra Barnes (2005) points out, cannot afford many things that most Americans take for granted as a part of life: getting divorced, having an unplanned pregnancy, developing medical problems, losing a spouse or partner without any life insurance, having a major car accident, being robbed, and so forth. To this list we can add legal problems in general, which are costly, and filing for bankruptcy, particularly after the 2005 bankruptcy laws were amended.

The 2005 bankruptcy laws made it more expensive, difficult, and time-consuming to file for bankruptcy (Porter 2010). Research shows that this new set of policies caused significant increases in the amount of debt that households accumulated before seeking bankruptcy relief and increases in the percentage of households that postponed filing for bankruptcy. Essentially, the reforms created barriers that caused couples to struggle for longer periods of time while trying to repay their debts. Ronald Mann (2006) argues that a primary objective of the reforms was to delay filings, thus increasing lenders' profits by trapping borrowers in a "sweat box" of debt. This is in part because bankruptcy costs anywhere from several hundred to three thousand dollars, depending on the complexity of the filing. It can be done without an attorney; however, the risks of filing without an attorney raise the risk of problems significantly (Littwin 2012). As Littwin describes:

> Faced with rising legal fees, some debtors may want a do-it-yourself bankruptcy, but the system thwarts the attempts of even the most sophisticated. The complexity of the process leaves debtors with two inadequate options: pay $1,000 to $3,000 for a bankruptcy lawyer—on top of court fees and other administrative costs—or try bankruptcy on their own and face high odds of losing their homes, their cars, or their discharge from debt. (158)

Beyond just the expense, bankruptcy has further ramifications that alter one's economic standing for years. Having to file for bankruptcy acts as a magic wand, but a bad one; it freezes a household or individual's financial status into a negative credit status for years. Bankruptcy remains on a credit report for ten years, and employers who require bondable employees and scrutinize credit reports generally shun job applicants who have recently declared bankruptcy. Bankruptcy also raises potential costs for lending for cars, which are often critical for getting to work, and for other consumer financial products, leading to challenges to asset building. In short, the situation for those facing bankruptcy is daunting and carries high costs as well as risks. Adding to the problem is that medical debt, divorce, and other legal issues are also costly to address, and the working poor face significant costs in trying to clear simple legal hurdles that are necessary.

The freezing of one's legal status has broad affects on the labor market. Financing of a car may fall through, getting a job in certain occupations may be impossible, breaking a lease or moving may be difficult, and settling custody issues, a requisite for CalWORKs, may be impossible. In the interim, costs mount up. Spouses may argue over discharging debt for months through a divorce without ever reaching a settlement, and then both parties end up with poor credit ratings and a limited capacity to pay off their debts, as the entire process drags out, and late fees and interest charges mount. Complicating matters, financial pressures are the number 1 reason for divorce, and often poor couples going through divorce are also struggling with debt payments and potentially bankruptcy; this process holds both people and their economic standing up until a settlement is reached.

How do entwined legal and financial problems affect economic mobility? Beyond the clear damage to credit reports, the cost of filing, and the cost of reduced income when families split up through divorce, there are a host of other challenges that emerge. People facing these types of legal hurdles may have a hard time moving or switching jobs until their legal and financial standing is settled further. Also, bankruptcy and other legal issues may limit the ability of someone to get an apartment until the process is completed. These problems are, in effect, limiting the ability of people to move on to new jobs, residences, and so forth. Thus, while the U.S. economy has been pushing for greater and greater flexibility on the part of workers for decades now, at the same time, policies like bankruptcy reform and the costs of legal filings make moving to take a new job or changing family composition more difficult.

RETHINKING BARRIERS TO OCCUPATIONAL MOBILITY

Research on occupational mobility among the working poor and urban poor in particular has tended to view barriers to labor force attachment and success in very reductionist terms, socially, culturally, and economically. Thus, much of the research from sociology and anthropology views barriers for the urban poor as either cultural ("the wrong attitudes" or a "culture of poverty") or social (limited social capital, social networks, or sufficient motivation to work, etc.). Other research on the spatial or skills mismatch theories also views barriers as either a purely geographic problem (the jobs have left the inner city for the suburbs) or as a human capital issue (people do not have the right skills for the "new economy" jobs). Other research demonstrates that employers discriminate based on race or gender and that minority job candidates are not seen as having the soft skills necessary for many types of jobs (Conrad 1999). While this scholarship has illuminated important barriers to occupational mobility, they all tend to reduce the problems to ones of space, skills, attributes, and so forth, without looking at the job-seeking behavior in process.

As I demonstrate here, when viewing job-seeking and job-retention behavior, along with efforts for attaining more education and training qualitatively, new barriers emerge that are underappreciated or poorly understood. In this chapter, I argue that one of the salient barriers to labor force entry, attachment, and mobility is a set of employment- and skills-enabling resources, or "mobility enabling" resources. These inevitably require time and, critically, money. These are important for lower-wage workers in the U.S. economy, precisely at a time when social support programs are being cut back. To further illustrate the point, I'll recount a conversation I had with a case worker, Stacey, a forty-five-year-old who has worked for nearly ten years at a job readiness program that serves primarily African Americans and Latinos, including a significant number of ex-offenders who are going through reentry and job-training programs.

After discussing a number of these very challenges, and how financial assistance, particularly up front at the start of employment, would help a lot of the clients, I asked Stacey what she would do if she were facing some of these challenges.

> QUESTION: "What would you do if you lost your job and were having problems finding a new one?"
>
> ANSWER: "Well, I have an MSW [Masters in Social Work], and there are jobs out there, but I could always relocate if necessary; my kid is in college now."
>
> QUESTION: "What if you woke up one day and found that your MSW was obsolete, or you needed some skills or education to keep your job or move up in salary, would that be doable?"
>
> ANSWER: [laughing] "I don't want to go back to school at my age, but yeah, that's doable."
>
> QUESTION: "No problems with getting there, paying for say a degree, or another year for a certification of something at a college?"

ANSWER: "No problem, well, depends, but generally paying wouldn't be a problem."

QUESTION: "What if your car broke down, how would you get to school?"

ANSWER: "It's under warranty from the dealer; we let them fix our cars."

QUESTION: "And if you needed a computer to take online classes, or apply for jobs, or communicate with an employer via e-mail, type up a résumé or something?"

ANSWER: "Ok, is this a set of joke questions or what?"

What I was trying to get at with this line of questions was that the resources available to someone with already well-established human capital and access to high-speed Internet, and a car that is under warranty and gets fixed by a dealer, and with plenty of resources to pay for a degree or credential, has far greater capacity for finding, getting, and keeping a job or moving up in a career ladder. Ostensibly, this is what so many of the excellent job-training and readiness programs do in service organizations, state programs, and nonprofits all across the country.

If we compare Stacey's situation to that of Salvador, still contemplating an HVAC career, one of the critical issues emerges here for low-income workers: risk. Risk in the context of trying to get ahead in the labor market means that one is encouraged by a variety of social pressures, and the labor market, to obtain more skills or qualifications, but these all require a significant investment. With any investment, investing in skills acquisition means risk. One risk is that the skills acquired will lose relevancy. This may be fine for someone who can retrain and has the time and resources to do so, but for someone like Salvador, unlike Stacey, he cannot afford too much labor market volatility. Retraining takes time and money. Expecting workers to simply retrain for better jobs at the whim of shifts in the labor market assumes that people are capable of absorbing the costs to do so, but this is clearly not the case, or it involves taking on too much more risk than what we might actually find financially responsible—taking out loans to study for a career with few job prospects, for example. Yet, this is precisely what the U.S. economy is demanding of workers in its search for flexibility and retrainability, without providing adequate resources to support such retraining. A second risk that workers take on is that once a course or program has begun, time and money have been invested; if something happens to force an individual to withdraw from the program, then that investment is lost. Again, this may not be a problem for someone with a stable middle-class income or the wealthy, but for someone who is barely at the self-sufficiency level, expecting them to bear this risk discourages lower-income workers from getting more skills and education. Finally, there is the risk of a job shift not being beneficial in the long run. Some fields may have greater wages and benefits, but less job stability.

A case in point regarding workers trying to make a move into a better career but having to take on the risk is Marcia, a thirty-five-year-old administrative assistant for a social service organization. Marcia worked as an administrative assistant for years until she got her associate's degree in business and got an entry-level job as a teller at a bank, looking to further her career in the financial sector. This was before the collapse of the housing market and the restructuring of many banks in California. She lost her job but was hired at another bank, but then told that she would have to work a long time as a teller before she could move up within retail banking. Compounding matters, she felt discriminated against at the new bank and left, eventually returning to work as an administrative assistant. In sum, she had taken a pay cut from her original administrative position to get into the banking sector, but then found that the career ladder was not as she expected, and with the recession there were few positions opening for her to move into above a teller position. She had no way of knowing any of these shifts in the industry were going to occur, and she took the risk of trying to shift careers, but in the end it did not pay; she in fact lost a significant amount of income compared to what she would have made had she just stayed in her administrative position. As Marcia's case illustrates, even moving horizontally within labor markets holds risk: if things do not work out as hoped, then wages and time may be lost, and low-income workers have a surfeit of neither. This set of challenges illustrates a broader point: lower-income workers may become very cautious, or risk averse, in the labor market, precisely because they cannot afford any disruption in their income. As an illustration, most low-wage Latinos in central San Diego, when asked about why they don't quit their job and look for something else, often reply with puzzled expressions. How can one take the risk of shifting jobs when children and perhaps family members in other countries are dependent on the limited earnings they bring in? Putting those wages at risk puts one or perhaps more family members at risk. Thus, being at the economic margins makes it more difficult to assume the risk of trying new avenues in the labor market.

The issue of risk aversion among lower-wage workers casts new light on the challenges of providing job-training opportunities for those seeking to move up in the labor market. Indeed, there are numerous problems with the way that these job-training programs approach the complex problems in relation to providing employment and mobility enabling resources. One of the biggest challenges is that most programs, like Jobs Corp, are limited to those under twenty-four years of age, but this is only a small segment of the labor market. What about those who have struggled in low-wage jobs for most of their working career? While some programs have attempted to tackle this challenging problem with direct payments and cash assistance to people who need it, these are few and far between. Additionally, most job readiness and retention programs only go as far as getting someone into a job; follow-up and keeping someone on the job or moving up a career ladder are left up to the individual. It is precisely in these moments, however, where individuals may have started well, but either run into barriers or slide back down a career track; little assistance is available for low-wage workers in these situations.

THE VALUE OF TEETH

Despite all our efforts as social scientists, despite all the modeling, data analysis, and randomized sampling, sometimes it is simply impossible to capture the depth and complexity of individual life circumstances, and the potential implications for our understanding of significant human challenges, without casting the models, theory, and data aside and simply listening to someone's story. To make the issue of mobility enabling resources empirically clear, we can take an example from someone who had spells of relatively long-term unemployment. Jennifer is a recovering addict and recently has been paroled. She went through a work-readiness program, a job-training program for people interested in becoming office assistants. She has been provided with interviewing skills and a computer-typed and printed résumé (albeit a short one). She even has a letter of recommendation attached to her résumé from her job-training program. One of the unfortunate consequences of her substance abuse in the past is that she has lost several teeth and needs work on some of her existing teeth. This has left her with somewhat of a speech impediment, and getting bridgework done is not financially feasible, nor is it covered by Medi-Cal dental. She feels strongly that this is one of the problems holding her back in job interviews, but there is no way she can afford to get her teeth fixed until she finds a job and becomes more economically stable. In following up with the human resources manager she had interviewed with recently, I was told that although she seemed nice and interested in "getting back on her feet," as the manager put it, "Jennifer had difficulty communicating during the interview, and we have a fast-paced office here, communication is critical, so we weren't an ideal fit." While the perspective of this HR manger is understandable, it does not change the situation for Jennifer, who feels "damaged" and depressed about her appearance and speech.

Fortunately, almost a year after being released from prison, Jennifer's sister and brother-in-law, along with some friends from their church, offered to help pay for her much-needed dental work. She accepted, but only on the condition that she took it as a loan and paid them back. Her family and friends stated that it was more important that she stay clean, continue to meet her parole obligations, and keep working. Getting her dental work done was a transformative experience. She describes the generosity and getting her new teeth, and her real voice back, as a "transformation. . . . I became the person I always new I was and should be." This event changed her complete sense of self, her confidence, and her ability not only to communicate, but to be more effective at work, so much so that she left her position for a better one as an assistant manager trainee in the shipping and receiving department for an online retailer. The prospect of going from an hourly employee with limited benefits to a salaried one with health insurance was an extraordinary opportunity. When asked about the impact of having new teeth, she stated, "It might have helped get the job, maybe not, you never know these things, but it certainly helped me, you know, because I'm a different person. Putting my teeth right again was like me burying my mistakes of the past, you know, moving on, finally turning that page and writing my own story now." The salient point of Jennifer's experience is that her turnaround from recovering, unwell, recently released addict to a gainfully employed management trainee with new dental care and health insurance is that it took extraordinary effort not just on her part, but on the part of social service organizations, job-training organizations, a generous social network, and a supportive employer who took a chance on her. Indeed, one of the reasons she feels she got the management trainee job was the relationship she had with her first employer out of prison; the social service organization that provided her with steady work for nearly a year allowed a great deal of leeway in her job performance but put faith in her so that she would be successful. As she describes it, "I wasn't the best employee, not by a long shot, when I started there, but by the time I left I really knew the ropes. I was good, but they gave me a lot of time and patience to get it right. Thank God they gave me that."

I have argued in this chapter that the poor and near poor often lack sufficient resources for getting ahead economically. They face barriers in hiring, adequate transportation to work, among other challenges. For those with complex and daunting issues such as substance abuse and criminal records, they may not have the same types of supportive resources to help them. Additionally, any minor problems during the postincarceration and addiction recovery period can lead to serious consequences. As a social worker in the community described to me the all-too-common occurrence of someone falling back into substance abuse, and then crime or jail time, and never getting any substantive rehabilitation or job readiness when they exit, only to wind up back in a never-ending cycle of substance abuse, crime, and incarceration. Keeping the cycle going is very easy—one small slip or uncontrolled event (a financial crisis even) can start it up—but keeping that from happening in people's lives, day after day after day, requires enormous supportive resources.

Conclusion

An Expanding Servant Class or a
Pathway to Prosperity?

ASSERTING THAT PEOPLE may have a hard time getting ahead economically, precisely because they start out poor or in a lower-income family, contradicts conventional wisdom. My point can be made by asking the question: do people have low income because they cannot get the skills and education needed to succeed in today's labor market, or do they have low skills and education that prevents them from earning better income because they are low income? To ask the latter means reversing conventional wisdom; barriers to economic mobility are typically not seen as income dependent. If this were the case, then it runs directly counter to the core ideas of American meritocracy: that people deserve what they get based on how hard they work; that if you are poor, the best thing to do is work hard, grab economic opportunity (as if it were something on a shelf to simply be grabbed or built out of hard effort), and stick to it. Growing evidence suggests, however, that economic mobility in the United States is stagnant or declining.

Lack of economic mobility in the United States is a growing problem across socioeconomic and racial/ethnic demographics. The central research question regarding economic mobility is why so many people in low-income families have a difficult time moving out of the bottom rungs. For instance, reviewing the recent scholarship on the topic, Hertz (2006) finds that the likelihood of being born in a lower-income household and remaining there is quite high, approaching 50 percent, while those in the top quintile have nearly the same chance of staying there throughout their lifetime. In short, whether you are born rich or poor does matter. This runs in sharp contrast to the American mantra of meritocracy and the opportunities afforded in the particularly volatile type of capitalism the United States has embraced. Explanations for limited mobility are, as a result, often linked to a culture of poverty, laziness, welfare dependency (although welfare was largely eliminated in the mid-1990s), and so forth. Research on mobility and its causes has not fared much better; we have ample and unequivocal evidence that this is a growing problem (Corak 2012; Corcoran 1995), but when decomposing or breaking down the variables in our research on economic mobility, it appears that the most important factor is "unexplained" (Hertz 2010). In short, we simply do not have a full picture of why economic mobility is so difficult for low-income Americans. Addressing the issue of economic mobility is critically important and requires a radical rethinking of many assumptions about how low-income workers can achieve greater degrees of mobility.

For those working in the expanding servant class, I have argued that there are significant structural forces that can limit economic opportunity in three critical areas: the labor market, as discussed in the first part of the book; the workplace, detailed in part II; and the local economy, which includes financial services, issues related to investing in more human capital, and so on. Moreover, the qualitative cases provide insight into how the decisions people make to maintain some level of economic stability or to gain greater economic mobility upward often entail significant costs and risk. These structural forces form an interactive set of challenges, woven into the very operation of the economy, and often mutually reinforcing each other. As a result, economic problems that may start out small can escalate into much larger problems. The chutes and ladders metaphor is apt here; for the urban working poor, there are far more paths down, and they are very easy to fall down, and to fall down fast; in contrast, there are few ways up, and they are arduous, risky, and sometimes expensive. The prevailing mythology in American society, of course, is that this is not the case; the story is that there are ladders everywhere—one just needs to latch on and climb up.

CONNECTIONS

What we also find from looking closely at low-wage service workers in the inner city is that there are strong connections among the various aspects of their economic lives. These relationships are often direct, very strong, and have an enormous impact on other aspects of people's economic circumstances. These linkages are in part what contribute to the overall cumulative economic adversity that can easily set an individual or family back very quickly in their effort to move up economically. For instance, landscaping workers often rely on personal transportation; they bring their own lunches, spare clothes, and boots to specific job sites. Unless they are going to a landscaping firm that drives them out to the job sites, they get there on their own. This is the case certainly with those working informally; a personal vehicle is necessary for their work. If something happened to the car or truck, paying for repairs might require borrowing on very expensive credit, or purchasing a new vehicle would again potentially require high borrowing costs. The high cost of credit and high cost of transportation make the landscaper assume significant financial risk if anything happens to their car or truck. We can add to this the limited career ladders or training available to landscaping workers. Landscaping services have a nearly flat occupational staffing pattern; as there are only two or three, possibly four different occupations within a landscaping firm, and almost no real chance for moving up into the one or two supervisory positions for landscaping workers, we can see how limited the options are for economic improvement.

Similarly, reliance on high-cost financial services and difficulty in accumulating assets or having poor credit may make it difficult to pay for further education or specialized training. For-profit colleges and training programs can be very costly. Applying for private loans requires a credit check; federal loans may or may not be available to many borrowers or cover the entire cost of the program. Additionally, there is a range of other potential barriers for someone from the low-wage service sector in the inner city seeking additional education or training. What needs to be involved to ensure workers can pursue these goals? A range of possible supports: child care, elder care, transportation, affordability of the courses and program of study, time to actually enroll in the courses, the ability to risk time and money on additional education that may or may not actually be beneficial in the end. I recall a conversation I had with an experienced welder, Robert, who became injured on the job and had to quit welding. He then went back to school to study computer software applications for business, but soon found that the job market was already flooded with college graduates with far more skills and experience. He shifted focus to network administration because of the good salary and apparently high demand on the job market. He looked into a network administrator diploma program at a for-profit college, but the program costs were more than $20,000 with financial aid, if he could get it, covering less than half the cost, maximum, and still with no real assurance that once he completed the program he would get a job. With an annual median salary of $49,000, network administrator is a reasonably good job in San Diego, but again, the concern Robert has is the educational cost, and the worry that there are already so many graduates with the experience that he may not get a job and will have to do something else to make him more attractive to employers. As it stands, he remains employed part time at a social service organization and does odd jobs, earning less than $25,000 per year.

The broader conclusion to be drawn here is that resource scarcity or a lack of opportunity in one area can spill over and have effects in others. This seems obvious, but it is not the case with policy debates and research on the urban poor and working poor. The policy debates around how to help the urban poor and working poor almost always revolve around two themes: increase wages, and promote education. Conservatives tend to push for an expanded EITC, while those on the left tend to push wage-floor policies like raising the minimum wage. These are often discussed entirely separate from educational policy, which has largely ignored the challenges facing the urban and working poor, and focused almost exclusively on affordability through expanding financial aid programs, which still remain inadequate. The problem is that debates this narrowly focused are merely superficial. These types of policy debates and prescriptions do not address the deeper, structural, and often mutually constitutive forces that batter the low-wage servant class workers in today's inner cities.

What often occurs then, to return to the spatial metaphors of chutes and ladders, is that for those individuals or families that may fall off the knife edge of economic insecurity, they often experience what I have termed cumulative disadvantage. This means that as adverse events occur in labor markets, with finances, with unplanned bills, or with family or transportation issues, the costs both short and long term can rise and accumulate until someone is pushed into a more and more disadvantageous position.

A further conclusion to be drawn from this study of how labor markets, the workplace, and economic circumstances in low-income communities intersect is a greater appreciation and understanding of the limited or at least structurally constrained agency of the poor and working poor. One of the reasons for the decades-old, woefully inadequate and often implicitly racist description of the urban poor as having the "wrong values" or a "culture of poverty" is that the assumptions about the behaviors and decision-making of the poor are completely misunderstood. Context, institutions, social structure, and other factors all influence the range of possible outcomes and responses that individuals and families can make in the context of poverty and low-wage jobs. The data in this study of San Diego's inner-city poor show clearly that it is not cultural norms or "bad values" that constrain people's actions and outcomes, but rather the fact that more often than not, the range of available actions and possible outcomes are not necessarily productive. They may, in fact, be counterproductive. When faced with an unexpected expense that forces a family head to resort to a payday loan, which then grows into a larger debt, and eventually begins to become a serious threat to that family's financial stability, who should be to blame for the impending financial catastrophe? Is the family head not doing the responsible thing by taking on the higher-cost loan in order to pay the bill (say, for a funeral of a family member)? Should the payday lender, who has to charge exorbitantly high rates to cover the higher risk and far higher default rate, be to blame? What if the household head winds up not being able to fully pay back the payday loan with interest and fees and then has their credit score damaged and cannot apply for even a cashier job to earn extra money because defaults on a credit score usually disqualify someone from working as a cashier? Who should be to blame for the inability of that person to earn extra income in that scenario? Clearly, the assumption that as a society we simply have to hold people accountable for their choices and economic behaviors may sound good rhetorically, but it does little good empirically in light of the fact that often the urban poor and working poor *do not have any good choices that can be made!* The real problem is the broader context and the structural inequities of the economy that engender a universe of economic decisions that often lead to bad consequences. These contexts and structures are part and parcel of the urban capitalist economy, not the culture of the urban poor. Higher interest rates and fringe banking are market driven; the dramatic expansion of low-wage and contingent work are market driven (though in the case of San Diego, with the aid of public resources for redevelopment); and the high transaction costs throughout urban poor communities for nearly everything are market driven. These more theoretical conclusions lend themselves to rethinking policies for the urban poor and working poor, as well as urban economic development and inner-city revitalization in particular.

THE POLICY DEBATE

Rugged individualism, self-sufficiency, and self-enterprise are deeply embedded within American culture. This cultural disposition tends to inhibit sympathy for those who are poor or less well off, and it produces great antipathy toward state programs to aid less-fortunate members of society. An inability to escape low-wage work or to accumulate assets such as those through homeownership is often pinned on individual failings, sloth, or bad decisions. In central San Diego, like any other inner city in urban America, or any suburb for that matter, people can and do make bad decisions. Instead of buying health insurance or paying down a credit card, someone may instead purchase fancy rims for a car. Poor decisions and bad luck can contribute to a host of problems for the urban poor and near poor, but in this book I have not focused on the mythical poor, urban "welfare queen" who abuses drugs and uses food stamps to buy cigarettes, quite simply because such cases are actually a tiny minority of San Diego's inner city.

The greatest challenges facing the inner city are not a product of individuals' poor decisions, but decisions that have been made for them: conditions that are a product of both market forces and policy changes over the past forty years of urban restructuring and inner-city revitalization. These conditions include changes to urban economic development; changes in contracting welfare and social safety net provisions; changes in the labor market and job quality; changes in access to affordable health care, banking, and other important services; and skyrocketing housing costs and fraudulent mortgage lending. As a result of these changes, and in some ways responses to them (such as working in the informal economy, which provides lower wages on average for the poor but subsidizes services and goods for more affluent consumers), polarization and inequality become even more entrenched, and upward economic mobility is diminished.

Which Future? Policy Recommendations for the Servant Class and Working Poor

Decades of research on the dramatic growth of the working poor, urban poverty, the effects of welfare reform, and challenges facing American workers, particularly those in the lower-wage/lower-skill distribution, demonstrate clearly that these issues are complex and interrelated. Policy recommendations are widely debated, and within very detailed studies of the working poor these recommendations are laudable and quite comprehensive.

The difficulty is, however, that no matter how laudable, the laundry list of policy recommendations to address the issues of urban poverty, the working poor, and economic mobility/inequality are only partial. They will only potentially affect one small part of what is clearly an immensely complex set of intersecting and often mutually reinforcing forces that structure and influence people's life trajectories. For instance, in one of the most widely cited and discussed studies of the working poor, Katherine Newman (2009) points to a need for a whole range of productive policies—wage and tax breaks that are targeted for those in need, place-based policies like local hiring initiatives, public–private ventures with targeted hiring, not undermining unions or workplace empowerment at every turn, providing adequate child care and health care (it remains to be seen how adequate the Affordable Care Act will be to the working poor)—as well as listing some good examples of successful urban workforce development and hiring programs. Similarly, Dan Zuberi's (2006) comparative study of the working poor suggests a range of policies from increasing the EITC to creating parental leave programs and providing subsidized day care. Studies of welfare reform and the challenges of working mothers and parents attempting to escape poverty all point to the same litany of problems the working poor face: inadequate child care, inadequate transportation, expensive housing, poverty-wage jobs, limited or nonexistent career ladders within those jobs, chronic economic and financial insecurity, predatory and exploitive financial services, inadequate educational and training opportunities, and so forth (Collins and Mayer 2010; Marchevsky and Theoharis 2006; Waquant 2009). This might lead to the erroneous conclusion that the poor and working poor need assistance with everything. This is not the case; rather, as I have documented, there are key areas that can potentially have a significant positive impact because they allow the decisions that people make to be productive and contribute to greater economic empowerment, rather than work against them.

Rethinking Policies to Empower the Urban Poor and Working Poor

In the introduction I described how popular discourses of poverty and the poor more generally are overly simplistic. They are rooted in a set of basic assumptions about human agency and the structures of opportunity in society: conservatives tend to embrace a Horatio Algerism wherein anyone can be successful if they are honest, work hard, and persevere. A lack of success is often explained by individual attributes (laziness) or governmental distortions of behavior (welfare dependency). We know definitively from years of research on economic mobility, welfare use, and the working poor in the United States that this belief surrounding individual opportunity is a myth. Inequality is very high and very persistent, regardless of how hard people may or may not work. On the other hand, more progressive approaches to poverty and the working poor emphasize structural problems that can be overcome with specific social policies. Both of these approaches to the policy debate have an inaccurate view of human agency and social structure and the relationship and effects of decision-making involved in mediating both. In this book I have documented how at different institutional and structural levels, conditions are such that regardless of the effort of the decision-making, often the end result is that an individual or family remains stuck or has very few options. A greater understanding of this is needed in order to inform the policy debate and move beyond merely penalizing the poor and working poor on the one hand or simply expanding the social safety net and federal policies on the other.

My own approach to understanding the persistent and growing challenges of urban poverty and the dramatic growth of the working poor in San Diego suggests that the working poor in San Diego face a variety of challenges that are embedded structurally within the broader economy in three critical areas: the labor market, the workplace, and the local economy. There are two empirical findings here worth highlighting that help illuminate the complexity of economic mobility and opportunity structures in central San Diego. The first is the idea of cumulative disadvantage. While we have clear findings that urban poverty and marginality can be intergenerational and that the damage of growing up poor or working poor makes it very difficult to break out (Sharkey 2013), the mechanisms through which this occurs on a social and individual level are harder to parse out. My approach looks at this process through the construct of cumulative disadvantage, the idea that once someone has moved to a position of relative deprivation or economic hardship, it tends to make even greater challenges in moving away from this position of marginality. Indeed there is a variety of research demonstrating this effect. Workers who experience low-wage employment, for instance, tend to have more unemployment as well. Low-wage jobs act as conduits for repeat unemployment and considerably increase its probability, while higher-wage jobs reduce the increased risk of repeat unemployment to insignificance (Stewart 2007). Having to resort to a payday loan raises the risk that one will fall into a vicious debt cycle, escaping from which may be extremely costly (Stegman 2007).

Where should policies move in order to address the complex, cumulative, and growing problems of San Diego's urban poor and working poor? As the occupations with some of the largest shares of growth in the future are estimated to be in low-wage service work, what policies might work to promote greater economic opportunity and economic stability? No policy suggestions come without the caveat that political will needs to be established to accomplish anything, but an honest discussion of the empirical merits of such policies is a first step to getting there. Virtually every book about the poor or working poor (in this case both) that ends with policy recommendations typically lists a range of well-conceived, analysis-based policy suggestions. Many of these provide a detailed list of improvements to social safety nets. I would include such a list here, but this is a well-trodden policy debate, so in the following section I provide suggestions that are more specific to the findings of this book, and which in some cases may not at all be a part of the current policy debate surrounding poverty, the working poor, and economic opportunity.

POLICY RECOMMENDATIONS

Economic Development and Urban Policy

Single, silo policies will accomplish very little unless there is a comprehensive effort to address the inadequacies of market-driven development. As the case of San Diego clearly shows, billions of dollars of public–private investment, gentrification, rising property values, and thousands of jobs created does not mean revitalization. There is a massive need for better labor market institutions and workplaces (which I discuss more below), a need for supportive services from child care and elder care to better public transportation. The critical point is that we won't see much improvement until all the gaps in the critical institutions and infrastructure for working families and the poor are filled.

The aforementioned suggestions require that there be far greater collaboration between different economic institutions at multiple levels. For example, we should not expect many low-wage workers who need and want more education and training to sign up for it if the costs are exorbitant and the potential to get a job that earns enough to make the costs worthwhile are unclear or very limited. In such instances we need far greater collaboration and coordination among educational and training institutions, employers, and funding sources, which may include foundations or federal, state, and local sources. There are excellent examples of these programs, including some workforce development initiatives, but they are inadequate to address the scale and complexity of a growing servant class.

The now decades-old approach to inner-city and downtown revitalization by throwing incentives at tourist/convention/entertainment and retail industries must be evaluated thoroughly. Billions of dollars of public assistance to attract-low-wage, primarily service-sector jobs is not a sound economic development policy. We have known this for years given all the extant research, but short-sighted urban planning, a lack of understanding of the effects of a narrow industry focus, and a growth-machine, politically driven system of development need to change.

It must be recognized that job quality is a public policy issue. Labor market policies are nearly invisible in urban public policy when it comes to economic development and redevelopment. As a result, so is job quality. This needs to change. There are organizations like Goodjobsfirst that are attempting to get this to happen, but cities need to take the lead, not just follow advocacy organizations.

We must develop better evaluations of economic development to capture labor market impacts. Nearly every city promotes self-congratulatory job-creation numbers when something is built, especially if it is in a low-income community. These figures are based on overly simplistic employment density functions that are often inaccurate and say *nothing* about job quality. As I have argued in this book, a thousand low-wage retail or hotel jobs do *not* represent economic development. I have developed and used some new job quality metrics in this study. Data are available, and analytics are available to provide the public and policy makers with far better information about labor market impacts when economic development occurs; these should be used by city staff, consultants, and the economic development and planning professions, respectively.

Addressing job quality directly is one of the hardest to implement because it often expressly hits at employers. Richard Florida (2010) has written that it would be good for cities if retailers paid their workers more, but this is wishful thinking at best for those of us who have worked in advocacy organizations and on living wage campaigns. Ultimately, whether they are wage-floor policies, or other high-road economic development policies, there are plenty to choose from based on different approaches around the United States. The problem is political will. I am convinced, however, that if communities are organized and the public is educated about the dire costs and consequences of low-wage job growth, then political will can be attained to directly tackle the problem.

Job Quality

Job quality needs to become central to policy debates when economic development is concerned. Not having a strategy to balance different industries, wage structures, and types of jobs can lead to situations like San Diego where the trend toward low-skilled, low-paying, service-sector employment has been driven in part by public policy.

Career ladders need to be evaluated more fully in industries. While there are some cases where these may be very productive and beneficial, such as in the health care field, career ladders as I have documented also may be flat or becoming more polarized. If economic growth continues toward industries with flatter and flatter career paths, then we have an even greater problem with socioeconomic mobility than generally recognized.

There is mounting evidence that job quality varies more by firm than by industry. Encouraging those firms that engage in new, innovative ways to improve overall job quality and provide more opportunities should be a policy priority. Instead of tax breaks and other incentives simply to create jobs, incentives should also be provided for those that improve jobs.

Encouraging productive partnerships can help. Labor unions and the hotel and restaurant industry provide numerous cases of local hiring, training, and other programs that not only improve job quality, but have other more far reaching benefits as well.

Even "servant class" jobs can be upgraded, but it takes prodding and resources. When retail workers serve merely to stock shelves, there is limited value that can be added to the firm and limited pay that can be allocated to the worker. Improving the job can add value to the firm and make it possible to increase productivity, profitability, and pay. Discount retail such as at Walmart is one example where job quality could be dramatically improved, but this would run counter to a business model that seeks to keep labor costs as low as possible and more or less serve as a warehouse for goods, with occasional store staffing. Trying to improve the quality of a job in that type of a business model will require significant change to the model.

Workforce development is inadequate in terms of matching job seekers to training programs and job openings. These need to be rethought and reworked on a much larger scale.

Developing Alternatives to Fringe Banking and Promoting Asset Building

The poor and working poor can only save money and build assets if they already have an income stream. On the assumption that they do, it would be of great help for them to accumulate assets and savings to gain a greater degree of economic security and ability to invest if there were better mechanisms to do so. There are a range of programs being used with some degree of success, and these should be expanded and tested more widely. It goes without saying that banking regulation or alternative financial services regulation can protect consumers better from predatory lending and other forms of fringe banking, but these require political power and mobilization. There are programs that have demonstrable effects, like IDAs. To help the urban poor gain greater access to reasonable financial services, the following should be considered:

- Promote and establish IDAs in lower-income communities by piloting projects that have proven effective elsewhere.
- Encourage novel approaches of mutual credit associations like lending circles.
- Offer federal incentives to retail banks for providing alternative financial services at lower costs by absorbing and socializing some of the risk. This type of program could expand FDIC coverage of depositors to also cover potential losses for lower-income resident accounts that are either free or relatively low cost.
- Push for tighter regulation of alternative financial services.

Promoting Greater Socioeconomic Mobility

It goes without saying that greater social supports and programs across the entire spectrum of human needs—health, education, child care, housing, and so forth—are needed by the poor and working poor. Covering all of these with specific policy suggestions is, as I indicated, a well-established policy debate. Ultimately, of course, these are questions of political will, and hence political mobilization.

THE FUTURE OF POLICY

I have argued that conventional approaches to improving economic stability and opportunity for the urban poor and working poor are far from inadequate because they misunderstand the depth and complexity of the problem. We can see that simply following a supply-side-driven model of urban revitalization—enterprise zones, redevelopment, and growth machine pressures to push for development as fast as possible—may not have much impact on the working poor and those in poverty. In fact, it may be that the new jobs are those that predominantly demand large segments of the labor force remain low-wage, legitimized by the long-disproven mantra that hard work and greater education leads to greater economic stability and mobility. Nor is it acceptable, however, simply to push for wage-floor policies; it is important to promote industries that have some semblance of career ladders, and to promote greater access to education when the majority of economic growth is occurring outside of industries with career ladders (in areas like the retail sector) and the majority of occupational growth is in jobs where only a high school diploma or less are the necessary qualifications.

We must have a far more honest discussion about restructuring the class system in the American economy. The growing ranks of the servant class, as I describe it in American cities, are not jobs that are tertiary to the U.S. economy. They are positions that include personal care aides (taking care of the elderly and handicapped) and child care workers (taking care of our youngest members of society). Why should the growing need for people to fill these critically important occupations be structured in such a way that nobody can devote themselves to these careers unless they are willing to live in relative poverty, or can work in the job as a "luxury" because they have a household or partner with a greater income to support them?

Toward a Critical Urban Policy

We also need, I argue, a far more honest debate about the role of policy and how effective it is. Virtually every book-length publication on the urban poor, working poor, or low-wage workers that ends with policy recommendations offers a litany of well-meaning, laudable policy prescriptions to help those whose work the labor market does not adequately reward. These policies typically include improvements to wage floors, career ladders, more funds for job training, better workforce investment practices, and so on. There are three serious challenges I want to raise in regard to policy recommendations, and this goes for the ones I have suggested as well.

The first concern is the lack of political engagement in urban policy. It is virtually impossible to pass any policies at a municipal level without political power. City council votes, the mayor's office, and even city staff members all have to be behind something to get it passed. This often requires very real organizing and political mobilization, two things that many poor and politically disenfranchised communities do not have. Thus, there is a very real relationship between political inequalities and realities and the demands of the policy world. Not recognizing these symbiotics is a huge failing of current policy debates and practice.

The second concern I have is the limited debate about how effective policies are. This is also a call for greater political engagement. The problem can be illustrated by a case in point. In a very erudite and welcome discussion of theories of poverty and potential approaches through community development, Bradshaw (2007, 9) describes how different policies can have an impact on geographically demarcated poor urban communities. He specifically offers the following list of policy recommendations:

- Improved local industry competitiveness through cluster development or development of creative communities
- Enterprise zones, redevelopment, and other tax-based incentive programs to promote economic development and channel private investments
- Inclusionary zoning, affordable housing, and similar programs that place conditions on development
- Downtown revitalization and civic improvements that increase amenities and make areas more attractive to stimulate employment and tax revenues
- Investment in infrastructure, including interstate highways, parks, water, waste disposal, schools, and other public facilities
- Community organizing

All of these were used in San Diego over a more than twenty-five-year period, and with very limited impact, even when combined! In other words, even in a dream scenario where each of these strategies was used intensively, their effect was not only paltry but fell far short of the overwhelming demand. In fact, the neoliberal model of bringing in not millions, but billions of dollars of private-sector investment actually did very little to affect poverty or the rates of the working poor. As I have argued in this book, the issues are not public policies, but the profound, deep, and widening inequities of contemporary capitalism and the urban economies engendered by it. Why, then, should we be promoting private-sector-driven strategies when the problems of inequality and working poverty are caused by private-sector market forces?

Furthermore, why should we assume that community organizing or public-sector expansion and investment will actually have any significant impact in terms of long-term, sustainable equity and economic opportunity? For decades, very well-meaning progressive nonprofit and foundation-backed programs and policies were put in place in Detroit, but what devastated Detroit was the massive restructuring of capitalism and a long-standing hallmark of the Fordist era: the automotive industry. Perhaps a better way to clarify my concern is through a metaphor: our collective house has a roof fire. The roof is on fire! And while it burns, our collective policy efforts amount to tinkering with a faulty light bulb hanging in the garage. Regardless of the era of federal-urban devolution and its aftermath, our efforts at substantive urban economic revitalization are staggeringly inadequate and require a complete rethinking of how we should structure the economy.

The third concern centers on what I term the urban policy industrial complex. Far too much work occurs within a large industrial complex of funders, government agencies, think tanks, institutes, and academia centered around urban policy, without demonstrable impact. Many community-based organizations are critical of careerist policy professionals who are more concerned with their own career trajectories than with a community in trouble. Within academia, we are guilty as well. Syllabi, master's programs, faculty, and researchers are primarily focused on small, silo projects or evaluations, or debating methods, and the real work of transforming society is left up to people "out there" somewhere in the "real world." This policy industrial complex is highly insular and self-reproducing. There are few incentives to be progressive, and indeed, the status quo appears to be generating, implementing, and evaluating policies and programs over and over without any real effort to substantively alter the upstream conditions of urban capitalism that are often leading to the problems in the first place.

So what do I mean then by a critical urban policy? I define critical urban policy as a process for the development, implementation, and evaluation of urban policies that aim at *both* specific social and economic problems, but also the broader structural conditions that contribute to them and that must be addressed in order to prevent recurrences of the problem in the future. This is more akin to public health practice and preventive medicine than what is traditionally considered social policy, and this is precisely the point. Social policy is always playing catch-up, always trying to fix "downstream" problems, and never capable or politically engaged enough to move upstream. Critical urban policy, therefore, must move upstream politically, methodologically, epistemologically, and ethically. This means tackling real, challenging, and seemingly insurmountable issues: racism, discrimination, political disenfranchisement, and other problems that prevent substantive social and economic empowerment. We have seen how the paradigm for urban revitalization based on a neoliberal model fares; the future demands better.

Appendixes

APPENDIX A: THE COMMUNITIES

The communities in this study were chosen for several reasons. First, they are geographically in the center of the urban core, which is both a historically impoverished area that has just undergone a remarkable transformation through redevelopment downtown, and a diverse, multi-ethnic area. The study area is demarcated by the three zip codes: 92101, 92102, and 92113 (see Map 1 at the end of this appendix). These include the Centre City Plan Area (the area of most of the redevelopment activity) as well as the neighboring communities to the east and southeast of that area. I refer to these collectively as central San Diego; it is in essence what some might refer to as the "inner city." Choosing this area, therefore, allows a closer examination of the redevelopment and revitalization of an inner city over a long period. We can directly see the effects of redevelopment, the changes in labor market data, and the shifts in census data over time. The second reason to choose this area was for data gathering purposes: zip code level analyses allow the use of a large range of data over time, as well as a growing breadth of different types of data. Third, regarding the evaluation of the impact of redevelopment, these areas are adjacent to the largest job creation effort in the city; thousands of new jobs have been created in the urban core of 92101. According to most economic models, this should generate catalytic effects in adjacent and nearby communities as more people move into the booming downtown to work, or at least commute to work there. Sampling from these adjacent zip codes allows the testing of this catalytic model.

One of the most striking aspects of even a cursory look at the census data for these communities shows that further analysis is needed to understand what is happening with the inner city in terms of economic opportunity and unemployment. Table A.1 provides a statistical snapshot of selected economic characteristics of the study area during the period between 1990 and 2000. These data raise a host of questions that I pursue in other chapters in the book.

First and foremost, the period between 1990 and 2000 saw some of the greatest job creation in the inner city. Redevelopment in 92101 generated an estimated 15,000 permanent jobs in the downtown area (CCDC 2004), yet during the same time period, though unemployment dropped from 12.6 to 7.6 percent, poverty actually increased from 15 percent to 20 percent. This may be due to an influx of far more poor residents—such as those moving into SRO housing, on disability, or on fixed incomes, but increases in housing for these occupants are not adequate to explain the change. To put the question more simply, why would redevelopment and job creation *increase* poverty? The problem, however, becomes more serious if we look at adjacent zip codes: the poor communities with historically high unemployment in 92102 and 92113. In those areas the poverty rate remained nearly unchanged (dropping

TABLE A.1. Selected Economic Characteristics of Central San Diego, by Zip Code

	92101	92102	92113
Poverty (1990)	15%	32%	39%
Poverty (2000)	23%	32%	37%
Poverty (2012)	22%	28%	38%
Unemployment (1990)	12.6%	12.0%	14.7%
Unemployment (2000)	7.6%	9.6%	15.1%
Unemployment (2012)	7.9%	8.9%	16.3%
Working poor (income at 2× FPL) (1990)	46%	65%	70%
Working poor (income at 2× FPL) (2000)	50%	66%	71%
Working poor (income at 2× FPL) (2012)	39%	57%	72%
Households with public assistance income (2000)	2%	11%	15%
Households with public assistance income (2012)	1.7%	4.3%	8.3%

SOURCE: U.S. Decennial Census 1990 and 2000; ACS 2012 five-year estimates.

3 percent in 92113), while unemployment both dropped and increased. While this is not a full and thorough analysis of the impact of redevelopment and urban revitalization, this simple statistical overview does raise the broader question, one that this book addresses: why did the creation of so many new jobs not have a great impact on the communities?

Another way to view these communities is by looking at not simply the poverty rate, which is high, but the percentage of those who are working poor, that is, who have incomes up to 200 percent of the poverty rate. This amount, double the poverty line, is a critical threshold. It is still too little to provide a level of self-sufficiency for many families and individuals, and yet it is also the level at which most people will become ineligible for most public services. This rate is often termed the "working poor" by scholars who study low-wage work. Central San Diego has a staggering 68 percent of residents who are within this income range. In short, this is a poor set of communities, even though the downtown area, 92101, is dramatically changed from fifteen years ago, with a far higher income group moving in to take advantage of new high-rise housing.

Another difference with the study of San Diego's urban core when compared with older, Midwest and East Coast cities is that the debates about urban poverty in the latter have largely been centered on African American communities, while the emerging Sunbelt cities are more diverse in terms of the demographics of concentrated poverty and the working poor.

These communities are also heavily immigrant-dense and contain a significant portion of the city's African American residents, but they are predominantly Latino; overall, nearly two-thirds of the resident community is Latino, much of it from recent immigration. The only exception to this is the downtown area, 92101, which has seen a significant amount of gentrification and influx of nonminority residents over the past two decades. While the area is a long-standing historical destination for Latin American and Asian immigrants, it is Latinos who are by far the largest ethnicity in the area, and as a segment of the local population they have grown significantly over time. Overall, central San Diego is 64 percent Latino, with the vast majority being in the two more eastern portions of the inner city. As Table A.2 shows, this growth in population is also a shift, out of the revitalized downtown of 92101, eastward into the other two zip codes. This is largely due to the gentrification effects of

TABLE A.2. Portion of Latino Population over Time, by Zip Code

	92101	92102	92113
Latino 1990	24%	54%	65%
Latino 2000	22%	62%	74%
Latino 2012	22%	62%	74%

SOURCE: U.S. Decennial Census 1990 and 2000; ACS 2012 five-year estimates.

urban redevelopment in the downtown area. Rents have jumped significantly and pushed up housing costs as one travels east.

Overall, central San Diego remains a poor area, relatively speaking, though the transformation of the downtown area has changed the overall demographics significantly. The picture emerging in the new, postindustrial, redeveloped, revitalized metropolis is one where the older characteristics of urban poverty and ghettoes have given way to urban renewal and historically low unemployment and crime, but yet growing poverty and growing numbers of the working poor. These are families and individuals who have left welfare, entered the workforce, and by all accounts are "playing by the rules" but who are losing in the game. Their chances for occupational and income mobility are increasingly limited, and the "new" urban economy is not one where there are any clear avenues out of the ranks of "just getting by." Instead of chronic unemployment, we have chronic underemployment; instead of chronic substance abuse and gang violence, we have chronic illicit entrepreneurialism, which has provided an alternative to violent and property crime but is still an entirely deregulated and risky form of economic activity.

APPENDIX B: SERVANT CLASS OCCUPATIONS IN SAN DIEGO

The occupations in Table A.3 are those that earn less than a self-sufficiency wage for 2013 in San Diego and are exclusively service producing rather than goods producing.

APPENDIX C: SURVEY DATA AND METHODOLOGY

Surveys were conducted for this study between 2002 and 2013 in consecutive waves, sampling the three zip codes of 92101, 92102, and 92113. Sampling was restricted to residents eighteen to sixty-five years of age. In-person interviews as well as mail-in surveys were conducted through

TABLE A.3. Servant Class Occupations in San Diego

Occupation	Wage ($)
Retail salespersons	10.54
Cashiers	9.95
Waitstaff	9.00
Food preparation and serving workers, including fast food	9.19
Laborers and freight, stock, and material movers, hand	11.29
Janitors and cleaners, except maids and housekeeping cleaners	11.83
Stock clerks and order fillers	11.38
Cooks, restaurant	11.59
Security guards	11.53
Maintenance and repair workers, general	17.87
Landscapers and groundskeepers	11.69
Maids and housekeeping cleaners	10.00
Food preparation workers	9.66
Dining room and cafeteria attendants and bartender helpers	8.85
Cooks, fast food	9.12
Counter and rental clerks	12.55
Counter attendants, cafeteria, food concession, and coffee shop	9.45
Bartenders	9.19
Personal care aides	10.31
Dishwashers	9.17
Childcare workers	11.13
Hosts and hostesses, restaurant, lounge, and coffee shop	9.03
Home health aides	11.00
Cleaners of vehicles and equipment	10.39
Amusement and recreation attendants	9.12
Recreation workers	11.23
Hotel, motel, and resort desk clerks	11.98
Food servers, nonrestaurant	10.04
Hairdressers, hairstylists, and cosmetologists	12.38
Parking lot attendants	9.21

SOURCE: BLS Industry and Occupation Wage Data 2013.

multiple waves and pooled to a final sample of 421 residents. A randomly selected three-digit sequence was used at each survey interval to determine census block groups from which to sample, and every *n*th residence.

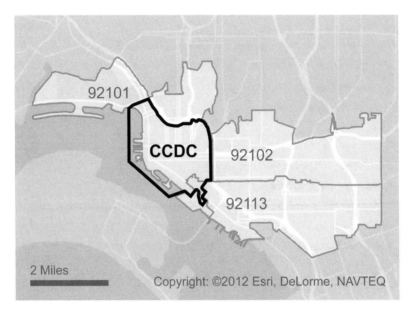

Map 1

Bibliography

Abowd, John M., and Richard B. Freeman 1991. *Immigration, Trade and the Labor Market*. Chicago: University of Chicago Press.

Abutaleb, Yasmeen. 2013. "Caregivers: Two-Fifths of U.S. Adults Care for Sick, Elderly Relatives." *Reuters*, June 20. http://www.reuters.com/article/us-usa -health-caregivers-idUSBRE95J03X20130620.

ACS (American Community Survey). 2013. *American Community Survey Multi-Year Data Release*. Washington, D.C.: Census Bureau.

Alaimo, K., C. M. Olson, E. A. Frongillo Jr., and R. R. Briefel. 2001. "Food Insufficiency, Family Income, and Health in U.S. Preschool and School-Aged Children." *American Journal of Public Health* 91, no. 5: 781–86.

Allan, Emilie Andersen, and Darrell J. Steffensmeier. 1989. "Youth, Underemployment, and Property Crime: Effects of the Quantity and the Quality of Job Opportunities on Juvenile and Young Adult Arrest Rates." *American Sociological Review* 54, no. 1: 107–23.

Althauser, R. P., and A. L. Kalleberg. 1981. "Firms, Occupations, and the Structure of Labor Markets." In *Sociological Perspectives on Labor Markets*, ed. I. Berg, 119–49. New York: Academic Press.

Alvarez, Lizette. 2012. "No Savings Are Found from Welfare Drug Tests." *New York Times*, April 17.

Anderson, Elija. 2000. *Code of the Street: Decency, Violence, and the Moral Life of the Inner City*. New York: W. W. Norton.

Anderson, K. H., J. S. Butler, and F. A. Sloan. 1987. "Labor Market Segmentation: A Cluster Analysis of Job Groupings and Barriers to Entry." *Southern Economic Journal* 53: 571–90.

Anderson, Patricia M., and Philip B. Levine. 1999. "Child Care and Mothers' Employment Decisions." NBER Working Paper no. 7058. Washington, D.C.: National Bureau of Economic Research.

Appelbaum, Eileen. 1992. "Structural Change and the Growth of Temporary and Part-Time Employment." In *New Policies for the Part-Time and Contingent Workforce*, ed. V. L. duRivage, 1–14. Armonk, N.Y.: M. E. Sharp.

Appelbaum, Eileen, Annette Bernhardt, and Richard J. Murnane, eds. 2006. *Low-Wage America: How Employers Are Reshaping Opportunity in the Workplace.* New York: Russell Sage Foundation.

Avery, Robert B., Raphael W. Bostic, Paul S. Calem, and Glenn B. Canner. 1997. *Changes in the Distribution of Banking Offices.* Washington, D.C.: Federal Reserve Bulletin, 83: 1–24.

Bailey, Susan, and Nathan Whittle. 2004. "Young People: Victims of Violence." *Current Opinion in Psychiatry* 17, no. 4: 263–68.

Bailey, Thomas, and Annette Bernhardt. 1997. "In Search of the High-Road in a Low-Wage Industry." *Politics and Society* 25, no. 2: 179–201.

Barker, Kathleen, and Kathleen Christensen. 1998. *Contingent Work: American Employment Relations in Transition.* Ithaca: Cornell University Press.

Barnes, Sandra. 2005. *The Cost of Being Poor: A Comparative Study of Life in Poor Urban Neighborhoods in Gary, Indiana.* Albany: State University of New York Press.

Bates, Beth T. 1999. "No More Servants in the House." *Review of Black Political Economy* 26, no. 3: 33–49.

Baxamusa, Murtaza. 2012. "Need for Housing Is Greater Than Ever Before." *Voice of San Diego,* August 6. http://www.voiceofsandiego.org/fix-san-diego/need-for-housing-is-greater-than-ever-before/.

Berg, Nate. 2012. "The Most and Least Affordable Housing in America." *The Atlantic,* January 24.

Bernhardt, Annette, Laura Dresser, and Erin Hatton. 2003. "The Coffee Pot Wars: Unions and Firm Restructuring in the Hotel Industry." In *Low-Wage America: How Employers Are Reshaping Opportunity in the Workplace,* ed. Eileen Appelbaum, Annette Bernhardt, and Richard J. Murnane, 33–76. New York: Russell Sage Foundation.

Bernstein, Jared. 2006. *All Together Now: Common Sense for a Fair Economy.* San Francisco: Barret-Kohler.

Blank, Rebecca M., and Michael S. Barr, eds. 2009. *Insufficient Funds: Savings, Assets, Credit, and Banking among Low-Income Households.* New York: Russell Sage Foundation.

BLS Industry and Occupation Wage Data. 2013. Washington, D.C.: Bureau of Labor Statistics.

BLS Industry Location Quotient Data. 2013. Washington, D.C.: Bureau of Labor Statistics.

BLS Industry Occupation Matrix. 2011. Washington, D.C. Bureau of Labor Statistics.

Blumenberg, Evelyn, Steve Moga, and Paul Ong. 1998. "Getting Welfare Recipients to Work: Transportation and Welfare Reform—Summary of Conference Proceedings." Los Angeles: UCLA Lewis Center for Regional Policy Studies.

Bookman, Ann, and Delia Kimbrel. 2011. "Families and Elder Care in the Twenty-First Century." *Future Child* 21, no. 2: 117–40.

Borjas, George J. 1994. "The Economics of Immigration." *Journal of Economic Literature* 32, no. 4: 1667–717.

———. 1995. "The Economic Benefits from Immigration." *Journal of Economic Perspectives* 9, no. 2: 3–22.

Borjas, George J., Richard B. Freeman, and Lawrence F. Katz. 1992. "On the Labor Market Effects of Immigration and Trade." In *Immigration and the Work Force: Economic Consequences for the United States and Source Areas*, ed. George J. Borjas and Richard B. Freeman, 213–44. Chicago: University of Chicago Press.

Boyer, Christine M. 1992. "Cities for Sale: Merchandising History." In *Variations on a Theme Park*, ed. M. Sorkin, 181–204. New York: Noonday Press.

Bradshaw, Ted K. 2007. "Theories of Poverty and Antipoverty Programs in Community Development." Rural Poverty Research Center Working Paper no. 06-05. Columbia, Missouri.

Brandwein, Ruth. 1999. *Battered Women, Children, and Welfare Reform: The Ties That Bind*. Thousand Oaks, Calif.: Sage Publications.

Brisson, Marc, Malanie Drolet, and Talia Malagon. 2013. "Inequalities in Human Papillomavirus (HPV)–Associated Cancers: Implications for the Success of HPV Vaccination." *Journal of the National Cancer Institute* 105, no. 3: 158–61.

Brooks, Jennifer, and Kasey Wiedrich. 2013. *Assets and Opportunity Scorecard*. Washington, D.C.: Corporation for Enterprise Development.

Brooks-Gunn, Jeanne, and Greg J. Duncan. 1997. "The Effects of Poverty on Children." *The Future of Children* 7, no. 2, Children and Poverty: 55–71.

Buffie, Nick. 2015. "Inequality in Benefits: Low-Wage Workers Have Little Access to Paid Leave." *CEPR Blog*, December 16. http://cepr.net/blogs/cepr-blog/inequality-in-benefits-low-wage-workers-have-little-access-to-paid-leave.

Burawoy, Michael. 1975. "The Functions and Reproduction of Migrant Labor: Comparative Material from Southern African and the United States." *American Journal of Sociology* 81, no. 5: 1050–87.

Butler, Stuart. 1989. "Enterprise Zones at Last May Be Ready to Combat Urban Decay." Executive Memorandum no. 230. Washington, D.C.: Heritage Foundation.

Bynner, John, and Sofia Despotidou. 2001. "The Effects of Assets on Life Chances." Report on file. London: Center for Longitudinal Studies, Institute for Education.

Cacho, Lisa M. 2000. "'The People of California Are Suffering': The Ideology of White Injury in Discourses of Immigration." *Cultural Values* 4, no. 4: 389–418.

CALA (California Assisted Living Association). 2012. "2009 Assisted Living Summit: Expanding Options." Report on file.

Calavita, Kitty. 1984. *U.S. Immigration Law and the Control of Labor, 1820–1924*. London: Academic Press.

Caldwell, Patrick. 2012. "Romney's Race-Based Initiative." *American Prospect*, August 20.

California Association of Realtors. 2011. Market Study, San Diego. http://car.org/.

California Budget Project. 2002. "Voters Believe That Welfare Reform Should Move Families Out of Poverty." Sacramento: California Budget Project.

———. 2004. "What Happens after Welfare Recipients Leave CalWORKs?" Sacramento: California Budget Project.

———. 2012. "Key Facts about the CalWORKs Program." Sacramento: California Budget Project.

California Healthcare Foundation. 2012. *Annual Survey of the Working Uninsured.* Oakland, California.

Campbell, Jacquelyn C., and Karen L. Soeken. 1999. "Forced Sex and Intimate Partner Violence Effects on Women's Risk and Women's Health." *Violence against Women* 5, no. 9: 1017–35.

Card, David. 2001. "Immigrant Inflows, Native Outflows and the Local Labor Market Impacts of Higher Immigration." *Journal of Labor Economics* 19, no. 1: 22–64.

———. 2005. "Is the New Immigration Really so Bad?" *Economic Journal, Royal Economic Society* 115, no. 507: F300–F323.

Caroll, Hamilton. 2011. *Affirmative Reaction: New Formations of White Masculinity.* Durham: Duke University Press.

Carré, Françoise. J. 1992. "Temporary Employment in the Eighties." In *New Policies for the Part-Time and Contingent Workforce,* ed. V. L. duRivage, 45–87. Armonk, N.Y.: M. E. Sharp.

Carré, Françoise, and Chris Tilly. 2008. "Continuity and Change in Low-Wage Work in U.S. Retail Trade." Research report. Center for Social Policy, McCormack Graduate School of Policy Studies, University of Massachusetts, Boston.

———. 2009. "America's Biggest Low-Wage Industry: Continuity and Change in Retail Jobs." Center for Social Policy Working Paper no. 2009-6. University of Massachusetts, Boston.

Carré, Françoise, Chris Tilly, and Brandynn Holgate. 2010. "Competitive Strategies in the U.S. Retail Industry: Consequences for Jobs in Food and Consumer Electronics Stores." Center for Social Policy SP Working Paper no. 2010-1. University of Massachusetts, Boston.

Caskey, John P. 1994. *Fringe Banking: Check-Cashing Outlets, Pawnshops, and the Poor.* New York: Russell Sage Foundation.

Catanzarite, Lisa. 1998. "Immigrant Latino Representation and Earnings Penalties in Occupations." *Research in Social Stratification and Mobility* 16: 147–79.

———. 2000. "Brown-Collar Jobs: Occupational Segregation and Earnings of Recent-Immigrant Latino Workers." *Sociological Perspectives* 43, no. 1: 45–75.

———. 2002. "Dynamics of Segregation and Earnings in Brown-Collar Occupations." *Work and Occupations* 29: 300–345.

Catanzarite, Lisa, and Michael B. Aguilera. 2002. "Working with Co-Ethnics: Earnings Penalties for Latino Immigrants at Latino Job Sites." *Social Problems* 49, no. 1: 101–27.

CB Richard Ellis. 2013. *Real Estate Market Report.* San Diego, California.

CCDC (Centre City Development Corporation). 2004. *Annual Report.* San Diego: CCDC.

———. 2010. *Annual Report.* San Diego: CCDC.

———. 2011. *Annual Report.* San Diego: CCDC.

———. 2012. *Annual Report.* San Diego: CCDC.

Center for Responsible Lending. 2009. "Payday Loans: A Stepping Stone to Debt, Reduced Credit Options and Bankruptcy." Policy brief. Washington, D.C.: Center for Responsible Lending. http://www.responsiblelending.org /research-publication/payday-loans-stepping-stone-debt-reduced-credit-options -and-bankruptcy.

Central San Diego Survey. 2002–10. Author's data files.

CFED (Center for Enterprise Development). 2008. *Assets and Opportunity Scorecard*. Washington, D.C.

Chapin, Tim. 2002. "Beyond the Entrepreneurial City: Municipal Capitalism in San Diego." *Journal of Urban Affairs* 24, no. 5: 565–81.

———. 2004. "Sports Facilities as Urban Development Catalysts: Assessing Baltimore's Camden Yards and Cleveland's Gateway Complex." *Journal of the American Planning Association* 70, no. 2: 193–209.

———. 2007. "Local Governments as Policy Entrepreneurs: Evaluating Florida's 'Concurrency Experiment.'" *Urban Affairs Review* 42, no. 4: 505–32.

Child Care Aware. 2012. "Child Care in California." http://www.naccrra.org /sites/default/files/default_site_pages/2012/california_060612-3.pdf.

Chin, Pearl. 2004. "Payday Loans: The Case for Federal Legislation." *University of Illinois Law Review*, 723–54.

Chiswick, Barry. 1988. "Illegal Immigration and Immigration Control." *Journal of Economic Perspectives* 2, no. 3: 101–15.

Chiswick, Barry R., and Teresa A. Sullivan. 1995. "The New Immigrants." In *State of the Union: America in the 1990s*, vol. 2, *Social Trends*, ed. R. Farley, 211–70. New York: Russell Sage Foundation.

City of San Diego. 2012. *Centre City Planning Report*. City of San Diego Planning Department.

———. 2013. *Centre City Planning Report*. City of San Diego Planning Department.

City of San Diego District Attorney. 2011. Lawsuit against Countrywide Home Lenders. San Diego: City Attorney's Office.

Clark, Terry N. 2004. *The City as an Entertainment Machine*. Amsterdam: Jai/ Elsevier.

Clarke, Susan E., and Gary L. Gaile. 1998. *The Work of Cities*. Minneapolis: University of Minnesota Press.

Cohen, Robin A., Renee M. Gindi, and Whitney K. Kirzinger. 2011. "Financial Burden of Medical Care: Early Release of Estimates from the National Health Interview Survey, January–June." Washington, D.C.: Division of Health Interview Statistics, National Center for Health Statistics.

Collins, Jane, and Victoria Mayer. 2010. *Both Hands Tied: Welfare Reform and the Race to the Bottom in the Low-Wage Labor Market*. Chicago: University of Chicago Press.

Conrad, C. A. 1999. "Soft Skills and the Minority Workforce." Joint Center for Political and Economic Studies. Washington, D.C.

Corak, Miles. 2012. "How to Slide Down the 'Great Gatsby Curve': Inequality, Life Chances, and Public Policy in the United States." Center for American Progress, December 5. https://www.americanprogress.org/wp-content/uploads /2012/12/CorakMiddleClass-INTRO.pdf.

Corcoran, Mary. 1995. "Rags to Rags: Poverty and Mobility in the United States."
    Annual Review of Sociology 21: 237–67.
CPI (Center on Policy Inititatives). 2006. "Downtown for Everybody?" Research
    report. http://www.cpisandiego.org/downtown_for_everybody.
———. 2011. "Foreclosure: The Cost Communities Pay." By Corinne Wilson.
    June. http://d3n8a8pro7vhmx.cloudfront.net/onlinecpi/pages/331/attachments
    /original/1399853444/Foreclosure_4page_eng_web.pdf?1399853444.
CSI Market. 2014. Reports. San Diego: CSI.
Danziger, Sheldon, and Gottschalk, Peter. 1985. "The Poverty of Losing Ground."
    Challenge 28, no. 2: 32–38.
Dardia, Michael. 1998. *Subsidizing Redevelopment in California.* San Francisco:
    Public Policy Institute of California.
Datko, Karen. 2012. "Can Poor People Have HDTVs? Being Counted as Poor in
    America Doesn't Mean You're Doing without Cable, Air Conditioning and
    Video Games." *MSN Money,* August 2. http://money.msn.com/saving-money
    -tips/post.aspx?post=af23341f-50a1-4bd3-9cd1-412865aac16f.
Davidson, Chandler, and Charles Gaitz. 1974. "Are the Poor Different—A Com-
    parison of Work Behavior and Attitudes among the Urban Poor and Non-
    poor." *Social Problems* 22, no. 2: 229–45.
Davis, Kristina. 2010. "Crime Rate Continues to Plummet in San Diego." *San
    Diego Union Tribune,* January 27.
Di Piero, Thomas. 2002. *White Men Aren't.* Durham: Duke University Press.
Dohan, Daniel. 2003. *The Price of Poverty: Money, Work, and Culture in the Mexi-
    can American Barrio.* Berkeley: University of California Press.
Dolbeare, Kenneth, and Russell M. Lidman. 1985. "Ideology and Policy Research:
    The Case of Murray's Losing Ground." *Review of Policy Research* 4, no. 4:
    587–94.
Doeringer, Peter, Paul Feldman, David Gordon, Michael Piore, and Michael
    Reich. 1969. *Low Income Labor Markets and Urban Manpower Programs: A
    Critical Assessment.* Washington, D.C.: U.S. Department of Labor.
Doussard, Marc. 2013. *Degraded Work: The Struggle at the Bottom of the Labor
    Market.* Minneapolis: University of Minnesota Press.
D'Souza, Dinesh. 1996. *The End of Racism: Principles for a Multiracial Society.*
    New York: Free Press.
Duggan, Lisa. 2012. *The Twilight of Equality? Neoliberalism, Cultural Politics and
    the Attack on Democracy.* Boston: Beacon Press.
Duneier, Mitchell. 2000. *Sidewalk.* New York: Farrar, Straus and Giroux.
Dyer, Richard. 1997. *White: Essays on Race and Culture.* New York: Routledge.
Edin, Kathryn, and Maria J. Kefalas. 2007. *Promises I Can Keep: Why Poor Women
    Put Motherhood before Marriage.* Berkeley: University of California Press.
Editors. 2013. "Editorial: Food Stamps Second Chance: After the Farm Bill
    Defeat, an Opportunity for Real Reform." *Wall Street Journal,* June 21.
Ehrenreich, Barbara. 2001. *Nickel and Dimed: On (Not) Getting By in America.*
    New York: Metropolitan Books.
Eisinger, Peter. 1998. "City Politics in an Era of Federal Devolution." *Urban
    Affairs Review* 33: 330–31.

———. 2000. "The Politics of Bread and Circuses." *Urban Affairs Review* 35, no. 3: 316–33.

EPI (Economic Policy Institute). 2011. *The State of Working America*. Washington, D.C.: Economic Policy Institute.

Erie, Steven P., Vladimir Kogan, and Scott A. MacKenzie. 2011. *Paradise Plundered: Fiscal Crisis and Governance Failures in San Diego*. Palo Alto: Stanford University Press.

Evans, Gary. 2004. "The Environment of Childhood Poverty." *American Psychologist* 59, no. 2: 77–92.

Fainstein, Susan S. 2001. *The City Builders: Property Development in New York and London, 1980–2000*. New York: Routledge.

Fainstein, Susan, and Robert Stokes. 1998. "Spaces for Play: The Impacts of Entertainment Development on New York City." *Economic Development Quarterly* 12: 150–65.

Faludi, Susan. 1999. *Stiffed: The Betrayal of the American Man*. New York: Harper Perennial.

Farber, Henry S. 1998. "Employment Insecurity: The Decline in Worker-Firm Attachment in the United States." Center for Economics Policy Studies Working Paper no. 172. Washington, D.C.

Farley, Reynolds, Sheldon Danziger, and Harry J. Holzer, eds. 2000. *Detroit Divided: A Volume in the Multi-City Study of Urban Inequality*. New York: Russell Sage Foundation.

FDIC (Federal Deposit Insurance Corporation). 2012. *National Survey of Unbanked and Underbanked Households*. Washington, D.C.: FDIC.

Federal Financial Institutions Examination Council. 2012. HDMA Data from San Diego Filings. http://www.ffiec.gov.

Feige, Edgar. 1990. "Defining and Estimating Underground and Informal Economies: The New Institutional Economics Approach." *World Development* 18, no. 7: 989–1002.

Ferguson, Rod. 2003. *Aberrations in Black: Toward a Queer of Color Critique*. Minneapolis: University of Minnesota Press.

Fitzgerald, Joan. 2006. *Moving Up in the New Economy: Career Ladders for U.S. Workers*. Ithaca: Cornell University Press.

Florida, Richard. 2002. *The Rise of the Creative Class: And How It's Transforming Work, Leisure, Community and Everyday Life*. New York: Basic Books.

———. 2010. *Who's Your City?* New York: Basic Books.

Folbre, Nancy. 1994. *Who Pays for the Kids? Gender and the Structures of Constraint*. New York: Routledge.

Freeman, Richard B. 1999. *The New Inequality: Creating Solutions for a Poor America*. Boston: Beacon Press.

Frey, William H., and Reynolds Farley. 1996. "Latino, Asian, and Black Segregation in U.S. Metropolitan Areas: Are Multiethnic Metros Different?" *Demography* 33, no. 1: 35–50.

Friedberg, Rachel, and Jennifer Hunt. 1995. "The Impact of Immigrants on Host Country Wages, Employment, and Growth." *Journal of Economic Perspectives* 9, no. 2: 23–44.

Frieden, Bernard J., and Lynne B. Sagalyn. 1991. *Downtown Inc.: How America Rebuilds Cities.* Cambridge, Mass.: MIT Press.

Fukuyama, Francis. 1992. *The End of History and the Last Man.* New York: Free Press.

Funkhouser, Edward, and Stephen J. Trejo. 1995. "The Labor Market Skills of Recent Male Immigrants: Evidence from the Current Population Survey." *Industrial and Labor Relations Review* 48, no. 4: 792–811.

Gilens, Martin. 1999. *Why Americans Hate Welfare: Race, Media, and the Politics of Antipoverty Policy.* Chicago: University of Chicago Press.

Gittleman, M. B., and D. R. Howe. 1995. "Changes in the Structure and Quality of Jobs in the United States: Effects by Race and Gender." *Industrial and Labor Relations Review* 48: 420–44.

Glaeser, Edward. 2012. *Triumph of the City: How Our Greatest Invention Makes Us Richer, Smarter, Greener, Healthier, and Happier.* New York: Penguin.

Goldman Sachs. 2009. *Real Estate Submarket Report.* New York: Goldman Sachs Real Estate Analytics.

Goldsmith, William, and Edward Blakely. 2010. *Separate Societies: Poverty and Inequality in U.S. Cities.* Philadelphia: Temple University Press.

Gonos, George. 1998. "The Interaction between Market Incentives and Government Actions." In *Contingent Work: American Employment Relations in Transition,* ed. Kathleen Barker and Kathleen Christensen, 170–91. Ithaca: Cornell University Press.

Goodwin, Leonard. 1972. *Do the Poor Want to Work? A Social-Psychological Study of Work Orientations.* Washington, D.C.: Brookings Institution.

Gordon, D. M., R. Edwards, and M. Reich. 1982. *Segmented Work, Divided Workers: The Historical Transformation of Labor in the United States.* Cambridge: Cambridge University Press.

Gordon, Linda. 1994. *Pitied but Not Entitled: Single Mothers and the History of Welfare.* New York: Free Press.

Grodach, Carl. 2012. "Cultural Economy Planning in Creative Cities: Discourse and Practice." *International Journal of Urban and Regional Research* 37, no. 5: 1747–65.

Grogan, Paul S., and Tony Proscio. 2000. *Comeback Cities: A Blueprint for Urban Neighborhood Revival.* New York: Basic Books.

Guha-Khasnobis, Basudeb, Ravi Kanbur, and Elinor Ostrom. 2006. *Linking the Formal and Informal Economy: Concepts and Policies.* New York: Oxford University Press.

Gustafson, Kaaryn. 2009. "The Criminalization of Poverty." *Journal of Criminal Law and Criminology* 99, no. 3: 643–716.

Hacker, Jacob. 2006. *The Great Risk Shift: The Assault on American Jobs, Families, Health Care and Retirement And How You Can Fight Back.* New York: Cambridge University Press.

Hackworth, Ian. 2006. *The Neoliberal City: Governance, Ideology, and Development in American Urbanism.* Ithaca: Cornell University Press.

Hadass, Y. S. 2004. "The Effect of Internet Recruiting on the Matching of Workers and Employers." *Harvard Business Review,* February 10, 1–36.

Hall, Tim, and Phil Hubbard. 1998. *The Entrepreneurial City: Geographies of Politics, Regime, and Representation.* New York: Wiley.

Hancock, Ange Marie. 2004. *The Politics of Disgust: The Public Identity of the Welfare Queen.* New York: New York University Press.

Hannigan, John. 1998. *Fantasy City: Pleasure and Profit in the Postmodern Metropolis.* New York: Routledge.

Hart, J. K. 1973. "Informal Income Opportunities and Urban Employment in Ghana." *Journal of Modern African Studies* 11, no. 1: 61–89.

Harvey, David. 1989. *The Urban Experience.* New York: Blackwell.

Healy, Jane. 1998. *Failure to Connect: How Computers Affect Our Children's Minds—For Better and Worse.* New York: Simon and Schuster.

Hertz, Tom. 2006. *Understanding Mobility in America.* Research report. Washington, D.C.: Center for American Progress.

Himmelstein, David U., Deborah Thorne, Elizabeth Warren, and Steffie Woolhandler. 2009. "Medical Bankruptcy in the United States, 2007: Results of a National Study." *American Journal of Medicine* 122, no. 8: 741–46.

Hogan, Richard. 2003. *The Failure of Planning: Permitting Sprawl in San Diego Suburbs, 1970–1999.* Columbus: Ohio State University Press.

Hogler, Raymond L., Christine Henle, and Carol Bemus. 1998. "Internet Recruiting and Employment Discrimination: A Legal Perspective." *Human Resource Management Review* 8, no. 2: 149–64.

Holzer, Harry. 2001. "Spatial Mismatch and Costly Suburban Commutes: Can Commuting Subsidies Help?" *Urban Studies* 38: 1305–18.

———. 2007. "Collateral Costs: The Effects of Incarceration on the Employment and Earnings of Young Workers." Institute for the Study of Work Discussion Paper No. 3118. Bonn, Germany.

Holzer, Harry J., Julia I Lane, David B. Rosenblum, and Fredrik Andersson. 2011. *Where Are All the Good Jobs Going? What National and Local Job Quality and Dynamics Mean for U.S. Workers.* New York: Russell Sage Foundation.

Hondagneu-Sotelo, P. 2001. *Doméstica: Immigrant Workers Cleaning and Caring in the Shadow of Affluence.* Berkeley: University of California Press.

Hudson, K. 1999. "No Shortage of Nonstandard Jobs." Briefing paper. Washington, D.C.: Economic Policy Institute.

———. 2001. "The Disposable Worker." *Monthly Review* 52: 43–55.

Jargowsky, Paul A., and Rebecca Yang. 2005. *The "Underclass" Revisited: A Social Problem in Decline.* Washington, D.C.: Brookings Institution, Metropolitan Policy Program.

Jessop, Bill, and Nick Sum. 2000. "An Entrepreneurial City in Action: Hong Kong's Emerging Strategies in and for Interurban Completion." *Urban Studies* 37, no. 12: 2287–313.

Joassart, Pascale, and Daniel Flaming. 2002. *Workers without Rights.* Los Angeles Economic Roundtable. Los Angeles California.

Johnston, David Cay. 1995. "The Nation: The Servant Class Is at the Counter." *New York Times*, August 27. http://www.nytimes.com/1995/08/27/weekinre view/the-nation-the-servant-class-is-at-the-counter.html.

Judd, Dennis R. 1999. *The Tourist City*. New Haven: Yale University Press.

Kaiser Family Foundation. 2011. *Immigrant Status and Health Care Coverage*. Los Angeles: Kaiser Family Foundation.

Kalleberg, A. L. 2001. "Review: Farewell to Commitment? Changing Employment Relations and Labor Markets in the United States." *Contemporary Sociology* 30, no. 1: 9–12.

———. 2011. *Good Jobs, Bad Jobs: The Rise of Polarized and Precarious Employment Systems in the United States, 1970s to 2000s*. New York: Russell Sage Foundation.

Kalleberg, A. L., E. Rasell, N. Cassirer, B. F. Reskin, K. Hudson, D. Webster, E. Appelbaum, and R. Spatler-Roth. 1997. *Nonstandard Work, Substandard Jobs: Flexible Work Arrangements in the U.S.* Washington, D.C.: Economic Policy Institute and Women's Research and Educational Institute.

Kalleberg, A. L., B. F. Reskin, and K. Hudson. 2000. "Bad Jobs in America: Standard and Nonstandard Employment Relations and Job Quality in the United States." *American Sociological Review* 65: 256–78.

Kalleberg, A. L., M. Wallace, and R. P. Althauser. 1981. "Economic Segmentation, Worker Power, and Income Inequality." *American Journal of Sociology* 87, no. 3: 651–83.

Kaplan, H. Roy, and Curt Tausky. 1972. "Cadillac: The Function of and Commitment to Work among the Hard-Core Unemployed." *Social Problems* 19, no. 4: 469–83.

Karjanen, David. 2008. "Gender, Race, and Nation in the Making of Mexican Migrant Labor in the United States." *Latin American Perspectives* 35: 51–63.

———. 2010a. "The Informalization of the Economy: Subcontracting and Cash-in-Hand Work in the U.S. Service and Construction Sectors." Paper presented at UCLA, Institute for Research on Labor and Employment.

———. 2010b. "Opposition to the Living Wage: Discourse, Rhetoric, and American Exceptionalism." *Anthropology of Work Review* 31: 4–14.

Kasarda, John. 1989. "Urban Industrial Transition and the Underclass." *Annals of the American Academy of Political and Social Science* 501: 26–47.

Katznelson, Ira. *When Affirmative Action Was White: An Untold History of Racial Inequality in Twentieth-Century America*. New York: W. W. Norton.

Keating, William D., and Norman Krumholz, eds. *Rebuilding Urban Neighborhoods*. Thousand Oaks, Calif.: Sage Publications.

Kimmel, Jean. 1998. "Child Care Costs as a Barrier to Employment for Single and Married Mothers." *Review of Economics and Statistics* 80, no. 2: 287–99.

Kolko, Jed, and David Neumark. 2009. *Do California's Enterprise Zones Create Jobs?* Sacramento: Public Policy Institute of California.

Korenman, Sanders, and Jane E. Miller. 1997. "Effects of Long-Term Poverty on Physical Health of Children in the National Longitudinal Survey of Youth." In *Consequences of Growing Up Poor*, ed. Greg J. Duncan and Jeanne Brooks-Gunn, 70–99. New York: Russell Sage Foundation.

Kuhn, Peter, and Mikal Skuterud. 2000. "Job Search Methods: Internet versus Traditional." *Monthly Labor Review*, October, 3–11.

Kuznicki, Jason. 2009. "Never a Neutral State: American Race Relations and Government." *PowerCato Journal* 29, no. 3: 417–53.

Lamb, Michael E., and Lieselotte Ahnert. 2007. "Nonparental Child Care: Context, Concepts, Correlates, and Consequences." In *Handbook of Child Psychology*, vol. 4, *Child Psychology in Practice*, ed. K. Ann Renninger and Irving E. Sigel, 3–23. New York: Wiley.

Lambert, Susan J. 2008. "Passing the Buck: Labor Flexibility Practices that Transfer Risk Onto Hourly Works." *Human Relations* 61, no. 9: 1203–27.

LeRoy, Greg. 2005. *The Great American Jobs Scam.* San Francisco: Berrett-Koehler.

Lee, Morgan. 2012. "San Diego Gas Prices among Highest in Nation." *San Diego Union Tribune*, February 27.

Leff, Mark H. 1973. "Consensus for Reform: The Mothers'-Pension Movement in the Progressive Era." *Social Service Review* 47, no. 3: 397–417.

Lewis, Oscar. 1975. *Five Families: Mexican Case Studies in the Culture of Poverty.* New York: Basic Books.

Lipsitz, George. 1998. *The Possessive Investment in Whiteness.* Philadelphia: Temple University Press.

Littwin, Angela K. 2012. "The Do-It-Yourself Mirage: Complexity in the Bankruptcy System." In *Broke: How Debt Bankrupts the Middle Class*, ed. Katherine Porter, 157–74. Palo Alto: Stanford University Press.

Lubove, Roy. 1968. "Economic Security and Social Conflict in America: The Early Twentieth Century, Part II." *Journal of Social History* 1, no. 4: 325–50.

Mahler, Sarah. 1995. *American Dreaming: Immigrant Life on the Margins.* Princeton: Princeton University Press.

Mann, Ronald, J. 2006. "Bankruptcy Reform and the 'Sweat Box' of Credit Card Debt." *University of Illinois Law Review.* Law and Economics Research Paper No. 75. University of Texas Law.

Mann, Ronald J., and Jim Hawkins. 2007. "Just until Payday." *UCLA Law Review* 54. Law and Economics Research Paper No. 83. University of Texas Law.

Marcelli, Enrico, Colin C. Williams, and Pascale Joassart. 2010. *Informal Work in Developed Nations.* New York: Routledge.

Marchevsky, Alejandra, and Jeanne Theoharis. 2006. *Not Working: Latina Immigrants, Low-Wage Jobs, and the Failure of Welfare Reform.* New York: New York University Press.

Massey, Douglas. 1995. "The New Geography of Inequality in Urban America." In *Suburbs and Cities: Changing Patterns in Metropolitan Living*, ed. Domestic Strategy Group, 27–37. Washington, D.C.: Aspen Institute.

———. 2009. "Globalization and Inequality: Explaining American Exceptionalism." *European Sociological Review* 25, no. 1: 9–23.

Massey, Douglas, and Nancy Denton. 1993. *American Apartheid: Segregation and the Making of the Underclass.* Cambridge, Mass: Harvard University Press.

Massey, Douglas S., and Mitchell L. Eggers. 1993. "The Spatial Concentration of Affluence and Poverty during the 1970s." *Urban Affairs Review* 29, no. 2: 299–315.

Matza, David. 1966. "The Disreputable Poor." In *Class, Status and Power: Social Stratification in Comparative Perspective*, ed. Reinhard Bendix and Seymour Martin Lipset, 289–302. 2nd ed. New York: Aldine.

———. 1971 "Poverty and Disrepute." In *Contemporary Social Problems*, ed. Robert Merton and Robert Nisbet, 619–69. 3rd ed. New York: Aldine.

McCoy, Patricia. 2005. "A Behavioral Analysis of Predatory Lending." *Akron Law Review* 38, no. 4: 725–39.

McPhail, Ruth, and Ron Fisher. 2008. "It's More than Wages: Analysis of the Impact of Internal Labour Markets on the Quality of Jobs." *International Journal of Human Resource Management* 19: 461–72.

Mead, Lawrence. 1992. *The New Politics of Poverty: The Nonworking Poor in America*. New York: Basic Books.

———. 2008. *Beyond Entitlement: The Social Obligations of Citizenship*. New York: Simon and Schuster.

Mincy, Ronald, ed. 2006. *Black Males Left Behind*. Washington, D.C.: Urban Institute Press.

Moretti, Enrico. 2012. *The New Geography of Jobs*. New York: Houghton Mifflin Harcourt.

Moss, Philip, and Chris Tilly. 1996. "'Soft' Skills and Race: An Investigation of Black Men's Employment Problems." *Work and Occupations* 23: 252–76.

Mossberger, Karen, Caroline J. Tolbert, and Mary Stansbury. 2003. *Virtual Inequality: Beyond the Digital Divide*. Washington, D.C.: Georgetown University Press.

Mullainathan, S., and E. Shafir. 2009. "Savings Policy and Decisionmaking in Low-Income Households." In *Insufficient Funds: Savings, Assets, Credit and Banking, among Low-Income Households*, ed. M. Barr and R. Blank, 121–45. New York: Russell Sage Foundation.

Murray, Charles. 1984. *Losing Ground*. New York: Basic Books.

Murray, Charles, and Richard Hernstein. 1996. *Bell Curve: Intelligence and Class Structure in American Life*. New York: Free Press.

Myrdal, Gunnar. 1944. *An American Dilemma: The Negro Problem and Modern Democracy*. Reprint. New York: McGraw-Hill, 1964.

Naples, Nancy. 1997. "The 'New Consensus' on the Gendered Social Contract: The 1987–1988 U.S. Congressional Hearings on Welfare Reform." *Signs: Journal of Women in Culture and Society* 22, no. 4: 907–45.

———. 2003. *Feminism and Method: Ethnography, Discourse Analysis, and Activist Research*. New York: Routledge.

Nelson, Richard, R. 1956. "A Theory of the Low-Level Equilibrium Trap in Underdeveloped Economies." *American Economic Review* 46, no. 5: 894–908.

Neubeck, Kenneth J., and Noel A Cazenave. 2001. *Welfare Racism: Playing the Race Card against America's Poor*. New York: Routledge.

Newman, Katherine. 1999. *Falling from Grace: Downward Mobility in the Age of Affluence*. Berkeley: University of California Press.

———. 2009. *No Shame in My Game: The Working Poor in the Inner City*. New York: Vintage Books.

Newman, Katherine, and Victor Chen. 2007. *The Missing Class: Portraits of the Near Poor in America*. Boston: Beacon Press.

Nielsen, Marsha L., and Kristine M. Kuhn. 2009. "Late Payments and Leery Applicants: Credit Checks as a Selection Test." *Employee Responsibilities and Rights Journal* 21: 115–30.

Nissim, Sharon G. 2010. "Stopping a Vicious Cycle: The Problems with Credit Checks in Employment and Strategies to Limit Their Use." *Georgetown Journal of Poverty Law and Policy* 28, no. 1: 45–71.

Noll, Roger G., and Andrew Zimbalist. 1997. *Sports, Jobs, and Taxes: The Economic Impact of Sports Teams and Stadiums*. Washington, D.C.: Brookings Institution Press.

O'Connor, Alice. 2001. *Poverty Knowledge: Social Science, Social Policy, and the Poor in Twentieth-Century U.S. History*. Princeton: Princeton University Press.

O'Connor, Alice, Chris Tilly, and Lawrence Bobo. 2003. *Urban Inequality: Evidence from Four Cities*. New York: Russell Sage Foundation.

Office of Family Assistance. 2010. TANF Annual Enrollees. Washington, D.C.: Office of Family Assistance.

Offner, Paul, and Harry Holzer. 2002. *Left Behind in the Labor Market: Recent Employment Trends among Young Black Men*. Washington, D.C.: Brookings Institution, Center on Urban and Metropolitan Policy.

Ong, Paul, and Evelyn Blumenberg. 1998. "Job Access, Commute and Travel Burden among Welfare Recipients." *Urban Studies* 351: 77–93.

Osterman, Paul. 1999. *Securing Prosperity: The American Labor Market: How It Has Changed and What to Do about It*. Princeton: Princeton University Press.

———. 2008. "Improving Job Quality: Policies Aimed at the Demand Side of the Low-Wage Labor Market." In *A Future of Good Jobs? America's Challenge in the Global Economy*, ed. Timothy J. Bartik and Susan N. Houseman, 203–44. Kalamazoo, Mich.: W. E. Upjohn Institute.

Osterman, Paul, and Beth Shulman. 2011. *Good Jobs America: Making Work Better for Everyone*. New York: Russell Sage Foundation.

Pager, Devah, and Hanna Shepherd. 2008. "The Sociology of Discrimination: Racial Discrimination in Employment, Housing, Credit, and Consumer Markets." *Annual Review of Sociology* 34: 181–209.

Pardo, Italo. 1996. *Managing Existence in Naples: Morality, Action, and Structure*. New York: Cambridge University Press.

Peck, Jamie. 1998. Geographies of Governance: TECs and the Neo-liberalisation of 'Local Interests.'" *Space and Polity* 2, no. 1: 5–31.

———. 2001. *Workfare States*. New York: Guilford.

Petersen, David. 1996. *Sports, Convention, and Entertainment Facilities*. Washington, D.C.: Urban Land Institute.

Phillips, Julie A., and Douglas S. Massey. 1999. "The New Labor Market: Immigrants and Wages after IRCA." *Demography* 36, no. 2: 233–46.

Pierce, Charles P. 2012. "Our Mr. Brooks Finds Another Very Important Thinker." *Esquire*, January 31. http://www.esquire.com/news-politics/politics/a12538/david-brooks-charles-murray-6649112/.

Piore, Michael J., and Peter Doeringer. 1971. *Internal Labor Markets and Manpower Adjustment*. New York: D. C. Heath and Company.

Polivka, Anne E. 1996. "Contingent and Alternative Work Arrangements, Defined." *Monthly Labor Review*, October, 3–9.

Porter, Katherine M. 2010. "Life after Debt: Understanding the Credit Restraint of Bankruptcy Debtors." *American Bankruptcy Institute Law Review* 18, no. 1: 1–42.

Port of San Diego. 2012. "Board Takes Action Advancing Proposed San Diego Convention Center Expansion." Unified Port of San Diego, September 21. https://www.portofsandiego.org/convention-center-expansion-project/3158 -board-takes-action-advancing-proposed-san-diego-convention-center-expan sion.html.

Quadrango, Jill. 1996. *The Color of Welfare: How Racism Undermined the War on Poverty*. New York: Oxford University Press.

Rangarajan, Anu. 1996. *Taking the First Steps: Helping Welfare Recipients Who Get Jobs Keep Them*. Washington, D.C.: Mathematica.

———. 2001. "Staying On, Moving Up: Strategies to Help Entry-Level Workers Retain Employment and Advance in Their Jobs." In *Low Wage Workers in the New Economy*, ed. Richard Kazis and Marc S. Miller, 91–110. Washington, D.C.: Urban Institute Press.

Raphael, Steven, and Lorien Rice. 2002. "Car Ownership, Employment, and Earnings." *Journal of Urban Economics* 52: 109–30.

Raphael, Steven, and Michael Stoll. 2003. *Modest Progress: The Narrowing Spatial Mismatch between Blacks and Jobs in the 1990s*. Washington, D.C.: Brookings Institution, Center on Urban and Metropolitan Policy.

Reardon, Sean F., and Kendra Bischoff. 2011. "Growth in the Residential Segregation of Families by Income, 1970–2009." Report from the Russell Sage Foundation. New York: Russell Sage Foundation.

Rector, Robert, and Rachel Sheffield. 2011. "Understanding Poverty in the United States: Surprising Facts about America's Poor." Heritage Foundation report. http://www.heritage.org/research/reports/2011/09/understanding-pov erty-in-the-united-states-surprising-facts-about-americas-poor.

Reder, Stephen. 2007. *Adult Education and Postsecondary Success*. Owensboro, Ky.: Council for the Advancement of Adult Literacy.

Roberts, Susan M., and Richard H. Schein. 1993. "The Entrepreneurial City: Fabricating Urban Development in Syracuse, New York." *Professional Geographer* 45, no. 1: 21–33.

Romero, Mary. 1992. *Maid in the USA*. New York: Routledge.

Sachs, Wolfgang, ed. 1992. *The Development Dictionary: A Guide to Knowledge as Power*. London: Zed Books.

Sallis, James F., Judith J. Prochaska, and Wendell C. Taylor. 2000. "A Review of Correlates of Physical Activity of Children and Adolescents." *Medicine and Science in Sports and Exercise* 32, no. 5: 963–75.

Sanders, Heywood T. 2002. "Convention Myths and Markets: A Critical Review of Convention Center Feasibility Studies." *Economic Development Quarterly* 16, no. 3: 195–210.

San Diego Apartment Association. 2010. Vacancy and rental rate survey.

San Diego County Centralized Eligibility List. 2012. Program guidelines. San Diego: County of San Diego.

Sassen, Saskia. 1991. *The Global City: New York, London, Tokyo.* Princeton: Princeton University Press.

Schneider, Daniel, and Peter Tufano. 2007. "New Savings from Old Innovations: Asset Building for the Less Affluent." In *Financing Low-Income Communities,* ed. J. S. Rubin, 13–71. New York: Russell Sage.

Schorr, Lizabeth B., and Daniel Schorr. 1988. *Within Our Reach: Breaking the Cycle of Disadvantage.* New York: Anchor Press/Doubleday.

Schoen, Doug. 2012. "Newsweek/Daily Beast Poll Finds Majorities of Americans Think Country Divided by Race." *Daily Beast,* April 7. http://www.thedaily beast.com/articles/2012/04/07/newsweek-daily-beast-poll-finds-majorities-of -americans-think-country-divided-by-race.html.

Schreiner, Mark, and Michael Sherraden. 2007. *Can the Poor Save? Saving and Asset Building in Individual Development Accounts.* New Brunswick, N.J.: Transaction.

SDCC (San Diego Convention Center). 2010. *Annual Report 2010.* San Diego: SDCC.

Sharkey, Patrick. 2013. *Stuck in Place: Urban Neighborhoods and the End of Progress toward Racial Equality.* Chicago: University of Chicago Press.

Shipler, David. *The Working Poor: Invisible in America.* New York: Random House.

SHRM (Society for Human Resource Management). 2010. Annual member survey. Alexandria, Va.: Society for Human Resource Management.

———. 2012. Annual member survey. Alexandria, Va.: Society for Human Resource Management.

Simpson, Isaac, and Art Tavana. 2015. "Is Gentrification Ruining Los Angeles, or Saving It? Pick a Side." *LA Weekly,* January 29. http://www.laweekly.com /news/is-gentrification-ruining-los-angeles-or-saving-it-pick-a-side-5342416.

Soss, Joe, Richard C. Fording, and Sandord F. Schram. 2011. *Disciplining the Poor: Neoliberal Paternalism and the Persistent Power of Race.* Chicago: University of Chicago Press.

Spalter-Roth, Roberta M. 1997. *Managing Work and Family: Nonstandard Work Arrangements among Managers and Professionals.* Washington, D.C.: Economic Policy Institute.

Stack, Carol. 1975. *All Our Kin.* New York: Basic Books.

Stegman, Michael A. 2007. "Payday Lending." *Journal of Economic Perspectives* 21, no. 1: 169–90.

Steinberg, Ronnie J. 1990. "Social Construction of Skill, Gender Power and Comparable Worth." *Work and Occupations* 17, no. 4: 449–82.

Stewart, Mark B. 2007. "The Interrelated Dynamics of Unemployment and Low-Wage Employment." *Journal of Applied Econometrics* 22, no. 3: 511–31.

Stiglitz, Joseph. 2013. *The Price of Inequality. How Today's Divided Society Endangers Our Future.* New York: W. W. Norton.

Stoll, Mihael A. 1999. "Spatial Mismatch, Discrimination, and Male Youth Employment in the Washington, D.C. Area: Implications for Residential Mobility Policies." *Journal of Policy Analysis and Management* 18, no. 1: 77–98.

Strom, Elizabeth. 2002. "Converting Pork into Porcelain: Cultural Institutions and Downtown Development." *Urban Affairs Review* 38, no. 1: 3–21.

Sullivan, James X. 2008. "Borrowing during Unemployment: Unsecured Debt as a Safety Net." *Journal of Human Resources* 43, no. 2: 383–412.

Swan, Richelle, Linda Shaw, Sharon Cullity, Joni Halpern, Juliana Humphrety, Wendy Limbert, and Mary Roche. 2008. "The Untold Story of Welfare Fraud." *Journal of Sociology and Social Welfare* 35, no. 3: 133–51.

Taylor, Brian D., and Paul M. Ong. "Spatial Mismatch or Automobile Mismatch? An Estimation of Race, Residence and Commuting in U.S. Metropolitan Areas." *Urban Studies* 32, no. 9: 1453–73.

Terhune, Chad. 2012. "1.2 Million Californians Lost Employer Health Benefits since 2009." *Los Angeles Times*, October 25.

Theodos, Brett. 2010. *Characteristics of Users of Refund Anticipation Loans and Refund Anticipation Checks*. Collingdale, Calif.: Diane Publishing.

Tilly, C. 1996. *Half a Job: Bad and Good Part-Time Jobs in a Changing Labor Market*. Philadelphia: Temple University Press.

Tolbert, C. M. 1983. "Industrial Segmentation and Men's Career Mobility." *American Sociological Review* 47: 457–77.

Tolbert, C. M., P. M. Horan, and E. M. Beck. 1980. "The Structure of Economic Segmentation: A Dual Economy Approach." *American Journal of Sociology* 85: 1095–116.

Tolman, Richard M., and Daniel Rosen. 2001. "Domestic Violence in the Lives of Women Receiving Welfare Mental Health, Substance Dependence, and Economic Well-Being." *Violence against Women* 7, no. 2: 141–58.

Trachta, Ali. 2010. "Le Cordon Bleu Culinary School Faces Class Action Lawsuit." *LA Weekly*, October 11.

Tucho, Admasu E. 2000. "Factors Influencing the Successful Completion of the General Education Development (GED) Program at Community College of Philadelphia as Perceived by the GED Students." E.D. diss., Temple University.

Tufano, Peter, and Daniel Schneider. 2009. "Using Financial Innovation to Support Savers: From Coercion to Excitement." In *Insufficient Funds: Savings, Assets, Credit and Banking among Low-Income Households*, ed. M. Barr and R. Blank, 149–90. New York: Russell Sage Foundation.

Tully, Shawn. 2006. "Welcome to the Dead Zone Real Estate Survival Guide: The Great Housing Bubble Has Finally Started to Deflate, and the Fall Will Be Harder in Some Markets Than Others." *Fortune*, May 5. http://money.cnn.com/2006/05/03/news/economy/realestateguide_fortune/?cnn=yes.

Turner, Margery Austin, Michael Fix, and Raymond Struyk, eds. *Opportunities Denied, Opportunities Diminished: Racial Discrimination in Hiring*. Washington, D.C.: The Urban Institute.

Uggen, Christopher, and Jeremy Staff. 2001. "Work as a Turning Point for Criminal Offenders." *Corrections Management Quarterly* 5, no. 4: 1–16.

UNITE/HERE. 2012. "Hotel Industry Fact Sheet." http://www.unitehere2.org/wp-content/uploads/The-Hotel-Industry-on-the-Rebound-A-Fact-Sheet.pdf.

U.S. Decennial Census. 1990–2010. Washington, D.C.: Census Bureau.

USEIA (U.S. Energy Information Administration). 2011. Residential energy consumption survey. Washington, D.C.: USEIA.

U.S. Senate. 1988. Hearings on welfare reform. Washington, D.C.: Congressional Records Office.

Valdez, Zulema. 2010. *The New Entrepreneurs: How Race, Class, and Gender Shape American Enterprise.* Palo Alto: Stanford University Press.

Valenzuela, Abel. 2001. "Day Labourers as Entrepreneurs?" *Journal of Ethnic and Migration Studies* 27, no. 2: 335–52.

———. 2003. "Day Labor Work." *Annual Review of Sociology* 29: 307–33.

Venkatesh, Sudhir Alladi. 2009. *American Project: The Rise and Fall of a Modern Ghetto.* Cambridge, Mass.: Harvard University Press.

Wacquant, Loïc. 2009. *Punishing the Poor: The Neoliberal Government of Social Insecurity.* Durham: Duke University Press.

Waldinger, Roger. 1996. "From Ellis Island to LAX: Immigrant Prospects in the American City." *International Migration Review* 30, no. 4: 1078–86.

Warhurst, Chris, Françoise Carré, Patricia Findlay, and Chris Tilly, eds. 2012. *Are Bad Jobs Inevitable? Trends, Determinants, and Responses to Job Quality in the Twenty-First Century.* New York: Palgrave Macmillan.

Warren, Elizabeth, and Amelia Warren Tyagi. 2003. *The Two-Income Trap: Why Middle-Class Mothers and Fathers Are Going Broke.* New York: Basic Books.

Warschauer, Michael. 2004. "Of Digital Divides and Social Multipliers: Combining Language and Technology for Human Development." In *Information and Communication Technologies in the Teaching and Learning of Foreign Languages: State of the Art, Needs and Perspectives,* 46–52. Moscow: UNESCO Institute for Information Technologies in Education.

Weinberg, Daniel H. 2011. "U.S. Neighborhood Income Inequality in the 2005–2009 Period." American Community Survey Reports. Issue Brief, ACS-16, October. Washington, D.C.: Census Bureau.

Wiatrowski, William J. 2011. *Changing Landscape of Employment-based Retirement Benefits.* Washington, D.C.: Bureau of Labor Statistics.

Wiegman, Robyn. 2003. My Name Is Forrest, Forrest Gump: Whiteness Studies and the Paradox of Particularity." In *Multiculturalism, Postcoloniality, and Transnational Media,* ed. Ella Shohat and Robert Stam, 227–55. New Brunswick: Rutgers University Press.

Williams, Claudia, Julie Hudman, and Molly O'Malley. *Challenges and Tradeoffs in Low-Income Family Budgets: Implications for Health Coverage.* Kaiser Commission on Medicaid and the Uninsured. Los Angeles: Kaiser Family Foundation.

Williams, Colin C., John Round, and Peter Rodgers. 2007. "Beyond the Formal/ Informal Economy Binary Hierarchy." *International Journal of Social Economics* 34, no. 6: 402–14.

———. 2009. "Evaluating the Motives of Informal Entrepreneurs: Some Lessons from Ukraine." *Journal of Developmental Entrepreneurship* 14, no. 1: 59–71.

Williams, Laura. 2012. *Housing Landscape.* Washington, D.C.: Center for Housing Policy.

Williamson, John B. 1974. "The Stigma of Public Dependency: A Comparison of Alternative Forms of Public Aid to the Poor." *Social Problems* 22, no. 2: 213–28.

Wilson, William Julius. 1991. *The Truly Disadvantaged: The Inner City, the Underclass, and Public Policy.* Chicago: University of Chicago Press.

———. 1996. *When Work Disappears: The World of the New Urban Poor.* New York: Alfred A. Knopf.

Winsberg, M. D. 1989. "Income Polarization between the Central Cities and Suburbs of U.S. Metropolises, 1950–1980." *American Journal of Economics and Sociology* 48: 3–10.

Wood, David. 2003. "Effect of Child and Family Poverty on Child Health in the United States." *Pediatrics* 112, suppl. 3 (September 1): 707–11.

Woolsey. Matt. 2007. "America's Most Overpriced Real Estate Markets." *Forbes Online*, May 4. http://www.forbes.com/2007/05/03/market-housing-overpriced-forbeslife-cx_mw_0504overpriced.html.

Zaslow, M. J., E. Oldham, K. A. Moore, and E. Magenheim. 1998. "Welfare Families' Use of Early Childhood Care and Education Programs, and Implications for Their Children's Development." *Early Childhood Research Quarterly* 13, no. 4: 537–64.

Zuberi, Dan. 2006. *Differences That Matter: Social Policy and the Working Poor in the United States and Canada.* Ithaca: Cornell University Press.

Zukin, Sharon. 1995. *The Cultures of Cities.* Cambridge, Mass.: Blackwell.

Index

Abowd, John M., and Richard B. Freeman, 80
Abutaleb, Yasmeen, 174
ACS (American Community Survey), 94, 264, 266
African Americans, 1, 60, 74, 77, 79, 101–3, 122, 136, 141, 184, 217, 218, 238, 265
Allan, Emilie Andersen, and Darrell J. Steffensmeier, 77
Anderson, Elijah, 21
Anderson, Patricia M., and Philip B. Levine, 172
Appelbaum, Eileen, 53
Appelbaum, Eileen, Annette Bernhardt, and Richard J. Murnane, 6, 63
asset building, 185, 204, 236, 256
Avery, Robert B., Raphael W. Bostic, Paul S. Calem, and Glenn B. Canner, 191

Bailey, Thomas, and Annette Bernhardt, 110, 112
bankruptcy, 159–61, 201–8, 227, 229, 235; and legal problems, 235–37
Barker, Kathleen, and Kathleen Christensen, 53
Barnes, Sandra, 185, 235

barriers to formal sector employment, 134, 141
Bates, Beth T., 101
benefits (job-related), 39, 80–81, 88; benefits and informal work, 147; benefits and job quality, 51–70; benefits in retail, 112, 124–25; discouraged workers and benefits, 142; in jobs created by revitalization, 43; public assistance benefits (*see* public assistance)
Bernhardt, Annette, Laura Dresser, and Erin Hatton, 87, 94, 91, 106
Blank, Rebecca M., and Michael S. Barr, 193
blight, 8, 10, 27, 30, 33, 37, 39, 90, 162
BLS (Bureau of Labor Statistics), 15, 48, 56, 95, 113, 114, 115, 267
Bookman, Ann, and Delia Kimbrel, 174
Borjas, George, 102
Borjas, George J., Richard B. Freeman, and Lawrence F. Katz, 102
Boyer, Christine, 28
Bradshaw, Ted K., 11, 259
Brandwein, Ruth, 180
Brooks, Jennifer, and Kasey Wiedrich, 187

287

D A V I D J . K A R J A N E N is associate professor of American studies at the University of Minnesota.